development anthropology

DEVELOPMENT
ANTHROPOLOGY

---

encounters in the
real world

Riall W. Nolan

Institute for Global Studies and Affairs
University of Cincinnati

Westview
PRESS
A Member of the Perseus Books Group

Copyright © 2002 by Westview Press, A Member of the Perseus Books Group

Westview Press books are available at special discounts for bulk purchases in the United States by corporations, institutions, and other organizations. For more information, please contact the Special Markets Department at The Perseus Books Group, 11 Cambridge Center, Cambridge MA 02142, or call (617) 252-5298.

Published in 2002 in the United States of America by Westview Press, 5500 Central Avenue, Boulder, Colorado 80301-2877, and in the United Kingdom by Westview Press, 12 Hid's Copse Road, Cumnor Hill, Oxford OX2 9JJ

Find us on the World Wide Web at www.westviewpress.com

A CIP catalog record for this book is available from the Library of Congress.
ISBN 0-8133-0983-0 (hc)—ISBN 0-8133-0984-0 (pbk)

Text design by Jane Raese

The paper used in this publication meets the requirements of the American National Standard for Permanence of Paper for Printed Library Materials Z39.48-1984.

10   9   8   7   6   5   4   3   2   1

contents

PART ONE
ANTHROPOLOGY AND DEVELOPMENT

PART THREE

THE WAY AHEAD

list of illustrations

Tables

Figures

Mini-Cases

preface

THIS BOOK IS ABOUT how anthropology is used in international development projects. Written from a practitioner's viewpoint, it is designed for people who are—or intend to be—active in planning and carrying out programs of directed change in culturally diverse environments.

Although anthropology has been involved with international development for decades, the discipline has yet to have a determinant influence on how development is done. Today, however, the field of development is in the midst of a major transformation that will present us—as all transformations do—with new challenges and opportunities. If anthropology is ready to meet these challenges and opportunities, it can play a key role in development work in the future.

Today, nowhere on earth is truly remote. It often appears, thanks to television and the Internet, that the world is growing more Westernized with every passing day. But differences remain, many of them more important than ever. Advances in transport and communication have simply brought us into closer contact with the different worlds that were always there and that continue to shape and inform human interaction. We now have to deal with difference directly, instead of at a distance.

Nothing illustrates this better than international development itself, which is really an extended and intimate form of cross-cultural conversation. Our ability to manage this interaction in mutually productive and satisfying ways will be crucial to achieving the outcomes we all hope for.

Development is our biggest global project. If successful, it will not only transform the lives of billions of people, but change the way the world operates in fundamental ways.

But wishing is not enough. The philosopher Reinhold Niebuhr reminded us: "The same strength which has extended our power beyond a continent has also . . . brought us into a vast web of history in which other wills, running in oblique or contrasting directions to our own, inevitably hinder or contradict what we most fervently desire. We cannot simply have our way, not even when we believe our way to have the 'happiness of mankind' as its promise."[1]

As this book will make clear, the development industry is at present generally ill-equipped to manage the demands of sustained and focused cross-cultural collaboration, a necessary condition for development success. In a fundamental sense, international development work is an encounter between different worlds. To succeed, development needs to incorporate diversity of viewpoint and to forge common understandings and purposes that both acknowledge and use this diversity.

The subtitle of this book is "*encounters in the real world.*" In truth, however, the so-called real world is not a single entity, but consists of multiple worlds, each culturally-constructed. Anthropology, with its emphasis on, and respect for, these different cultural worlds, can make a major contribution . . . " to developing humankind's ability to understand and manage difference as we work to move the development agenda forward. This book is an attempt to show how this can be done.

Within the development literature, few books exist that describe how anthropology can be used in the design and management of change. One consequence of this is that few anthropology graduates are well equipped to enter this field and succeed within it. Indeed, our academic conferences and journals, to the extent that they discuss development at all, almost invariably emphasize accounts of projects that failed or agencies that ignored our contributions.

This text is a modest attempt at changing that situation. It provides a description of how development work today is done, focusing on projects as the nexus of the encounter between different cultural worlds and offering illustrations and examples of how anthropologists can contribute to making these encounters successful. By examining how projects work, anthropologists can better understand how to help them succeed. Each chapter contains one or more mini–case studies, many of them drawn from actual projects.

The book is divided into three parts. Part One, "Anthropology and Development," contains three chapters that lay the groundwork for understanding how development takes place today and what role anthropology has in that effort. Chapter 1 presents an overview of anthropology as a discipline and outlines the essential components of the anthropological approach. Chapter 2 examines the growth of the development industry, looking particularly at changes over time in how development has been approached. Chapter 3 discusses applied anthropology, sketching its early development, noting shifts in emphasis, and outlining some of the issues that surround application today.

Part Two, "Development Projects Examined," consists of five chapters that look in detail at what projects are, how they are crafted, and how anthropology is used in that process. Chapter 4 examines how development projects are put together and how anthropology is used to do this. Chapter 5 looks at the role of information and local input in project work. Chapter 6 focuses on aspects of design. Chapter 7 concentrates on project management. Chapter 8 addresses project evaluation, and how agencies and organizations learn—or fail to learn—from project experience.

Part Three, "The Way Ahead," looks at the future of development efforts. Chapter 9 discusses how the development industry might be reformed to make it more effective. In like manner, Chapter 10 presents suggestions for changing how anthropology is taught to make its impact more pronounced. Chapter 11 outlines some thoughts on how a new paradigm to guide development might be created.

The appendix provides some suggestions for preparing for a career in development anthropology. A glossary of terms and list of sources cited complete the book.

Riall W. Nolan
Cincinnati, Ohio

ENDNOTES

1. Quoted in Kaplan (1997: 60).

acknowledgments

MANY PEOPLE HELPED with the ideas that formed this book. Dean Birkenkamp and Karl Yambert, in particular, extended support, offered suggestions and criticisms at key junctures, and managed, in their different ways, to keep this project on track, never losing patience with me. Michael Cernea, Michael Horowitz, and Thayer Scudder offered insights from their considerable professional experience, and suggestions on the manuscript as it developed.

Many other colleagues also offered suggestions and comments. Alexander Ervin, Allan Hoben, Jasper Ingersoll, John Mason, Donald Messerschmidt, Augusta Molnar, William Partridge, William Roberts, Linda Stone, Rob Winthrop, John Young—to these and many others, my sincere thanks for their support, advice, and encouragement.

Anthropology, international development, and cross-cultural learning have come to be my professional life. Three individuals in particular are responsible for the direction that my career took, and I would like to thank them most sincerely at this time for opening doors to me—and, at times, pushing me through them. Arnold Sio at Colgate University suggested the Peace Corps to me, an experience that was to irrevocably change my life and my view of the world. Souleymane Faye of the village of Khenene in Senegal patiently showed me how to see with someone else's eyes and heart. Peter Lloyd at the University of Sussex helped me understand how anthropology could be used in development work, and encouraged me to stick with it. To each of these three quite different individuals, who inhabit cultural worlds very far away from one another, I owe much more than I can ever repay, much less express.

This book is dedicated to them.

R.W.N.

PART ONE

---

anthropology and development

ANTHROPOLOGY NOT ONLY SHOWS US that there are different cultural worlds beyond our own; it helps us understand how to interact successfully with them. Encounters between the world's diverse cultures occur daily, on a variety of different levels, but none are more important or significant than those relating to international development. This book examines how anthropology is used in those encounters.

Part One, "Anthropology and Development," provides the background and framework for this examination by looking at anthropology, development, and the relation between them.

Chapter 1, "Anthropology as a Science of Discovery," examines the discipline itself and what makes it special. Chapter 2, "The Rise of the Development Industry," looks at the way in which international development began and evolved from its post–World War II beginnings. Chapter 3, "Putting Anthropology to Work," focuses on the application of anthropology outside the university and specifically within the development industry.

chapter 1

ANTHROPOLOGY

AS A SCIENCE OF

DISCOVERY

A DIFFERENT WAY OF SEEING

Anthropology enables us to discover the different cultural worlds that human groups create and inhabit, and to understand these worlds in terms other than our own. Anthropology helps us appreciate that each culture has its own distinctive ethos or worldview, each with its own logic and coherence. Anthropology therefore serves as a bridge across cultures, making one intelligible to the other, preserving the integrity of each.[1]

In the United States, anthropology has traditionally comprised four subdisciplines, or fields. *Physical anthropology* deals with human evolution and the biological aspects of contemporary human variation. *Social* or *cultural anthropology* focuses on contemporary human societies.[2] *Archaeology* examines cultural history, and *linguistics* looks at language and how it is used.

Social and cultural anthropology, which form the focus of this book, have traditionally generated two principal products or outputs: *ethnography*, the detailed written description of part or all of a particular culture or society, and *ethnology*, the comparative analytical study of two or more societies in an attempt to derive patterns and build theory.

3

The Primacy of Culture

Culture is a central concept in anthropology. With minor variations, culture has a generally accepted definition among anthropologists; it refers to the distinctive, shared way of organizing the world that a particular group or society has created over time.[3] This framework allows the members of that society to make sense of themselves, their world, and their experiences in that world—who they are, what they value, and where they are going in life. Culture provides groups with identities, ways and means, and ultimately destinations.

A human invention, culture has enormous implications for group evolution and survival. The cultural patterns developed over generations of interaction enable a group's members to organize their experience, make sense of it, and tell others what they know. Culture helps promote security and predictability in human affairs, thus freeing group members to be more productive and creative. Throughout history, culture has been instrumental in helping human beings adapt to—and influence—their surroundings. Groups value their culture, because it provides them with a way to structure their world, to give meaning to their experiences in that world, and to help them respond to events and circumstances. Cultures create different worlds, and just as people will protect their physical selves from assault, so too will they act, individually and collectively, to protect their symbolic selves—that is, their cultural worlds.[4]

There are three generally accepted components to culture: *artifacts* (the things we make), *behavior* (the ways we act), and *knowledge* (what we believe and know about the world). These facets of culture are manifest in every aspect of our lives. Often, all three are combined in particularly powerful *symbols*, such as a flag or a logo.

Culture is not static but dynamic and flexible. One of the most interesting things that anthropologists do is to look at the way in which groups and individuals manipulate their culture and its symbols in interactions, constantly negotiating or redefining cultural categories, meanings, and values.

Cultural Differences

All humans are fundamentally alike in some important ways: We share biological needs and functions, we use language, we form relationships. At the same time, however, each of us is a unique individual: No one else on earth has quite our particular collection of experiences, thoughts, and wishes.

Culture, however, groups some individuals together and excludes others; it makes some of us alike and some of us different in important ways. The way we dress, the gods we worship, the languages we speak, the food we eat, the things we value or despise—all of these are culturally derived, and serve to differentiate the members of one culture from those of another.

Such differences are learned. At birth, we are not American or Mexican or Japanese. As young children, we begin to acquire the framework of values, beliefs, and expectations that forms our cultural identity. As we gain experience with this framework, our behavior is reinforced by the people around us. By the time we are adults, our acquired culture is practically second nature to us.

So although we all develop distinctive individual personalities, we operate as individuals within our cultural framework. As Americans or Mexicans or Japanese, we use this framework to help us satisfy the same basic needs that all humans have, but in ways that are American, Mexican, or Japanese.

Across groups, cultural differences are immediately apparent in terms of the things people make (artifacts) and what they do (behaviors). Anthropologists, however, are particularly interested in the less visible aspects of culture that generate these observable differences. They pay close attention, therefore, to *cultural knowledge*—how members of a culture arrange their world, and what meanings and values people assign to aspects of that world.

People use their cultural knowledge to look at their surroundings and to organize what they see. They use their culture to arrive at judgments about what is happening in their world, to help them select appropriate responses to those happenings, and to draw conclusions about the results of these actions. Cultural knowledge is organized in complex but discernible patterns, and although these patterns are essentially arbitrary, they don't seem arbitrary at all to the members of a particular society. Instead, they appear as logical, normal, right, and proper.

Cultures in Contact

As useful as culture is to us in many ways, it can also create problems. Although people everywhere must contend with many of the same issues in life—for example, life, liberty, and the pursuit of happiness—they may define these things quite differently, and they will act to gain them in different ways.

Because we all grow up within a specific culture, its forms become almost second nature to us. Most people are unaware of their own cultural assumptions and biases and tend to take them for granted. Because our cultural frames of reference are so implicit, we tend to believe that the way our culture has taught us to see the world is the way the world really is. Anthropologists call this *naive realism.* "Pigs," as one child explained, "are called pigs because they're so dirty."

Just as culture creates a "we" identity for us, it also creates a "they" category for everyone else. We deal with "them," much of the time, through *stereotypes:* summary generalizations about other, culturally different groups. Although stereotypes can reduce the threat of the unknown by enhancing predictability, they are abstract and one-dimensional, and tend to obscure important information in new situations. If we apply stereotypes unthinkingly, we will eventually make serious mistakes. Not all American tourists overseas are loud and boorish, not all Frenchmen are charming, and not all English soccer fans are hooligans.

Culture also encourages individuals to be *ethnocentric;* to judge other cultures in terms of our own set of standards. An ethnocentric person assumes, in Shaw's words, that "the customs of his tribe and island are the laws of nature."[5] Again, this can lead to mistakes in perception. What is different is not always inferior.

All this can make contacts between one culture and another potentially difficult. As we shall see, international development is, above all, a cross-cultural encounter.

HOW ANTHROPOLOGISTS WORK

The Ritual of Fieldwork

Although many disciplines engage in fieldwork, none do it as intensively as anthropologists, and the importance of fieldwork for both the discipline and its adherents cannot be overstated. Fieldwork is a true rite of passage, heavily invested with value. Students leave familiar surroundings for unknown places where strangers teach them new lore. When sufficient knowledge has been gained, the neophytes reenter their original community, but as profoundly changed individuals.

Many anthropologists consider their fieldwork experience as one of the defining moments of their life; as the time when they became aware not only of another culture's significance, but of their own cultural premises and assumptions. Fieldwork also demonstrates one's commitment to the discipline; surviving fieldwork and the ensuing dissertation is considered a test of one's character, ability, and courage.

FIGURE 1.1   A Model for Cross-Cultural Learning

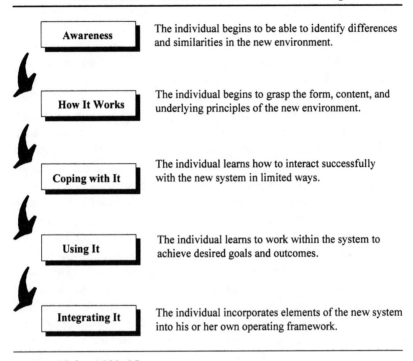

Awareness	The individual begins to be able to identify differences and similarities in the new environment.
How It Works	The individual begins to grasp the form, content, and underlying principles of the new environment.
Coping with It	The individual learns how to interact successfully with the new system in limited ways.
Using It	The individual learns to work within the system to achieve desired goals and outcomes.
Integrating It	The individual incorporates elements of the new system into his or her own operating framework.

SOURCE: Nolan 1999: 25.

Today, anthropological fieldwork is done within corporations as well as in remote villages. Whatever the setting, the anthropologist's goal is the same: to achieve an "out-of-culture" experience through immersion in another way of life; to transcend one's own cultural boundaries and limitations, and see—really *see*—new worlds through the eyes of others.

In this sense, fieldwork is similar to other cross-cultural learning situations, and involves a set of linked stages of comprehension. Figure 1.1 sets these out.

Fieldwork takes time, luck, skill, and patience. A period of fieldwork will last anywhere from three months to three years, and it is not unusual for a doctoral student to stay in the field for a year or more gathering data for a dissertation. By remaining in the field for long periods of time and entering as fully as possible into the lives of the people around them, anthropologists are able to build up a many-layered picture of what is happening, uncovering facts and connections between facts that survey work might never reveal.

Fieldwork takes as its premise that a culture's reality is socially constructed; that the members of a culture really *do* live in their own world, and that this cultural world differs in important ways from those of other cultures. The fieldworker seeks to discover and build up that reality inductively, based on what members of the community think, how they order and evaluate what is significant to them, and how they manipulate these things in daily interaction.

Anthropology therefore proceeds by a process of discovery rather than verification.[6] Although every field investigation begins with one or more hypotheses, a culture's categories, patterns, and values are not imposed or defined at the outset. Rather, they emerge over time as the anthropologist gains more familiarity with her surroundings. Fieldwork is therefore a type of emergent process, in which each data-gathering experience helps to structure subsequent interactions. In this respect, as we shall see, doing fieldwork is very similar to mounting a development project.

A map, for example, is a simple two-dimensional representation of a place on the earth. It contains a great deal of basic information, but very little cultural context. The anthropologist seeks to bring the map to life, as it were, by looking at how the inhabitants of the area see and use what is marked on it: which neighborhoods are regarded as desirable, for example, or as dangerous; which routes are quicker for the morning commute; and where to go for lunch. This "off the map" knowledge is precisely what most anthropologists are seeking when they go into the field.[7]

Do fieldworkers gain special or unique insight into a culture? Not really; on one level they simply come to understand what members of that culture already know. On another level, however, anthropologists come to understand a particular culture within a broader cross-cultural context. To an insider's, or *emic* perspective, is added the *etic*, or outsider's, viewpoint.[8] These combined perspectives help anthropologists to describe, predict, and analyze change in ways the members of the culture itself might not necessarily be able to do.

Participant Observation

Anthropologists acquire their knowledge from other people through *participant observation*. Participant observation is learning by doing to generate what one anthropologist termed a "living understanding" of the culture.[9] This usually requires knowledge of the local language. If culture is based on categories, rules, and values existing in people's minds, then it follows that one of the best ways to uncover these is through listening to what people say. Anthropologists therefore spend a great deal of time and energy trying to understand how people use language to talk about—and think about—what is important to them.

Learning the local language allows anthropologists to participate, observe, question, and measure using local terms and categories. Anthropologists in the field, far from being "objective" or "detached" observers, are extraordinarily dependent on the people around them for data, knowledge, and ultimately understanding. It is local people, in the end, who will determine the success or failure of the fieldwork enterprise. An example of language-based cultural misunderstanding learning that happened to me early in my career as a development planner is outlined in Mini-Case 1.1, "On the Road to Tunis."

Gaining an insider's understanding of another culture takes time and effort, as patterns fall into place one piece at a time. The process can be profoundly uncomfortable, physically and emotionally. Despite this, many fieldworkers have emphasized the intense creativity and passion of the experience, as a new culture opened itself before them, one day at a time. For many anthropologists, participant observation may begin as a field technique, but it eventually becomes a way of life, an approach to learning.

The knowledge gained and used during fieldwork is often unexpected; meanings and connections appear that might remain hidden to the more casual investigator. This includes serendipitous discoveries, made by simply being in the right place at the right time.

What is learned during fieldwork is often disconfirming in one way or another. That is, the reality of the culture almost invariably turns out to be different from what was assumed, and modifies—sometimes considerably—whatever original hypotheses or constructs the fieldworker began with. This is so well known within the discipline that most fieldworkers expect to have their initial ideas challenged, if not altogether disproved.

Relativism

Relativism is another key aspect of fieldwork methodology. Anthropologists believe that all people are fully and equally human, and that the only way to develop significant understanding of another culture is to judge it on its own terms. Because fieldworkers seek understanding from an insider's viewpoint, they adopt an attitude of relativism—the suspension of judgment about another culture's norms, values, or practices—the better to understand its internal logic and structure.

Each society has its own particular view of what is "normal," and the people in these societies come to accept this view of normality and act accordingly. What might strike outsiders as "irrational" or "inefficient"

MINI-CASE 1.1   ON THE ROAD TO TUNIS

Several days after I first arrived in Tunisia to begin a long-term contract, I was invited by another American development worker to take a drive in the country.

Both of us were new to Tunisia, both of us spoke fluent French, but neither of us spoke any Arabic, although I had arranged to begin Arabic lessons in a few weeks. We spent several hours driving through the beautiful Tunisian countryside, admiring the villages, the Roman ruins, the mountains, and the coast.

Late in the afternoon, we stood at a crossroads, wondering where on earth we were. We'd discovered, to our surprise, that once out of Tunis, mileposts were marked only in Arabic. It was growing late, and we needed to find the right road to get us back to the capital.

Fortunately, we spied a Tunisian farmer trudging up the road. "Bonjour, monsieur," my friend said. "Parlez-vous français?"

The farmer looked at us. "Bien sur," he said. "Of course I speak French. What can I do for you?"

My friend rubbed his hands together. "Great. We need to go to Tunis. Can you show us the right road to Tunis?"

The farmer's eyebrows went up. "You're already in Tunis, monsieur," he said.

My friend smiled indulgently. "Perhaps you didn't understand me," he said. "We want the road to Tunis."

The farmer smiled back. "I heard what you said, monsieur. Tunis is here."

My friend's smile grew somewhat tight. "No, no, no. We—want—the—road—to—Tunis. You know, *Tunis*. Where is it?"

(continues)

---

behavior usually makes sense within its own cultural framework, where rationality and efficiency are defined differently.[10]

Fiske provides an example from development planning:

Animal scientists attempting to introduce small ruminants (llama) in Peru were frustrated by Andean pastoralists' seeming irrational reluctance to cull their herds by slaughtering sick or old animals. The anthropologists . . . found that the principal reason for stock raising in the barren Andean highlands was actually for the end products, so to speak—manure for fuel and fertilizer. The critical products were not lambs, meat or fiber, as had been assumed from Western experience, and the Peruvians were not acting irrationally, because even old and sick animals produce the desperately needed products.[11]

MINI-CASE 1.1 (continued)

Speaking slowly and carefully, as if to a child, the farmer said, "Tunis, yes. I understand. You want to go to Tunis. You are here." Pause. "*It* is here. You—*are*—in—Tunis."

At this point, the exchange took on the aspect of a Laurel and Hardy skit. My friend grew red-faced, his voice creeping into a higher register, accompanied by waving arms, "*This* isn't Tunis, how could *this* be Tunis! I don't know where this is, but it's obviously *not* Tunis!" He was hopping up and down now. "So—one more time . . . where is the road to Tunis? It's not here, that's for sure! I don't *want* to be here, *I want to go to Tunis!* I—am—going—to—*Tunis*, do you hear?"

The farmer looked at him for a long moment. Then he shrugged. "Eh bien, monsieur, bon voyage." He picked up his tools and walked down the road, shaking his head.

We eventually found the right road, of course, and we spent quite a bit of our time on the long drive back to the city chuckling at the strange farmer. A few weeks later my Arabic instructor began our first language class with a geography lesson, and the shoe finally fell.

I raised my hand. "Let me get this straight," I said. "In Arabic, the word for the country of Tunisia and the word for the city of Tunis—they're the same?"

"Of course," said Hichem. "*Tunis.*" He wrote it on the board:

تـونس.

"Same word for the city, same word for the country. Everybody knows that, n'est-ce pas?" He smiled.

I smiled back, remembering our adventure in the country and the farmer who was now not so strange after all. "Of course," I agreed.

Although relativism may pose philosophical and ethical problems when carried to extremes, there is no doubt that the suspension of judgment is necessary during fieldwork to reach cross-cultural understanding. Imposing an outsider's framework on the culture you're trying to understand is a little like trying to fit square pegs into round holes—you might get them to fit, but only after you'd destroyed their original shape.[12]

Mini-Case 1.2, "Thinking Differently About Decisions," describes a project in West Africa where behavior by FulBe herders that seemed

MINI-CASE 1.2
THINKING DIFFERENTLY ABOUT DECISIONS:
DOUKOLUMA FULBE HERDERS IN WEST AFRICA

In the early 1970s, John Grayzel conducted fieldwork in rural Mali among FulBe herders, at a time when a USAID-funded cattle development project was being planned for the area. An important part of Grayzel's work involved understanding how the FulBe used the grazing resources of the local area. This included looking at decisions about the sale of animals, sizes of herds, the movement of these herds within the locally available pasturage, and the composition of herds.

Although Grayzel found that herd management followed essentially "rational" principles, he also discovered inconsistencies in the data, "broad variations in behavior among individuals that were not economically, managerially, or environmentally adaptive. Some practices made no contribution to sustaining maximum livestock production, while others appeared to have negative effects." These variations in practice, Grayzel concluded, could not be accounted for by any overarching generalizations about "rational" economic behavior.

The explanation, he felt, lay at the personal level, and could be understood by looking at the code of behavior and values, called *pulaade*, which characterized FulBe society as a whole. *Pulaade* comprises four main values: intelligence, beauty, wealth, and independence.

> The FulBe admired any demonstration of intelligence, and believed that they, as a group, were particularly well-endowed with this trait. . . . The FulBe attitude about physical beauty was similar; they considered themselves to be better looking and more intelligent than their neighbors. . . . The fundamental value of beauty was in the pleasure it gave the beholder. If the possessor was a woman, beauty was an avenue toward achieving the third most important FulBe value, wealth.
>
> Finally, freedom and independence were perhaps the most complex as well as the most important of all their values, and in a sense they incorporated all the others.

Grayzel then reexamined his data and found that the values inherent in *pulaade* did indeed help to explain individual variations in herder behav-

(continues)

<hr>

MINI-CASE 1.2 (continued)

ior. The pursuit of wealth or beauty, he notes, "often overrode economic benefit or family solidarity." In many cases, it appeared that a basic desire for independence—from family, community, and government—guided herders' choices. *Pulaade*, Grayzel noted, did not necessarily override economic and environmental factors, but it did influence a herder's response to them.

The proposed USAID project, as it appeared to be taking shape, would have contradicted *pulaade* in several important respects. Delimitation of the grazing area, the registration of herders and animals, the subordination of herders' decisions to those of outside technicians, and the bias toward maximizing returns with a smaller number of animals—these things were fundamentally inconsistent with FulBe attitudes toward the independent exercise of intelligence in pursuit of wealth, beauty, and emotional satisfaction. The FulBe worldview, as Grayzel dryly comments, "presents a thorny problem for those who tend to view life largely as a series of economic or production coefficients."

He continues:

> While certainly cognizant of their own needs for pleasure and comfort, in general development planners fail to include this sphere of human activities in their plans for others. On the contrary, they often attempt to subvert or destroy indigenous emotion satisfying institutions. Expenditures on folk festivals or religious structures are often labeled by planners as non-productive, and efforts are sometimes made to redirect these investments into shovels and fertilizer.

That a way of life—*pulaade* or any other—might be deeply satisfying emotionally to people, and might be considered an end in itself, appears to have been lost sight of in many development projects. Although local value systems, as Grayzel notes, are often cited as obstacles to the adoption of more "rational" practices, little attempt is made by planners to use such value systems as a basis from which to plan.

<hr>

SOURCE: Grayzel 1986.

irrational from a Western viewpoint was in fact perfectly consistent with the culture's own value system.

Holism

Holism is relativism's complement. Holism, simply put, is the notion that parts of a culture are connected in one way or another, often in ways that are not immediately visible. Fieldworkers therefore pay particular attention to the linkages between things. Like relativism, holism can pose problems at a philosophical or political level (seeming to justify, for example, situations of inequality, exploitation, or violence), but as a tool for gaining understanding of how a culture is put together, it is very useful.

One aspect of a culture—decisions about resource allocation, for example—can be studied and analyzed on its own, without any of the in-depth fieldwork we have been talking about. But one can never fully understand why people make the economic decisions they do without understanding much more about the rest of the culture to which these decisions are connected.

In the mini-case presented earlier, for example, to understand why FulBe herders made decisions about time and resources, it was necessary to understand FulBe notions of beauty, intelligence, independence, and other basic aspects of what might be called the FulBe worldview; the notion of what it was to be a FulBe at all. These essentially philosophical concepts had direct connections to the decisions that herders made on a day-to-day basis.

Mini-case 1.3, "One Thing Leads to Another," demonstrates in stark fashion the principle of holism as it details various far-reaching changes that occurred within an Australian Aboriginal society as the result of the introduction of a single item of new technology.

Domain Analysis

Anthropologists often use *domain analysis* to help them understand how people in a society define their world. Since all cultures use some system of categories to order experience, the anthropologist tries to determine what categories are important to people, how they are arranged, and what values are attached to them.[13] Figure 1.2 shows the basic process of domain analysis.

To begin the analysis, a significant cultural area, or *domain*, is identified. Once this has been done, the domain can be explored to uncover its

MINI-CASE 1.3
ONE THING LEADS TO ANOTHER:
STEEL AXES AND SOCIAL CHANGE

Lauriston Sharp conducted fieldwork in the early 1930s among the Yir Yoront, an Aboriginal group living on the west coast of the Cape Yorke Peninsula in northern Queensland. As part of his research, Sharp documented the effects of the introduction of a single piece of Western technology—the steel axe—into the social and economic system of the Yir Yoront.

Sharp began his explanation for what happened subsequently, and why, by looking at the traditional functions of the stone axes that the Yir Yoront had used until the time that steel axes became available from missionaries. The stone axe was crafted by men, using materials—wood, bark, and gum—freely available in their environment. The stone that formed the head of the axe, however, was not found in their territory, but much farther to the south. Yir Yoront men had therefore established long lines of male trading partners. In these exchanges, the Yir Yoront would trade stingray spears for stone axe heads. Such exchanges were particularly important during the dry season, when large Aborigine fiestas would take place. These fiestas centered around various rituals associated with totems or initiation, and attracted large numbers of people from different areas.

Once the axe had been crafted by men, it could be used by anyone, including women and children, but it always belonged to a man. Furthermore, the stone axe also had a place in Yir Yoront cosmology, and was associated with one of the several dozen clan groups in the society. The axe was essential to many important tasks, such as making wet-season huts, storage platforms, or shelters. The axe was also used in hunting, fishing, and food gathering. In only two areas was the use of the axe limited to men alone: for gathering wild honey and for fabricating ceremonial paraphernalia.

The axe, then, was not just a useful implement, but a definer and regulator of a host of social, economic, and symbolic relationships. Yir Yoront men depended on their far-flung trading partners for axe heads. Women and children wishing to use the axe needed to ask permission of a man, and this was done according to the group's rules of age and kinship. Indeed, Yir Yoront society was a complex of superordinate/subordinate relationships, wherein no one could be on an exactly equal footing with anyone else. The axe both symbolized and enforced this system.

Sharp notes that the introduction of the steel axe into this system posed no technological difficulties, and that steel axes appeared to be used in

(continues)

MINI-CASE 1.3   (*continued*)

Some Connections Between Axes and Other Aspects of Yir Yoront Society

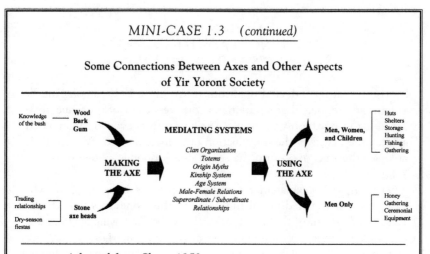

SOURCE: Adapted from Sharp 1952.

much the same way as stone axes had been, despite their supposed advantages. Sharp says:

> . . . the assumption of the white man . . . that his axe was much more efficient, that its use would save time, and that it therefore represented technical "progress" toward goals which he had set for the native was hardly borne out in aboriginal practice. Any leisure time the Yir Yoront might gain by using steel axes or other western tools was invested, not in "improving the conditions of life," and certainly not in developing aesthetic activities, but in sleep, an art they had thoroughly mastered.

In other respects, however, the changes brought by the axe were considerable. Axes were provided, not through trading links, but by missionaries. Not only were there many more axes than before; they were being given to younger men, women, and children. Acquiring a steel axe brought the Yir Yoront into closer contact with whites and resulted in new forms of relationship that fit uneasily with traditional superordinate/subordinate roles. Older men lost their monopoly of the axe, and with it, sex, age, and kinship roles began to change. Trading relationships with men outside the territory declined, together with attendance at the yearly dry-season fiestas.

Finally, the steel axe, having no place in the elaborate system of origin myths, which explain to Yir Yoront clans who they are and how they should behave, has had the effect of helping to undermine the overall

(*continues*)

MINI-CASE 1.3 (continued)

belief system. Sharp comments: "With the collapse of this system of ideas, which is so closely related with so many other aspects of the native culture, there follows an appallingly sudden and complete cultural disintegration and a demoralization of the individual such as has seldom been recorded for areas other than Australia."

Sharp's sobering analysis demonstrates the importance of holism in analyzing and understanding cultural patterns. Technology in any society is intimately connected at many points with other cultural subsystems—economics, kinship, and concepts of how life should be lived and why. Like a spider's web, disturbances in one part of the pattern will resonate elsewhere throughout the structure. Although these connections—and their consequences—will assume different patterns in different societies, the connections are always there.

SOURCE: Sharp 1952.

FIGURE 1.2   Domain Analysis

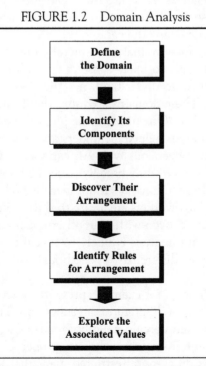

SOURCE: Adapted from Spradley 1979, 1980.

components, their arrangement, and the rules governing this arrangement. Once the structure of the domain is understood, the anthropologist can explore the values, expectations, and attributes that surround different components.

A cultural domain is any area of life that is of local importance. It is crucial that the fieldworker not define this domain in advance; rather, the domain should emerge from the concerns and interests of the people themselves. It is the fieldworker's task to discover which domains are culturally significant, rather than to impose her own.

Often, the outline of a domain is obvious. Modes of livelihood, for example, are probably universally important to people. So is the life cycle and its component stages. Categories of people and how they are grouped or differentiated is another. Typically, a fieldworker will be able to identify significant domains through interviewing, collecting life histories, and by observing members of the community interacting with each other.

Once a domain has been selected, interviewing and observation are used to determine how the domain is structured. How is the domain broken down into categories? How are these categories arranged? What is the rationale or basis for the arrangement? Finally, what values, beliefs, and expectations accompany the categories?

In many respects, domain analysis is merely a more careful form of a process that we use daily to make sense of new information. But fieldworkers are attempting to understand, not their own cultural domains, but those of others. These domains are often significantly different from our own. Mini-Case 1.4, "Organizing Principles in a Bassari Village," outlines how domain analysis helped me understand how village structure in a small and highly homogeneous West African society was put together.

Although cultures have many broadly structured domains, differences within the same culture in how subgroups identify and structure domains are also important. Fieldworkers are aware that the constructs they elicit are often highly specific, even within an otherwise homogeneous society. The process of domain analysis is likely to reveal the presence of subgroups that see things differently, even though they live in the same community.

A study of Los Angeles, for example, presented a series of maps of the city drawn by members of different urban subgroups. The maps drawn by affluent whites included upscale neighborhoods as well as recreational areas (beaches, mountains) outside the city proper. Urban blacks living near the Watts area drew more restricted maps that focused on streets

---

MINI-CASE 1.4
ORGANIZING PRINCIPLES IN A BASSARI VILLAGE

In the Bassari village of Etyolo in eastern Senegal, where I did fieldwork in the 1970s, I began by looking at how villagers were organized. "What kinds of people live here?" became the broad domain on which my efforts focused. Eventually, the outlines of village social structure became clear. Males and females, for example, occupied quite distinct ritual and economic niches. Within the male and female groups, an elaborate system of age-grades helped structure relationships between different cohorts. Each Bassari villager, furthermore, belonged to a matrilineage. Finally, each villager belonged to a residentially based labor exchange group.

Village Organizing Principles

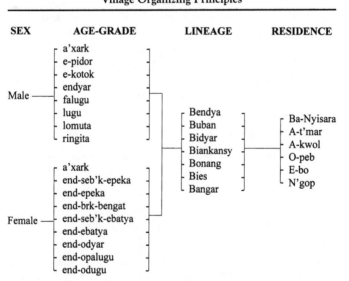

SEX	AGE-GRADE	LINEAGE	RESIDENCE
Male	a'xark / e-pidor / e-kotok / endyar / falugu / lugu / lomuta / ringita	Bendya / Buban / Bidyar / Biankansy / Bonang / Bies / Bangar	Ba-Nyisara / A-t'mar / A-kwol / O-peb / E-bo / N'gop
Female	a'xark / end-seb'k-epeka / end-epeka / end-brk-bengat / end-seb'k-ebatya / end-ebatya / end-odyar / end-opalugu / end-odugu		

These four principles—age, sex, lineage, and residence—served to structure almost every aspect of village life. Males and females owned different sorts of property (including land and agricultural produce) and controlled different but complementary aspects of ritual life. Age-grades had very specific rights and obligations vis-à-vis each other, as well as important ritual duties and communal labor responsibilities within a long-term pattern of intergenerational reciprocity. Lineage groups each owned certain ritual

(continues)

<u>MINI-CASE 1.4</u>   (continued)

sites and ceremonies, and determined marriage patterns. Residence-based labor exchange groups were an important source of economic support for families in good times and bad.

Such an analysis is interesting in itself; it presents a clear picture of how a West African society views itself, and gives an indication of some of the core values that are important to people in the society and that shape their lives. But having charted a system of categories does not, in fact, tell one very much about how a society actually works. Construction materials, as one investigator remarked, are not architecture. Of equal or greater interest, therefore, are the ways in which such categories are used by a society's members in their dealings with one another and with outsiders.

Over the course of three years of field study among the Bassari, for example, I was able to document how these basic organizing principles influenced their response to external opportunities presented by schooling, wage-labor employment, exogamy, migration, military service, and religion. The cultural categories and associated values were—and are—used by groups and individuals in Etyolo in a never-ending process of interaction, negotiation, and manipulation for desired ends.

SOURCE: Nolan 1986: 13–22.

---

leading to the city center. A Spanish-speaking group drew maps showing only their immediate area, city hall, and the bus station—their main way in and out of the city.[14]

James Spradley's work with urban nomads in Seattle, presented in Mini-Case 1.5, "The City Through Other Eyes," illustrates clearly how different the world can look to members of cultural subgroups within the larger society.

DEVELOPMENT AS
A CROSS-CULTURAL ENCOUNTER

Development has been defined in a variety of ways, but *improvement, empowerment,* and *participation* are key terms in almost any definition.

Improvement refers to betterment in ways that local populations understand, accept, and value. *Empowerment* means building local capacities for the planning and management of the changes associated with improvement. *Participation* means the involvement of different members of a society—groups and subgroups—in the decisions that will affect their lives, now and in the future.

Development—often emanating from outside—can pose a threat or challenge to existing cultural practices. Development opportunities, furthermore, do not arrive as discrete packages, but as part of a complex cultural system, with associated elements, values, and consequences.

Development is not a thing or a concept, it is a *process*—of negotiation and sometimes conflict—over whose goals and values will prevail in change, whose rules will apply. Groups use their culture as a resource—and sometimes, as a weapon—to help shape responses to such changes and opportunities. Stakeholders in a development encounter manipulate cultural categories in complex ways as they negotiate. If reality within one culture is in a sense constructed, then the reality of a development project is also a construction, arising from stakeholder interactions.

In this cross-cultural encounter, the potential for disappointment and disaster is high. Outcomes that satisfy neither development agencies nor local populations are all too frequent. Most of the time, development failures stem from a lack of fit between proposed changes and local cultural contexts, not a lack of finance, technology, or goodwill.

Content and Context in Development Work

Successful development work requires both content and context knowledge. *Content knowledge* includes specific details of processes, operations, and formulae—the procedures necessary to accomplish a task. *Context knowledge* refers to the understanding of a specific environment in which that task will be carried out.

Knowing the vocabulary and grammar of Arabic, for example, is a type of content knowledge. Understanding the appropriate thing to say in Arabic to a particular person at a particular time to produce a specific result is an example of context knowledge.

Gift giving is another example. The mechanics of shopping for a gift, paying for it, and wrapping and delivering it might be considered as a form of content knowledge. After all, stores, credit cards, and post offices work in roughly similar ways around the world. But as I've noted,

---

MINI-CASE 1.5
THE CITY THROUGH OTHER EYES:
URBAN NOMADS IN SEATTLE

What do people from different cultural groups actually see when they look at something? James Spradley, in an investigation of "urban nomads" in Seattle, used domain analysis to show how very differently these people conceptualize and use their surroundings.

Spradley notes that people do not live in the city so much as they live in their socially constructed versions of the city. When some people look at a downtown area, they may see places to work. Others see places to shop and eat lunch. Still others see places to park—or the lack thereof.

What do urban nomads see? As Spradley shows us, first and foremost, they see safe places to sleep. Spradley points out that any urban area will contain cultural subgroups and that a "normal" way of life for one of these groups will not necessarily characterize all the groups. Some groups engage in very different sorts of activity within the city. At other times, groups may engage in similar activities, but define them differently. Using domain analysis, Spradley attempted to discover what urban nomads see when they look out at the city, to build up what he calls a "cognitive map" of their world of experience.

Spradley began by defining significant domains. Based on interviews and observation, he hypothesized that "making a flop"—finding a place to sleep—was a highly significant domain for Seattle's urban nomads. Once he had identified this domain, he began to collect statements about it. Based on these statements, he began to derive possible categories, questions, and forms of contrast. By asking his informants a series of structured and semistructured questions, and by continuing to observe and listen, he was able to build up, from the informants themselves, a "taxonomy" of places to sleep. A selected portion of this appears below. In Spradley's study, the taxonomy is much more elaborate.

He noted several interesting features of this taxonomy. First, the categories of objects are arranged in terms of their function as places to sleep, and not in terms, say, of their physical form or any functions they might have for other people.

Second, the categories themselves are numerous—far more than most "ordinary" Americans would probably ever use or imagine. Indeed, Spradley comments that "places to sleep" does not appear to be a highly significant domain for most people in the mainstream culture.

Third, he points out that although we now have a map of places to sleep, this tells us little about how urban nomads actually use this map;

(continues)

MINI-CASE 1.5 (continued)

Kinds of Flops

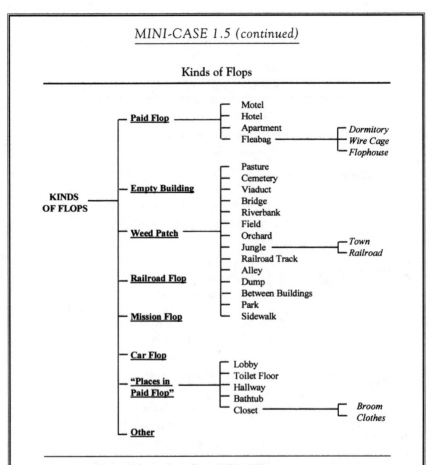

SOURCE: Adapted from Spradley 1972: 250.

about how, for example, they make decisions about where to bed down for the night.

To investigate this, he questioned his informants further, using sorting techniques, substitution frames, and contrast sets. Eventually he discovered that his informants used eight major considerations in deciding where to spend the night, considerations that directly reflect some of the most salient features of their daily life. Three of these appear below (again, Spradley's study provides much more detail).

Through this type of analysis, significant differences among groups can be explored, and ultimately mapped. By eliciting the principles, values, or factors that account for the categorizations, we can begin to understand

(continues)

MINI-CASE 1.5   *(continued)*

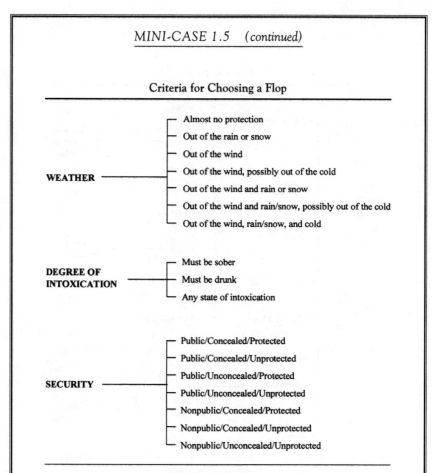

Criteria for Choosing a Flop

WEATHER
- Almost no protection
- Out of the rain or snow
- Out of the wind
- Out of the wind, possibly out of the cold
- Out of the wind and rain or snow
- Out of the wind and rain/snow, possibly out of the cold
- Out of the wind, rain/snow, and cold

DEGREE OF INTOXICATION
- Must be sober
- Must be drunk
- Any state of intoxication

SECURITY
- Public/Concealed/Protected
- Public/Concealed/Unprotected
- Public/Unconcealed/Protected
- Public/Unconcealed/Unprotected
- Nonpublic/Concealed/Protected
- Nonpublic/Concealed/Unprotected
- Nonpublic/Unconcealed/Unprotected

SOURCE: Adapted from: Spradley 1972: 250.

why the world of our informants looks the way it does. By further examining how informants use their cognitive maps, we gain additional insight into how culture—in this case, the culture of urban nomads—can be used as a problem-solving tool.

SOURCE: Spradley 1972.

each culture will have a different set of artifacts, behaviors, and associated values.

Many cultures give gifts, in other words, but not all cultures give the same gifts, not all cultures give gifts in the same way, and not all cultures value gifts in the same way. So although giving a gift looks simple in the abstract, what is chosen, who receives it, and how it is presented—all issues of context—will ultimately determine whether the gift is seen within that context as homage, tribute, thanks, appreciation, payment, tipping, a bribe, or perhaps as a deadly insult.

Development work tends to focus on matters of *content*—budgets, technical specifications, procedures, deadlines, and policies. Development specialists, whatever their discipline, therefore tend to share a common base of content knowledge that makes it possible for them to communicate effectively in many situations and to craft policy prescriptions at the macro level.

But when one moves from policy to practice, the common universe of discourse becomes more fragmented. The success with which macro policies actually work in the field depends far more on *context* than anything else—that is, on the extent to which cultural assumptions contained in the policy actually fit with those operating in the local environment. In development situations, the cross-cultural nature of the encounter means that the content knowledge that drives policy, finance, and technology almost always requires detailed context knowledge of the local situation to be both relevant and effective.

Regrettably, these two types of knowledge are often separated in the day-to-day operations of a development project. The engineer or architect may have little understanding of how villagers' use patterns affect the roads or buildings they construct; the doctor may not comprehend how local concepts of disease influence demands for health care; the economist may ignore symbolic or qualitative aspects of resource use and decisionmaking.

The local cultural context within which a development project is situated can be ignored, in other words, and often is. But it will not go away unless the people do. Cultures are flexible, resilient, and able to change, but they are also remarkably enduring. As fifty years of development experience has shown, development efforts that fit with their surroundings will work, whereas those that disregard salient aspects of context will usually fail, sooner or later. The question then becomes one of how context can be incorporated into development practice.

Anthropology and Development

In the development encounter, anthropology provides the means both for understanding context and for incorporating this context into planning and action in mutually satisfactory ways.

In some important ways, anthropologists are ideal development practitioners. Their inductive and nonjudgmental approach means that they enter a field situation with few preconceptions about what they will find there. Anthropologists are wary of generalizations, assumptions, or foregone conclusions. They are naturally interested in people rather than things, in what people do as well as in what they say. Anthropologists are aware that our own arrangements, with which most of us are so comfortable and secure, are essentially arbitrary, and indeed, exotic to others at times. We remind our colleagues that there are minds out there that think as well as we do, but differently.

Does anthropology really matter for development work? Or is the idea that cultures differ in significant ways and that everything in a culture is somehow connected to everything else, something that any talk show host already knows?

That the world looks different to people from different cultures is obvious. But how and why such differences affect the success or failure of development efforts is much less clear. This is where anthropology provides essential context-based insight.

Anthropology provides us with a way to look into other cultural worlds, to uncover and understand the shared meanings by which others act and react. It is through anthropology that we learn the things that aren't immediately obvious; that aren't revealed by surveys or quick site visits. Anthropology helps us understand how a culture is patterned, why changes in one part of the pattern may resonate elsewhere, and how norms and values affect plans, policies, and prescriptions. Anthropology, in short, helps us understand why actions, thoughts, and feelings make sense to people who inhabit cultural worlds often quite different from our own.

Anthropology provides a way of seeing that complements rather than challenges the kinds of knowledge generated by other disciplines. Anthropology does not conflict with these other approaches, but extends and enhances them. Learning to see through another's eyes is not a sufficient condition for effective and successful development, but it is a necessary one. One investigator, writing about the Kpelle village of Gbansu in Liberia, put it this way:

Listening to what Gbansu knows is the right way to begin. And that means seeing the forest, the bush and the swamps through the eyes of the different strata in Gbansu society. It means knowing what rice means and how it works, and thus not insensitively imposing swamp rice technology on a community which has good reasons for not accepting it. It means working at each level of development with those individuals, families and social groups that already operate at these levels. It means understanding how the village and the hamlets stand in the relation of producer and consumer, laborer and manager. It means seeing the central village as a microcosm of the 400 square km of forest, bush, swamp, river, trail, farm, hamlet and village, and seeing the totality of the land as the central village writ large.

But above all it means seeing that all of these work together to form a living system. It is not possible to tinker with one part of the system without affecting the remainder. Thus the outsider intervenes with fear and trembling, unless he or she is intent on destruction. Far better is to approach Gbansu quietly and patiently, waiting until it shows where it is going and where it wants to go.[15]

Anthropology not only uncovers different cultural worlds, it makes it possible for them to engage with each other. As a cross-cultural encounter, development is a protracted negotiation; unless both sides win, everyone must lose. As in life itself, success in development means coming to terms with different ways of seeing the world and learning how to create outcomes that draw on diversity as a source of intelligence and strength. Anthropology in development can help ensure that different cultural worlds that come together in projects and programs do so in ways that are mutually acceptable and satisfactory.

Development anthropology is anthropology applied, in a pure sense, but it is not traditional anthropology. The next two chapters examine this, looking first at the emergence of the development industry and then at the growth of applied anthropology.

SUMMARY OF CHAPTER 1

This chapter has looked at anthropology as a tool for exploring different cultural worlds. Culture, a key feature of all human societies, is a powerful organizing framework that helps human beings interpret their experience, plan action, and assess results.

Because culture creates a world for people that is very real and because different cultures embody different worlds, it is important to understand what happens when different cultural worlds encounter one another. Anthropologists are able to uncover a culture's patterns through fieldwork, using a variety of inductive research techniques.

Development projects are, in essence, situations of cross-cultural encounter. Development, which aims to improve people's lives, is not a thing but a process of negotiation between different ways of thinking, seeing, and valuing. In the negotiation process, although technology, finance, and management are important, knowledge of context is fundamental.

Anthropology, with its distinctive approach to investigation, provides the understanding of context that is needed for development. The anthropologist's ability to move between cultural worlds and facilitate their interaction through forms of brokerage enables partners in the development effort to achieve outcomes that are mutually satisfactory.

ENDNOTES

1. Spradley and McCurdy (1972: 9) put it this way: "[Anthropology] is a systematic attempt to discover the knowledge a group of people have learned and are using to organize their behavior. . . . Instead of asking 'What do I see these people doing?' we must ask, 'What do these people see themselves doing?' And we cannot answer this question with our own concepts, for that would implicitly introduce our view of their actions."

2. I know that some of my colleagues would vigorously dispute this statement. As someone who was educated in Britain and teaches anthropology in the United States, however, I am convinced that the similarities in approach and content far outweigh the differences.

3. Here again, others might differ with me, since there are almost as many definitions of culture as there are anthropologists. Many of these, to my mind, are distinctions without a difference.

4. Goldschmidt (2000: 11).

5. George Bernard Shaw, *Caesar and Cleopatra*, act 3.

6. E. Chambers (1985: 175–176). Finan (1996: 303) puts it this way: ". . . [cultural] knowledge is encoded in a local idiom with unique categories and classifications, which anthropologists are trained to recognize. The researcher thus faces a challenge of discovering this social knowledge in terms of its own internal logic, and then decoding this knowledge into more standardized categories that academics or change agents can mull over."

7. Turton (1988: 133).

8. The terms derive from linguistics, where phonetics refers to the range of sound that can be made by the human voice box, and phonemics focuses on those specific sounds associated with a particular language.

9. Belshaw (1976: 25).

10. A classic example of this is Laura Bohannon's well-known article "Shakespeare in the Bush" (Bohannon 2000), which describes how Tiv villagers in Nigeria reinterpreted the tale of Hamlet, Prince of Denmark, in terms that would be odd to most students of English literature, but that made perfect sense within the framework of Tiv society.

11. Fiske (1990: 20).

12. Moerman (1968) likens the imposition of an outside analytical framework to putting chocolate pudding in an egg crate. Although the material is neatly compartmentalized, its fundamental structure and composition remain a mystery.

13. This approach to field investigation is, with variations, widespread in anthropology. The clearest exposition of the methodology and its rationale probably remains James Spradley's *The Ethnographic Interview* (1979) and its companion volume, *Participant Observation* (1980).

14. Gould and White (1980).

15. Gay (1995: 285).

chapter 2

THE RISE OF
THE DEVELOPMENT
INDUSTRY

A WORLD OUT OF BALANCE

The World Bank defines poverty as living on one U.S. dollar per day or less. By this definition, some 1.2 billion people are poor. Raise the limit to two dollars per day, and two-thirds of the planet—over 4 billion people—live in poverty. Seventy percent of these are women.

Poverty is not simply a matter of income. Many millions are homeless, for example, or are living in inadequate or unsafe shelter. One and a half billion people have no access to safe drinking water. Nearly one-sixth of the world's population cannot read or write, and of these—again—almost 70 percent are women.

Although poverty is found throughout the world, inequalities across regions are particularly striking. Africa, in particular, seems especially hard-hit. Of the world's twenty poorest countries, eighteen are in Africa, where over 50 percent of the population lives at or below the dollar-a-day line. In 1993, for example, Africa's total gross national product (GNP) was less than that of the Netherlands, and Africa ranks low on many quality-of-life indicators.[1]

Technology has not redressed these disparities, and indeed, appears to be accentuating them in some cases. An astounding 97 percent of the world's computers are in wealthy industrialized countries, even though

TABLE 2.1 Defining Poverty (The World Bank divides countries into four groups [data used are for 1999])

Grouping	Annual per Capita GNP	Number of Countries	Examples	Percentage of World Population
Low Income	$785 or less	62	Afghanistan, Benin, Moldova, Vietnam	35%
Lower-Middle Income	$786–3,125	60	Algeria, Iraq, Russia, Panama, Sri Lanka	39%
Upper-Middle Income	$3,126–9,655	37	Botswana, Estonia, Mexico, Libya, Turkey	10%
High Income	$9,656 or more	53	Brunei, Japan, Slovenia, Greenland, Qatar	16%

SOURCE: Adapted from World Bank 1999.

these countries contain only 30 percent of the world's population. Africa, with some 13 percent of world population, has but 1 percent of the world's Internet users, with the overwhelming bulk of these in South Africa.[2]

The number of poor people in the world, furthermore, continues to grow. The income gap between rich and poor, already extreme, seems to be growing as well. World population rises by nearly 90 million people each year, which is an increase equal to the entire population of Mexico or Germany. Although birth rates are falling slowly across much of the world, enough people have already been born to ensure that population will continue to rise for at least the next half-century, possibly reaching 8–9 billion.

The overwhelming bulk of that increase is taking place in the poorer regions of the globe. In 1950, for example, sub-Saharan Africa's population was half Europe's. In 1985, it equaled Europe's, and by the year 2025, it will be three times Europe's.[3] By 2050, according to UN estimates, India will be the world's most populous country, with over 1.5 billion people, followed closely by China.

Population growth will occur primarily in cities. In the developing world, nearly one-third of the population is already urbanized, and this will increase to nearly two-thirds by 2025, when the world's urban population is projected to reach 5 billion. Ninety percent of that urban

TABLE 2.2   Quality-of-Life Indicators Compared: Africa and Asia

	Africa	East Asia
Children in Primary School	41.5%	59.5%
Literacy Rate	55%	82.7%
Life Expectancy at Birth	50.9 years	70.5 years

SOURCE: *New York Times,* June 6, 1996.

growth will be in developing countries.[4] In 1950, only New York and London, each with populations of 8 million or more, could be termed "megacities." By 2015, nine of the top ten megacities will be in the developing world.

DEVELOPMENT AS A GLOBAL PROJECT

Clearly, we live in a markedly unequal world, and by all accounts, the inequalities are getting worse. Although the human race has always known poverty, two things are different today: poverty today is highly visible and we now possess the means to bring it to an end, if we so choose.

Development is the word we use to describe the worldwide effort to eradicate poverty and its associated ills. Since the end of World War II, a veritable development industry has arisen, focused on improving life for billions of people around the world. Hundreds of thousands of people from all corners of the globe work in this industry, and enormous sums of money have been expended. As humanity's first global project, development is a test of our skill and commitment, and carries vast consequences for people everywhere.

But to succeed, development efforts must connect the diverse cultural worlds that we inhabit in ways that acknowledge the value of this diversity, at the same time generating results that are both sustainable and universally recognized as fair and satisfactory.

This is a very tall order. Pico Iyer has remarked: "Insofar as we aspire to be our brothers' keepers we have to acknowledge that we have five— soon eight—billion brothers, and that they are in Borneo and Bolivia and Benin. Insofar as we try to love our neighbors as ourselves, we have to admit that our neighbors are people with whom we share no common language, or past, or value."[5]

FIGURE 2.1   World Income Distribution

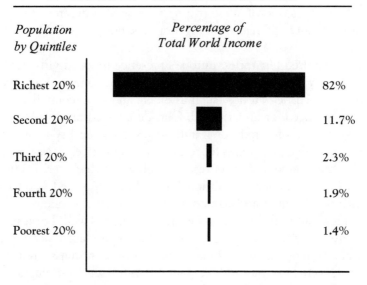

Population by Quintiles	Percentage of Total World Income	
Richest 20%		82%
Second 20%		11.7%
Third 20%		2.3%
Fourth 20%		1.9%
Poorest 20%		1.4%

SOURCE: Serageldin 1995: 114.

Successful development, as we shall see, requires people who plan and carry out development to learn a great deal about cultural worlds other than their own, and to use what they know intelligently. Until quite recently, the development industry has not really recognized this need to learn, but has concentrated instead on trying to impose an essentially ethnocentric view of progress on other countries, with highly variable results.

To understand why the development industry took shape the way it did, it is instructive to look briefly at its origins and past experience.

Antecedents

European empire-building transformed much of the non-Western world in ways that are still significant today. Spain reached the New World in 1492, and within fifty years, controlled territory from Mexico to Chile. Other European powers, including France, Holland, Portugal, and England, quickly followed suit. The discovery of the Americas and the opening up of Africa and Asia provided Europe with resources, which helped fuel further colonial growth and expansion. At the dawn of the twentieth century, Europe had established dominion over most of the globe. The imposition of Western rule took several different forms, but in nearly all cases, changes in indigenous societies were both rapid and drastic.

In the colonized territories, Europe's presence touched virtually every aspect of daily life for most people. Within local communities, the authority of established groups (such as elders and local councils) was replaced, challenged, or undermined. Outside administrators ruled alongside—or in place of—traditional authorities. New legal systems defined crimes, acceptable procedures for resolution, and the penalties for infractions. Rights to land and other resources changed character. Traditional forms of wealth and prestige, although not always displaced, had to compete with the demands and attractions of a wage-labor economy.

Social and cultural landscapes began to change as well. Local populations were counted, categorized, converted, or displaced, according to the circumstances. In some cases populations were massacred. Local boundaries were redefined and reorganized. In the schools brought by the Westerners, history was redefined and reinterpreted.

Western medicine saved many lives but led, in some areas, to population increases that put pressures on land, food, and other resources. Local practices offensive or foreign to colonial sensibilities, including cannibalism, infanticide, polygyny, and female circumcision, were banned or driven underground. Other practices such as bride price or initiation ceremonies were regulated. All of these changes had long- and short-term consequences for social and demographic patterns.

By the mid-twentieth century, the "developing world" had come into existence—poor, dependent, and for most of us, very far away.

Creating the Framework

World War II signaled the end of the age of empire, although the final breakup would take several decades more. By the time the war finally ended in late 1945, the economies of the colonial powers lay largely in ruins, several overseas dependencies were in active rebellion (with the near-certainty of more to follow), and a new and decidedly uneasy relationship was taking shape between the West and the Soviet Union.

Even before peace was concluded, the West recognized the need for a framework to meet the challenges of collective security and economic reconstruction, sure to dominate a postwar world. In July 1944, financial ministers from forty-four countries, led by the United States, met at a

fashionable resort in the mountains of New Hampshire to devise mechanisms for guiding postwar recovery and regulating economic relationships among states. The resulting Bretton Woods agreement created the
International Monetary Fund (IMF) and the International Bank for Reconstruction and Development (IBRD), better known as the World
Bank.

The Bretton Woods framework embodied and promoted an economic
approach to development in which rapid reconstruction and growth
were seen as essential to the establishment of national economic health.
The benefits of economic growth at the national level would be seen in
such gross indicators as higher export earnings, healthier balance of payment figures, and larger current accounts. These benefits, it was assumed,
would then filter down through the economy and be distributed across
groups and sectors. Political stability, greater democracy, and increased
participation would follow. First applied to war-torn Europe through the
Marshall Plan (see below), the Bretton Woods philosophy was soon extended to the emerging nations of the developing world.

By the mid-1950s, a new terminology had arisen to describe geopoliti-
cal arrangements. The poor countries of Africa, Asia, and Latin America, many of them colonies or former colonies, were now lumped together as the Third World. The term "Third World" (*tiers monde* in
French) is attributed to the French demographer Alfred Sauvy. First used
in 1952, it referred to countries belonging neither to the Western industrial democracies (the First World) nor to the centrally planned economies of the Soviet bloc (the Second World).

Third World countries varied enormously, but tended, on the whole,
to have a common profile: low per capita incomes, shorter life expectan-
cies, higher rates of infant mortality, and a higher population growth rate
than industrial countries. A high proportion of their population also
tended to work in agriculture. And as already noted, most Third World
countries had been former colonies, and were therefore equipped—or
saddled—with a range of Western-style institutions.

But in many respects, the term "Third World" has obscured more than
it has clarified. Third World countries were not and are not uniformly
poor, for a start. Their experiences with colonialism, thought by many to
be a fundamental common attribute, varied greatly. They also exhibited—and continue to exhibit—an enormous range of governments,
economies, and political ideologies.

In short, although it became fashionable during the 1960s and 1970s
to use the term to refer to a large group of countries that were neither

wealthy nor industrialized, neither wholly Western nor part of the Soviet bloc, the term provided little real insight into the nature of either poverty or development.

TODAY'S DEVELOPMENT INDUSTRY

Today, development is a multibillion-dollar industry comprising four main groups: multilateral agencies, bilateral agencies, nongovernment organizations, and private consulting firms.

Multilateral Agencies

Multilateral agencies are government organizations composed of two or more nations. Although development multilaterals do not, in principle, challenge or replace state sovereignty, they are active and powerful. Some multilaterals—such as the United Nations—are global in scope and membership. Others, like the Organization of American States, are regional or subregional.

Today, the bulk of the world's resources for development—money, ideas, information, and people—flow through a small number of multilaterals—in particular, the World Bank, the UN, and the various regional development banks.

The United Nations.   The UN is the world's most important multilateral development organization, with 90 percent of its resources devoted to the resolution of social and economic problems. Its operating budget has risen from $147 million in 1945, when it had fifty-one member states, to $1.3 billion dollars and 185 member states in 1995.[6]

Although the UN has many development-oriented agencies and groups under its broad umbrella, the most important is the United Nations Development Program (UNDP), founded in 1965. In each country, UNDP resident representatives coordinate technical assistance, funding, and relief efforts.

The World Bank and the IMF.   The World Bank and the IMF, although autonomous UN agencies themselves, deserve special mention. Each organization has its own charter and operates largely independently of other UN structures in terms of budgets, personnel regulations, and poli-

FIGURE 2.2   The World Bank Group

THE WORLD BANK GROUP

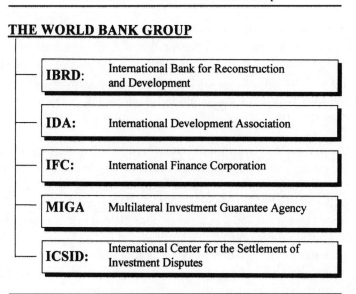

cies. In part because of this independence, these organizations have con-siderable power to influence other countries, and in many respects they resemble self-contained and sovereign states. Traditionally, the World Bank is headed by an American, the IMF by a European.

The IMF, with 184 members, is primarily a finance institution. It pro-vides temporary balance of payment assistance to countries and facili-tates currency conversion. It also provides a certain amount of technical assistance and collects information on financial matters. The World Bank, in contrast, is a development organization. It has 177 member countries and is comprised of five subagencies. Two of these, the IBRD and the International Development Association (IDA) (which makes loans to the poorest countries on concessional terms) constitute the largest single source of official funding for development. The World Bank also provides considerable technical assistance to countries.

As a result of its loans and technical assistance programs, the Bank possesses vast quantities of data on the countries it serves, together with a correspondingly high degree of influence on their development policies and practices. By the mid-1990s, the World Bank had over 7,000 staff members drawn from more than 130 countries. The United States sub-scribes about one-quarter of the Bank's total capital.

Bilateral Agencies

Almost all major industrial nations have one or more *bilateral agencies* involved in international development. Unlike multilaterals, which are composed of members from diverse nations, bilaterals represent the interests of one nation alone. For this reason, the policies of a bilateral agency usually reflect the particular political, social, or economic priorities of that country.[7]

USAID. The U.S. government has well over 100 agencies and departments with an international mandate, but its primary development agency is the United States Agency for International Development, commonly called USAID or simply AID. AID has existed in one form or other since the early 1950s, but has undergone a series of name changes and organizational reworkings. Today, it is part of the U.S. State Department. Like the UNDP, AID is made up of functional bureaus divided between administrative tasks and geographic regions. The regional bureaus are then linked to field missions in various countries.[8]

AID is accountable to the U.S. Congress, which in turn is influenced by a variety of interest groups, internal and external. Congress requires a great deal of accountability from AID, and it is said that the number of congressional reports required from AID is second only to that required from the CIA. Throughout its history, AID has had to contend with shifting political and economic priorities, and the agency is often expected to promote agendas that may have little to do with development directly.

One aspect of AID operation that is constant, however, is the need to move development money through the pipeline as quickly and smoothly as possible. Since AID runs on yearly congressional appropriations, and since there is perennial disagreement in Congress about the merits of foreign aid, it is in AID's interest to spend its money quickly, and in ways that can be presented as effective. In this effort, the agency faces a host of procedural problems stemming from its own labyrinth of regulations, which have grown, by accretion, over the years. It now takes several years to design and approve a new project or program.

AID's yearly budget appropriation typically consists of three main parts: *development assistance;* an *economic support fund* (which includes so-called "security assistance" for countries); and the *PL480 "Food for Peace"* program. Recent AID budgets appear in the table below.

TABLE 2.3   USAID Budgets FY 1997–FY 1999: Millions of Dollars

Major Categories	FY 1997	FY 1998	FY 1999 (requested)
Development Assistance			
Development Assistance	1,130	1,172	1,266
Child Survival and Disease Program	500	550	503
International Disaster Assistance	190	190	205
Credit Programs	12	11	14
Development Credit Authority	—	(8)	(15)
USAID Operating Expenses	518	508	517
Economics Support Fund			
Economic Support Fund	2,386	2,420	2,514
Eastern Europe	475	485	465
Newly Independent States	625	771	925
PL 480 (Food for Peace)	867	867	867
Total	6,703	6,974	7,276

SOURCE: USAID Fiscal Year 1999 Budget Request Summary: *www.info.usaid.gov.*

Overseas, an AID mission is part of a "country team" that includes representatives from the economic, political, and military offices in the embassy, as well as the Peace Corps, intelligence agencies, and so on. Each AID mission draws up a strategic development plan to guide programming decisions about how development aid will be used in that country. This, together with congressional guidelines, mandates, and requirements, forms the core of AID policy in each specific country, and is the basis on which programs, policies, and projects are crafted.

AID does not have sole authority for its programs, however, and its operations have always been heavily informed by diplomatic and security concerns. Although programming is done by AID, the coordination of AID programs with other overseas activities (military aid, for example) is done by the State Department, with review by the National Security Council. Should priorities conflict, diplomatic and security concerns usually prevail.

Nongovernment Organizations

Nongovernment organizations (or NGOs)—also known as nonprofits—are increasingly important as a source of ideas, funds, and technical assistance in development work.[9] Although the largest and most influential nonprofits are Western-based, increasing numbers of them are headquartered in the developing countries themselves. A number of universities, foundations, and think tanks also fall into the nonprofit, nongovernmental category.

There are several different types of NGOs. Some are traditional disaster relief or humanitarian agencies. Others specialize in various forms of technical assistance. Still others focus on education, community development, institution building, or policy formulation. They may have a particular character (for example, linguistic, political, cultural, religious) either in terms of their members and contributors, or in terms of the groups they target.[10]

NGOs proliferated throughout the 1970s and 1980s. Development-oriented NGOs registered in OECD (Organization for Economic Cooperation and Development) countries rose from 1,600 in 1980 to nearly 3,000 in 1996, but their actual number is probably much higher.[11]

Finance grew along with numbers. In the mid-1980s, NGOs spent between $3–4 billion yearly in the developing world, a figure double or triple what it had been in the 1970s. By the mid-1990s, the total had increased again: one estimate of OECD-registered NGOs put the annual expenditure for 1993 at nearly $6 billion.[12] World Vision, a faith-based NGO and the fourteenth largest fund-raising charity in the United States, raised over $200 million in donor support in 1993. Cooperative for American Relief to Everywhere (CARE) raised nearly $50 million in the same year, and Save the Children raised over $40 million.[13] Between 1990 and 1996, donations to major U.S. NGOs went up by an average of 36 percent.[14] Today, the twenty-five largest development NGOs probably channel 10 percent of all development aid money.[15]

NGOs raise the money they need in a variety of ways: through contributions, subscriptions, and grants. Increasingly, however, their funding is tied to budget allocations from the large multilateral and bilateral agencies, leading to worry about the degree of control that large agencies have over this supposedly independent sector within the development industry.

Private Consulting Firms

There are an enormous number of consulting firms in the United States alone that offer technical assistance services to the development industry.[16] AID, for example, does business with an estimated 3,500 consulting firms, and close to 80 percent of AID's grants and contract awards go directly to either consulting firms, individuals, or nonprofits.[17]

A group of these consulting firms, known as the "Beltway Bandits" because of their proximity to Washington, win the majority of contracts for U.S. agencies and for a substantial share of multilateral agency contracts. Mini-Case 2.1, "The Development Consulting Business," outlines how these firms operate.

Some consulting firms, in fact, have no other clients than the large development agencies. They offer a variety of services: architecture, engineering, regional and urban planning, education, health, agriculture, and so on. Outside the United States, every major industrialized country has a number of firms that also specialize in development work.

Development contracting is big business; in 1996, the top twenty-five development consulting firms in the United States were awarded over $2 billion in contracts.[18] Overall, the large development agencies award some $4 to 5 billion in contracts to firms and individual consultants each year. In addition to this, an estimated $30 billion in contracts are awarded by the countries that borrow aid funds from the large agencies.[19]

Integration Within the Industry

Although varied in size, purpose, and operation, the organizations that make up today's development industry are closely interconnected. These connections are of several different types.

One is through *funding*. As mentioned above, the smaller agencies, principally NGOs, often receive a substantial portion of their funding from the larger multilateral and bilateral agencies. Although some NGOs seek to remain relatively independent of the larger agencies, others have no problem with accepting funding from them. In most cases, of course, funding comes with a variety of attached strings.

Another important way in which the industry is interconnected is through the exchange of *personnel*. Development work is highly specialized, and it takes years to learn the ropes in most agencies. Sectoral ex-

---

MINI-CASE 2.1
THE DEVELOPMENT CONSULTING BUSINESS

Although some consulting firms provide specialized services to the development industry—such as mapping or data processing—other firms operate across the entire span of the project development cycle, from design and implementation to evaluation. Mickelwait's analysis of these firms would seem to place them in the category of a "mature" industry, whose products are increasingly undifferentiated, and where growth, profits, initiative, and innovation are low. Such firms fall into two main categories: those that focus on production activities, such as agriculture and small business development, and those that are centered on social services, such as health and education.

Micklewait traces the process whereby AID officials withdrew over time from hands-on contact with projects in favor of hired contractors. Although the number of firms offering contracting services to USAID grew, so did the competition, as well as the complexity of preparation and bidding procedures. Larger firms tend to dominate this market; smaller firms seek to form consortia or to enter into subcontracts with larger firms.

Because AID's needs are so specialized and its procedures are so unique and complex, firms have developed profiles and capabilities that tie them increasingly to this highly specific funding source: "Winning an AID contract requires that a firm produce support units, ranging from accounting and contract management to recruitment and overseas logistic support, whose staff is knowledgeable about AID regulations and is experienced in complying with them." In a mature industry, price tends to emerge as the market determinant:

(continues)

---

pertise, language ability, and cross-cultural experience are not acquired or developed overnight, and agencies tend to hire from within the industry itself when possible. Managers and technicians move from one agency to another, particularly in the NGO sector. In part, this is owing to the often short-term nature of development contracting, which makes it necessary to seek new assignments every few years, as projects are completed and move off line. Within the larger agencies, where there is a clear long-term career track, there is less turnover, but it is possible for an AID employee with twenty years of service, for example, to retire in his or her forties, and then to work as a consultant for other development agencies, either full- or part-time.

MINI-CASE 2.1 (continued)

Even in a mature industry, successful firms attempt to distinguish their product by claims to unique skills, successful corporate experience, sound financial controls, efficient project management, and corporate integrity. But AID often ignores these distinctions. It has always had an underdeveloped capacity to judge the competence of consulting firms, as evidenced by contract ranking systems, which rarely capture knowledge of past performance on similar contracts. Successful firms cling to the belief that doing the job correctly will pay off over the long term, but the sad truth is that there is generally little connection in any one competitive contest between corporate integrity, good will based upon past performance, and contract award.

The end result of the current system is that fewer firms have either the skills or the inclination to compete for AID contracts; those that do must either establish themselves as uniquely qualified in some respect or must price their services competitively—sometimes below break-even points. Although this may be good business for the federal government, it does little to build AID's understanding of how projects actually operate in the field, discourages innovation and risk-taking in development approaches, and focuses attention instead on the process and procedures associated with preparing proposals and winning bids.

SOURCE: Mickelwait, nd.

The development industry is also linked through the exchange of *information*. The major multilateral and bilateral agencies all maintain large databases and publish numerous reports and summaries. The World Bank, for example, has its own bookstore, and an impressive backlist of titles on virtually every aspect of development. Data from development agencies are now widely available on CD-ROMs and web sites as well. Agencies exchange much of their data on a regular basis, although the details of, say, World Bank negotiations and internal reports are usually not publicly released. Agencies also participate in many conferences, symposia, and training workshops, where people from different organizations meet each other and exchange information.

Finally, agencies *collaborate* with each other on specific projects. It is not unusual for two or more agencies to work together to plan and carry out a project. Smaller firms and NGOs will also join with each other in consortia to bid on and manage development projects for larger agencies. In some cases, agencies share responsibilities for the entire project; in others, agencies agree to work separately on different aspects of the project.

In one urban development project with which I was involved in Tunisia, for example, the World Bank funded the physical upgrading of the area, including roads, drainage, water, and electricity. AID funded the social and economic infrastructure, including loans to small businesses, vocational training, health education, and literacy. In turn, both larger agencies hired several consulting firms in the United States and elsewhere to work on specific aspects of the overall project.

Thus, although the development industry is composed of some quite different types of organizations, there is an overall sense in which they are all part, in one way or another, of a common enterprise with a remarkably uniform approach to development planning and implementation. Although some smaller NGOs have begun to develop more independent strategies in recent years, the vast bulk of development funding and other vital resources (personnel, information, and experience) is still tied to larger agencies and their partners. It is therefore worth looking in some detail at how development itself has developed in the decades since the end of World War II.

THE EVOLUTION OF DEVELOPMENT POLICY AND PRACTICE

To understand how the development industry grew and evolved and how it has attempted to address problems of world poverty, we need to begin with the underlying assumptions that characterized the early years and that played a crucial and determinant role in shaping what development was to become.

Framing Concepts

The structures put in place by Bretton Woods were originally intended to rebuild Europe, and in the process, to promote a framework, essentially economic, within which nations could operate with some degree of certainty and security. For a variety of reasons—including its initial success in Europe and the certainty it promised—economics came, very early on, to dominate development thinking.[20] Dealing with underdevelopment was seen as a technical problem, essentially one of making poor countries more like rich ones, and economics seemed to promise quick and clear solutions.

Classical Western economic theory explains underdevelopment simply and cleanly: low incomes produce low rates of saving; low rates of saving result in low rates of investment; and low rates of investment discourage growth in production, jobs, and—ultimately—income. Early development thinking therefore centered on the use of capital: where to put it and how to use it.

Development capital, furthermore, needed to come from outside— hence the term "foreign aid." The technology financed by the capital would also be external, in most cases. And the management systems used to raise production would, in turn, be derived from the successful models of the West.[21]

The problem of development thus came to be seen primarily as one of how to stimulate rapid, large-scale, and sustained economic growth. It was assumed that such growth would benefit the nation as a whole, that these benefits would be distributed in some relatively rational and equal fashion, and that this distribution would promote the general welfare. Planners hoped for some form of "takeoff" in which investment increases, manufacturing sectors grow and prosper, and supporting national institutions arise to sustain further growth.[22]

Although experts argued over whether balanced growth (spread over a range of sectors) or unbalanced growth (financing a few strategic sectors) was most effective, few questioned the axiom that increase was the goal. Keeping track of development results, logically enough, meant looking at key growth indicators, chief among which were measures of national output such as GNP.

What might be termed a *technicist* approach therefore guided development thinking from the outset. The *ends* sought were primarily material, *strategy* was derived from Western economic theory, and the *means* consisted of Western capital combined with Western technology and knowhow. Progress, of course, would be measured in economic terms, and industrialized societies would be the model to which weaker economies should aspire. Development, in this view, was essentially a unilineal evolutionary process that could be accelerated through the adoption of Western technology, models, and methods. The end point of the process would result in societies that, although perhaps outwardly different in terms of national dress, cuisine, or language, would operate and think largely along Western lines.

The implications of the technicist paradigm for development had a number of very important consequences. For one thing, it established Western industrial nations as the template or standard in planning and conceptualizing. Second, it tended to lump every other society into a residual category of "less developed," thus ignoring the range of differences existing between them, the specifics of their internal processes, and their particular problems or concerns. Most significantly, the technicist approach relegated social and cultural factors to the background, in many cases omitting them altogether from consideration. They were messy, too diverse, and essentially distracting. Culture, to many development theorists, simply did not matter.[23]

Finally, it was assumed that helping countries to develop would be a relatively simple matter. Western countries would provide finance, technology, and advice that the governments of the poorer countries would readily embrace, as countries in Europe had embraced the Marshall Plan. Within a few short years—certainly within a generation—we would, it was hoped, see takeoff.

The Impact of the Cold War

If economics was instrumental in shaping development thinking, politics played an equally important role, given the growing tensions between the West and the Soviet bloc. Although Cold War concerns helped shape virtually every Western country's development policies, this was particularly true in the United States.

Development assistance quickly came to be seen as a way for the United States to counter Soviet threats—real or perceived—in the newly emerging nations of the world. These nations, short on cash and trained manpower, readily accepted foreign assistance from both sides, and quickly learned to bargain for aid within the framework of superpower rivalry. Within a few years, *security assistance* had become an important subcategory of development aid.

Superpower rivalry helped explain why so much American aid in the 1950s and 1960s went to countries like Taiwan, South Korea, the Philippines, South Vietnam, Egypt, and Israel. In each case, aid was intended to counter the threat of communism, either within the recipient country itself (as in the case of the Philippines or South Vietnam) or in the region (as in the case of Israel or Taiwan). Development aid in the United States quickly became linked with America's broader diplomatic, military, and strategic interests.

The Packaging of Development Aid

A set of basic aid structures and procedures soon emerged to guide the way development would be done. Development agencies crafted *policies* to guide funding decisions and *programs* for various countries, embodying these policy guidelines. The programs were then implemented at the grassroots level through individual *projects*.

The project approach quickly became the preferred method for delivering development assistance, whether in the form of money, equipment, or technical expertise. Projects were designed primarily by donors or by donor-paid contractors, and managed, for the most part, by expatriates who were also paid by donors. Project funding took place either through *loans* carrying various rates of interest, or through *grants*, which did not normally have to be repaid.[24]

Projects focused on specific *development sectors*—some aspect of national life seen as important for development. Transportation, education, manufacturing, agriculture, or health are all examples of development sectors. Projects typically were designed in terms of one or more guiding *development approaches* that determined how the project was actually done. A project in the agricultural sector, for example, might adopt an approach that focused on women farmers and used low-level technology. Another agricultural project, however, might emphasize mechanization and cash-crop production. The development industry has tried a variety of approaches over the years.

Most development aid came with strings attached. This was termed *conditionality*, and could be of several different types. One was simple quid pro quo—if we do something for you, then you should do something for us (like staying away from the Russians). Another was *tied aid*; money that could only be used for very specific purposes. Many countries, for example, have traditionally tied their bilateral aid to commodity purchases, transportation on national carriers, and hiring their own technical experts. A third form of conditionality (discussed in more detail below) involved policy reform and structural adjustment. Whatever the mechanisms, development agencies retained a large measure of control over what was done with their funding, right down to decisions made at the field level.

Driven by economics and Cold War politics, and using a project-centered approach linked to various forms of conditionality, development policy and practice has gone through a series of four important transformations in the past fifty years, and is now in the midst of a fifth. Each of these will be briefly discussed below.

Postwar Reconstruction:
Early Success in Europe (1945–1955)

The initial phase of development activity focused on rebuilding postwar Europe. Spearheaded by the United States, the Marshall Plan (1949–1952) was intended to help war-damaged countries get their economies going again. The success of the plan—designed in part to forestall a Communist takeover in Europe—seemed to demonstrate that national economic growth could be stimulated quickly and relatively simply through the infusion of large amounts of money. This success explained in part the optimism with which the West then later approached the task of promoting development among the emerging nations of the world. It also gave credibility to the notion that aid could be used as an effective barrier against the growth of Soviet influence.

By 1948, the World Bank was making loans to Latin American countries.[25] A year later, in his inaugural address, President Truman urged the Americans to "embark on a bold new program for making the benefits of our scientific advances and industrial progress available for the improvement and growth of underdeveloped areas." This proposal, which came to be known as Point Four, was America's first coordinated attempt to provide aid to underdeveloped countries. Point Four concentrated primarily on the provision of technical assistance for large infrastructure projects, mainly in East Asia. The Act for International Development, which in 1950 authorized the Point Four program, also created the Technical Cooperation Administration, AID's precursor.

By the start of the 1950s, therefore, essential bureaucratic structures and policies were emerging. Finance was flowing, and the emerging nations of the world, anxious to raise living standards, were willing to join in partnership with the West to achieve economic growth and prosperity. "Development" as a global project had been launched.

Tech-Fix: The Growth of the
Development Industry (1955–1970)

From this point on, the development industry grew quickly. In the United States, the Mutual Security Act (1953–1961) and its successor, the Foreign Assistance Act (1962–1972) provided the mandate and the means to move ahead. The U.S. Agricultural Trade Development and Assistance Act of 1954 (usually known as PL480) created the Food for Peace program. And in the early 1960s, the Peace Corps came into being.

The United States was the clear leader during this early phase of development. Emerging from World War II with an intact industrial base but alarmed at growing Soviet power, the United States saw alliances with the emerging nations of the world as essential for its own continued growth and security. Most influential development theoreticians of the day linked the fate of the United States, Europe, and Japan to that of the less-developed world.[26]

Development efforts focused on macro-economic planning designed to boost aggregate production in key sectors. Donors favored large projects in infrastructure and technology, designed to promote industrialization, transportation, and large-scale agriculture. Western-style education was also a priority, so in addition to airports, harbors, and highways, money also went into schools.

Much of this was enthusiastically welcomed by Third World nations that, for the most part, had little money, minimal infrastructure, and few trained specialists of their own. Centralized state planning was something most of them were already used to, and foreign aid allowed them to strengthen the center and extend control over groups within the country. Regions, villages, and populations that accepted state power would receive access to development resources, in much the same way that the new nations themselves, by playing the Cold War game, could gain resources from the West.

The approach that characterized this period of development was, for all its faults, confident, optimistic, and forward-looking. The people of Europe and the United States, exhausted after a century with two world wars, a depression, and the rise of the Soviet Union, were attracted to the notion of a modern-day crusade where the West could once again lead the world. In reality, of course, the development effort was quickly enlisted into the service of the budding Cold War, and foreign aid became a reward for states that chose our side.[27]

Money and technology, it was assumed, could solve the problems of the developing world, particularly if they were coupled with Western management models. The development problem was essentially one of smooth and efficient transfer, and once this transfer had been accomplished, the job would be done. AID, indeed, was set up as a temporary agency, to be disbanded when the task was completed.

Development efforts were bankrolled, led, and controlled by multilateral and bilateral agencies headquartered in the West. Local resources, almost by definition, were seen as inadequate or inappropriate to the tasks at hand. Development was also seen, of course, as a way for the West to challenge the Soviet bloc, by providing more money, more machinery, and faster results. Within the technicist model for development that drove planning, local knowledge, customs, and traditions were seen mainly as obstacles to change.

Only a few people in the development industry questioned the rightness of this approach. Mini-Case 2.2, "The Ugly American and His Transformation," presents one famous case of disagreement.

New Directions: The Limitations of Donor Aid (1970–1980)

By the early 1970s, however, development planners had become less optimistic. Problems with the original approach to development had appeared, starting with the fact that it didn't seem to be working very well in many countries. Despite heavy investments in infrastructure and technology, some economies were simply not taking off in the ways predicted by the models. In other cases, growth was occurring, but the benefits of growth were somehow not finding their way into all corners of the economy.

With Robert McNamara's appointment to World Bank leadership in 1968, a greater concern for equity issues in development work began to appear, together with more of a focus on the needs of the very poor.[28] Within AID, a similar shift in thinking was taking place. The U.S. Foreign Assistance Act of 1973 contained a *New Directions* mandate, aimed at providing people with a minimum level of basic human needs—food, shelter, jobs, medical care, clean water, and so forth. By focusing more on poverty and deprivation, planners hoped to create conditions for economic growth, at the same time promoting the idea of equity in terms of the distribution of growth's benefits.

The types of projects and programs funded by the large agencies now changed. Although some large infrastructure projects continued to be financed, much greater emphasis went to projects that focused on poverty alleviation, job creation, small farmer agriculture, capacity building with local organizations, and so on.

Indeed, the 1970s was a decade of innovative approaches to grassroots development. The notion of *integrated rural development* (or what would now be called regional planning) was tried. Decentralization of services and of decisionmaking was a feature of many projects. Community participation in planning and implementation became watchwords. There

MINI-CASE 2.2
THE UGLY AMERICAN AND HIS TRANSFORMATION

In 1958, William Lederer and Eugene Burdick wrote a book about what was then happening in Southeast Asia. They called it *The Ugly American*. A polemic, the book's targets were the U.S. "country team" members fielded by our government: diplomats, military attachés, economic and political experts, and technicians. The book savagely criticized U.S. officials for their ignorance, their arrogance, and their lack of professionalism. Although much of the book was a thinly disguised call to arms in the fight against creeping communism, much of it also dealt directly with issues of local-level development.

Everyone in the book—a loosely structured narrative set in Vietnam, Cambodia, and the mythical kingdom of Sarkhan—seems larger than life, either a hero or a villain. Ambassador MacWhite, Joe Bing, Colonel Hillendale, Tex Wolchek, and others exist as stereotypes in a development morality play, unfolding against the backdrop of the impending Vietnam War.

Homer Atkins, the Ugly American, does not make an appearance until chapter 17, but his character clearly serves as a leitmotif for much of the book. Homer is a gruff and plainspoken engineer from Pittsburgh, and he is not a handsome man: "His hands were laced with prominent veins and spotted with big, liverish freckles. His fingernails were black with grease. His fingers bore tiny nicks and scars of a lifetime of practical engineering. The palms of his hands were calloused."

Clearly, Homer doesn't fit in. Here he is at a meeting with embassy officials, explaining to them why their ideas for foreign aid are all wrong: "Atkins was aware of the fact that he was the only man in the room not wearing a tie. In fact, he was wearing a rough khaki shirt, khaki pants, and old Marine field boots. He still had the smell of the jungle about him; the other men, Vietnamese, French, or American, all smelled of aftershave lotion."

Homer and his wife—who is as ugly as he is—live in a small cottage in a suburb of Haidho, the Sarkhanese capital. "They were the only Caucasians in the community. Their house had pressed earth floors, one spigot of cold water, a charcoal fire, two very comfortable hammocks, a horde of small, harmless insects, and a small, dark-eyed Sarkhanese boy about nine years old who apparently came with the house." Homer's wife learns to cook local food, and Homer learns to operate in the local environment. Both of

(continues)

MINI-CASE 2.2   (continued)

them learn to speak the local language. Homer's obsession is a hand-powered water pump to irrigate the local rice paddies. He's insistent, however, that the solution be a local one: "Now look, dammit, I've explained to you before," Atkins said. "It's got to be something they use out here. It's no good if I go spending a hundred thousand dollars bringing in something. It has to be something right here, something the natives understand. . . . Whenever you give a man something for nothing the first person he comes to dislike is you. If the pump is going to work at all, it has to be their pump, not mine."

Atkins spends time talking to the locals, trying to understand the context in which the pump will be used. "He talked to the headman, a venerable man of seventy-five, without an interpreter. It was not easy, but he could tell that the headman was pleased that Atkins was making the effort to talk the language. With infinite courtesy, the old man sensed what words Atkins was searching for, and politely supplied them."

Eventually, Homer Atkins meets Jeepo, a local mechanic. Together, they tackle the problem of the pump. Finally, by pooling their skill and knowledge, they find a workable solution. The pumps are wildly successful. At about this point, a "technical adviser" from the U.S. embassy shows up.

[He] called at the warehouse and watched quietly for several hours. The next day the counselor of the Embassy called. Taking Atkins to one side, he pointed out to him that for white men to work with their hands, and especially in the countryside, lowered the reputation of all white men. He appealed to Atkins' pride to give up this project. Moreover, he pointed out that the French, most experienced of colonizers, had never allowed natives to handle machinery. Atkins' reply was brief, but it was pointed, and the counselor drove away in anger. Atkins returned joyfully to his work in the warehouse.

(continues)

was more concern with women's issues in development and a greater emphasis on the environment in all aspects of planning.

Although many people in the development community welcomed the changes in emphasis, there was also some concern within the large agencies that they were moving away from the technical and financial issues that they knew best and into largely uncharted waters where they had little direct expertise.[29] The idea of working directly with the poor, after

---

MINI-CASE 2.2 (continued)

Later, Mrs. Atkins, using an approach similar to her husband's, introduces long-handled brooms to her Sarkhanese women neighbors.

Although the story of the Ugly American and his wife occupy only three chapters of the book, these are almost the only foreigners portrayed in a positive light. In their epilogue to the book, Lederer and Burdick draw attention to people like Atkins, who ". . . speaking the language, [are] able to go off into the countryside and show the idea of America to the people. These characters are based on actual Americans known to the authors. There are others like them; but by and large they are not beloved of the American officials in the various Asian capitals, and are a wild exception to the rule."

They conclude their book this way: "We do not need the horde of 1,500,000 Americans—mostly amateurs—who are now working for the United States overseas. What we need is a small force of well-trained, well-chosen, hard-working, and dedicated professionals. They must be willing to risk their comforts, and—in some lands—their health. . . . They must speak the language of the land of their assignment, and they must be more expert in its problems than are the natives."

This angry and uneven book caused a stir when it was published. Reread today, its descriptions reflect—in an eerie fashion—some contemporary development situations. But the Ugly American, alas, has today been transformed from a hero into a villain. The public has forgotten the gruff engineer who spoke the language, respected the village people, and worked side by side with them to find local solutions to their problems. Today, the label of "Ugly American" refers to an overweight and boorish tourist who flaunts both his affluence and his lack of cross-cultural sensitivity. It is a strange and sad legacy indeed for a book which had, years ago, a very different purpose.

SOURCE: Lederer and Burdick 1958.

---

all, required development specialists to actually know something about them.

At the same time, however, the agencies were becoming increasingly bureaucratized. Reviews, approvals, appropriations, and reporting—all of these had now become much more complex and time-consuming. Agencies began to hire more outside contractors and consultants to actually design and carry out projects in the field, while their own staff remained

in the office, taking care of the necessary paperwork. These two seemingly contradictory trends—a concern for the grass roots coupled with an
increase in bureaucracy—opened up major opportunities for anthropologists interested in development work.

The Debt Crisis and Policy-Based Lending
(1980–2000)

By the 1980s, however, more problems had appeared, centering on Third
World debt. Although the World Bank's IDA, set up in the early 1960s
to serve the poorest countries, had provided up to a quarter of Bank financing on concessional terms throughout the 1960s and 1970s, most
development lending was at market or near-market rates. And much of
it, as time went on, was not being repaid. Borrowing had always been the
cornerstone of development aid, but the debt levels of many poor countries now posed a major threat to the system.

  Overoptimistic lending by multilateral agencies was one trigger for the
debt crisis; the oil price shocks of the 1970s were another. Awash in
money, OPEC (Organization of Petroleum Exporting Countries) countries transferred large sums to Western banks. These banks, in turn,
needed to put the money to work. They did this, in part, by lending
money for doubtful projects to countries whose ability and willingness to
repay them was often equally doubtful. By 1982, when Mexico, Argentina, and Brazil defaulted on their loans, the debt crisis had officially
arrived.[30]

  In 1970 Third World countries spent approximately ten cents of every
dollar earned from exports on debt repayment. By 1986, this had doubled. In that year, Third World debt amounted to about $1 trillion.
There was now more money coming to the West in debt repayments
than there was going to the Third World in loans and investments.[31]

  Debt was not the only problem with the development business, however. Donor fatigue—a combination of cynicism, weariness, and a lack of
new ideas—was mounting in some quarters, as continued aid efforts produced few dramatic—or even visible—results. Poverty alleviation on any
significant scale was proving to be very difficult, and in many countries
whatever gains had been made were swallowed up by rising levels of debt
and continuing population growth. In the United States, President
Ronald Reagan's administration changed the official mood in Washington in favor of market forces and altogether less intervention by govern-

ment. The stage was now set for yet another reconceptualization of development policy.

It arrived in the form of *structural adjustment*. Structural adjustment, also known as policy-based lending, supported the new trend in development thinking toward privatization, private enterprise, and market reform.[32] Mini-Case 2.3 outlines the essentials of structural adjustment.

Structural adjustment did not sweep away other development concerns, however. Projects still continued to be the vehicle through which most development assistance was delivered. Previous development priorities, including rural development, the environment, and women, still continued to command both attention and resources. To these was added a new concern with urban development.

In these and other areas, more attention was being paid to issues of management and policy, giving rise to a new term in the development lexicon: *governance*, referring to the manner in which power was used internally to manage a country's resources for development purposes.[33]

In some countries, it had quickly became clear that structural adjustment alone would not transform the economy, as long as decisions were being made in the same ways as before. Governance was seen as the key to creating the long-term stability necessary to nurture and sustain economic turnaround.

Governance projects, beginning in the 1980s and extending into the 1990s, emphasized public-sector accountability, the decentralization and deconcentration of government, election reform and the creation of political parties, the encouragement of a free press, more open policies on information, the encouragement of private voluntary organizations, and legal reform, including alternative dispute resolution. Although agencies maintained that the governance agenda was nonpolitical, the approach clearly favored openness, participation, lessened state power, and an altogether more laissez-faire economy.

Mini-Case 2.4, "Means and Ends in Development Policy," summaries the various shifts and changes that took place in the development industry from the end of World War II to the present.

The 1990s posed challenges to the development industry on a number of fronts, bringing both opportunities and further problems.

The breakup of the Soviet Union opened dozens of countries to the West, and hundreds of millions of people—many of them very poor—were added to the ranks of the developing world. Aid agencies in the West scrambled to provide programs and projects in places where few of them had ever worked before. At the same time, the end of the Cold

---

MINI-CASE 2.3
WHAT IS STRUCTURAL ADJUSTMENT?

Structural and sectoral adjustment loans are aimed at helping countries re-vamp their economic policies and structures to redress balance of pay-ments problems. Their purpose, in effect, is to change the structure of a na-tion's economy, balance the books, and thereby free up resources internally that can be used for development. Structural adjustment lending began at the World Bank and the IMF in the 1980s. Under A. W. Clausen, McNa-mara's successor, adjustment lending increased significantly, up from 9 per-cent of the bank portfolio in 1983 to 23 percent by 1987.

Structural adjustment, also termed policy-based lending, has the effect of drawing recipient countries closer into the global economy and reori-enting their internal economic policies so they are more compatible with the needs and goals of this global economy.

Structural adjustment's message was quite simple: Governments should spend within their means, abolish most if not all subsidies, let businesses operate freely, close inefficient state operations, let prices rise to market levels, and keep exchange rates realistic.

Such loans proved popular with large agencies, in part because their de-sign requirements were relatively straightforward (that is, not linked to a specific local sociocultural context), and because they allowed agencies to move large amounts of money quickly. From 1980 to 1992, over seventy countries were subject to the structural adjustment measures prescribed by the World Bank and the IMF.

(continues)

War also meant the disappearance of superpower rivalry as a major com-ponent of development strategy.

Despite some successes with structural adjustment, debt problems con-tinued to plague many countries. In 1996, the World Bank identified some forty nations as "heavily indebted poor countries" with "unsustain-able" debt. Most of these countries were in Africa, where debt service was having a major impact on national budgets.

Tanzania, for example, has a literacy rate of only 50 percent, but spends a third of its national budget on debt repayment, and four times more on debt than on primary education. Niger, where life expectancy is less than fifty years, spends more on debt repayment than on health and education combined.[34]

Even for hard-liners within the development industry, the implica-tions of such debt levels were starting to sink in. By the end of the 1990s,

---

MINI-CASE 2.3 (continued)

Policy-based lending is quite simple in concept: In exchange for cash transfers into a country's central treasury, the recipient government agrees to make fairly significant changes in its economy, its administration, and the way it does things. Whereas a *project loan* may release funding for specific costs associated with a specific undertaking, and a *sector loan* may do the same for a linked series of projects of the same general type, a *structural adjustment loan* is contingent on nationwide (or perhaps sectorwide) changes in things like interest rates, exchange rates, or tariffs. The money is not used to pay for project expenses, but usually pays for imports. It is therefore quite different from other forms of development assistance.

Structural and sectoral adjustment loans began to be used increasingly to channel development finance and technical assistance and to leverage an agency's influence with the recipient country. Policy-based lending—although in principle tailored to each individual country's specific circumstances—tended to promote a remarkably uniform set of prescriptions, including austerity measures (for example, reduction in the civil service, curbs on government spending); the privatization and deregulation of state-run enterprises; trade liberalization; changes in monetary policy (such as devaluation and credit reform); and the decentralization of administration.

SOURCES: Hellinger et al. 1988: 147; McMichael 1996: 132; Staudt 1991: 164–165.

---

calls for debt forgiveness—hitherto considered treason within the development industry—were being heard with increasing frequency.

Despite the debt issue (and in part because of it), pressures for internal reform in developing countries continued to come from donors. Reforms emphasized privatization, the role of open and free markets, and the encouragement of the institutions of a "civil society"—for example, a free press, stock markets, access to information, and local participation.

In many countries, such changes were welcomed, but not in all. The West's insistence that growth and prosperity could be achieved only through democratic institutions and practices, hitherto accepted as axiomatic, was now starting to be challenged by the obvious success of states like Singapore and Malaysia—and more recently, China. In these places, government, although still controlling many aspects of life, was also delivering record levels of growth and steadily increasing prosperity.

MINI-CASE 2.4
MEANS AND ENDS IN DEVELOPMENT POLICY

Although there appears to have been little in the way of progress in development thinking across five decades, policy shifts and changes have not been altogether chaotic. Four major goals or ends have tended to characterize most of the policies adopted by major agencies, and within these broad groups, specific types of programs, or means, have been adopted by the same agencies in an attempt to translate policies into action.

The four major goals include:

- Growth in the national and regional economy, as measured by broad indicators such as GDP
    - Management of activities designed to promote development, on the regional and national levels
    - Equity, referring to the distribution of development benefits
- Participation, meaning the involvement of diverse groups of people in development decisions.

The various approaches or strategies that have formed the basis for particular development programs can then be located within the matrix.

Approaches that characterized the early years of development included an emphasis on centralized state planning, capital investment, and industrialization. These strategies favored economic growth and management.

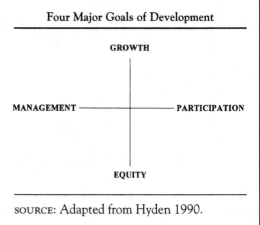

Four Major Goals of Development

GROWTH

MANAGEMENT ———————— PARTICIPATION

EQUITY

SOURCE: Adapted from Hyden 1990.

(continues)

MINI-CASE 2.4 (continued)

Development Strategies

SOURCE: Adapted from Hyden 1990.

Later on, development strategies shifted from growth per se into a pre-occupation with the equitable distribution of development benefits. Emphases now included decentralization of planning and integration of planning efforts in rural areas. Development efforts centered on the provision or enhancement of needs such as food, shelter, and basic services (health, education, and so forth) in an effort to create preconditions for growth.

Later, keeping the emphasis on equity, planning approaches began to pay more attention to issues of participation in development planning. Such approaches included attempts to use intermediate technology in development planning, building local capacity for planning, implementation and assessment of development, and the encouragement of nongovernment organizations (NGOs) as partners in the development effort.

Finally, development policy began to shift back toward a concern with macro-level growth issues, this time through programs centered on governance, structural adjustment, and attempts to create (or re-create) viable national institutions.

SOURCE: Adapted from Hyden 1990; Serageldin 1995: 64.

These emerging Asian success stories challenged the development orthodoxy of the large agencies, but they were by no means the only challenge that appeared in the 1990s. Although there had always been criticism of the development industry and its development models, this had been confined, for the most part, to the academy, or embodied in various peripheral movements with little or no real impact on policy and practice.[35]

Now, however, this changed; attacks began to come from mainstream groups within industrialized Western countries themselves. For some critics on the left, development was simply another form of exploitation of the poor and weak by the rich and powerful—as effective as colonialism, but cheaper. Others, more to the right, saw foreign aid as little more than a form of international welfare at best, or at worst, outright bribery—the poor people of the rich countries helping the rich people of the poor countries. Still others, simply weary of seeing pictures of starving children and miserable refugees on the television each night, felt that little could be done.

The most telling attacks, however, came from unlikely coalitions of workers, businesspeople, environmentalists, and ordinary citizens, all of whom sensed that problems of world poverty and inequality were linked to their own political and economic futures. Their concerns, though diverse, were nonetheless highly coherent, centering around environmental degradation, population pressure, famine, regional insecurity, and disappearing jobs, declining wages, or both.[36]

The conditions under which running shoes or children's clothes were produced in far-off countries, as only one example, triggered demonstrations and boycotts in local shopping malls in the United States, Canada, and Europe. Protesters saw a marked lack of progress in solving the world's problems, and had concluded that the policies of the development industry were at least partly to blame. The 1994 "Fifty Years Is Enough" campaign in the United States drew public attention to the World Bank to a degree hitherto unknown, and the World Trade Organization (WTO) protests in Seattle in 1999 focused that attention even more sharply on how multilateral institutions work.

Insightful observers drew attention to the relative poverty of thinking within the development industry, pointing out that in past decades, funding had flowed mainly into easy options—areas that development specialists felt comfortable and familiar with—and that little effort had been made to develop new insights into the nature of Third World poverty, the better to attack it. Such critics noted that although lip service was often given to the particularities of each country's situation, development agencies appeared to treat all developing nations in much the same way. Structural adjustment programs, in particular, were singled out as "cookie-cutter" blueprints, imposed by large agencies with little regard for local circumstances. Ironically, however, *within* each country one would often find a bewildering array of donor agencies, each jockeying for position and influence, each with its own specific set of procedures, requirements, and goals.

As the 1990s drew to a close, it was clear that the paradigm that had guided development policy and practice for decades was in need of a substantial overhaul. Although considerable progress had been made in some countries, the role of development assistance in promoting that progress was by no means clear. Even in areas where development efforts had clearly made a difference in certain sectors, regions, or communities, there was scant evidence of any overall impact on the ominous and growing gap between rich and poor, both within countries themselves and across the regions of the globe in general.

SUMMARY OF CHAPTER 2

This chapter has provided a broad overview of the international development industry and how it operates in response to global problems of poverty.

I began with the emergence of the developing world after the Second World War, and the creation, at the same time, of a new economic framework by Western nations to promote reconstruction and promote regional security; a framework that formed the basis for the development industry.

I then looked at the constituent parts of this industry: multilateral and bilateral agencies, together with a growing number of nongovernment organizations of several kinds. Multilateral agencies dominate development work, although all parts of the development industry are closely connected through finance, personnel, information, and collaboration on a variety of projects.

Several sections were devoted to looking at changes in development policies over the past fifty years. These have undergone several major transformations, from a concern with large-scale infrastructure investment designed to promote rapid economic through a series of attempts to promote equity and participation in development to attempts in the 1980s and 1990s to reshape national economies through programs of governance and structural adjustment. Until quite recently, these policies were heavily influenced by Cold War rivalries.

At the end of the twentieth century, as the development industry continued to search for more effective ways to fight poverty and promote equitable development, dissatisfaction with the results of five decades of effort began to grow. As the world entered the new millennium, it was clear to many people that the time had come for a new development paradigm.

ENDNOTES

1. See *New York Times*, March 17, 1996; *The Economist*, September 25, 1993.

2. Eade (1997: 161); *New York Times*, July 8, 1999: D8.

3. Serageldin (1995: 9–10).

4. See, for example, *New York Times*, June 6, 1996; *The Economist*, October 7, 1995: 120; *The Economist* 21, March 1998.

5. Pico Iyer (1994).

6. See Yoder (1988); *New York Times*, October 22, 1995: 8.

7. See Tendler (1975) and Hoben (1980) on USAID, Bruneau et al.(1978) on Canada's CIDA, and Conlin (1985) on Britain's Overseas Development Administration.

8. Porter (1990) provides a case study of AID, outlining the history of AID policy.

9. Gorman (1984) provides an overview of NGO involvement in development efforts. Paul and Israel (1991) focus on NGO involvement with the World Bank.

10. See Staudt (1991: 184).

11. See Gardner and Lewis (1996: 107); Smillie (1995: 2); Hackenberg and Hackenberg (1999: 6); Lewis (1988); Feeney (1998: 25).

12. Gardner and Lewis (1996: 107); Hellinger et al. (1988: 100); Brodhead (1987: 1).

13. Smillie (1995: 117).

14. Smillie and Helmich (1998: 25).

15. Feeney (1998: 25).

16. See Bodley (1994: 339); Micklewait (nd).

17. USAID (1998: 2).

18. Berrios (2000: 46–47).

19. *New York Times*, May 25, 1996.

20. The precise way in which economics managed to capture the development enterprise has not, to my knowledge, ever been explicitly documented, but the essentials of what happened are clear. Bennett (1988) for example, says

this: "Economics as a profession has a social agenda: to develop the Economy, not merely to research economic facts and construct theories. Sociology has something of an agenda, to improve Society, but it is vague and no one quite knows how to do it. Anthropology has no historic agenda: its task was pure research, the construction of cultural portraits." Ferguson (1997: 165) would no doubt agree: ". . . given the institutional needs of development bureaucracies, the anthropological talent for demonstrating the complexity of development problems (and for disclaiming certainty in offering prescriptions) could hardly compete with the universalistic, context-independent projections and prescriptions so confidently dispensed by the economist or the agronomist."

21. Korten (1997: 159) puts it this way: "When stripped of complexities and qualifications, the basic premise that has shaped most international assistance can be summarized as follows: Economic growth is the key to alleviating poverty, reducing population growth, protecting the environment, and strengthening civil order. Economic growth is a function of investment, which poor countries are too poor to generate through domestic savings. Therefore, their growth depends on the transfer of savings from abroad, either in the form of foreign aid and/or foreign investment. The larger the amount of foreign aid and/or foreign investment, the more rapid their growth (development) and the faster poverty will be eliminated, population stabilized, the environment preserved, and civil order maintained."

22. See Rostow (1960) for the classic explication of the "takeoff" theory of economic development.

23. Hoben and Hefner (1991: 25).

24. For a comprehensive overview of various aspects of development aid, see S. Browne (1990).

25. Hellinger et al. (1988: 14).

26. See, for example, Rostow's comments in 1954, quoted in McMichael (1996: 54).

27. See Sagasti (1997).

28. The effects on Bank policy of McNamara's accession are discussed in some detail in Ayres (1983).

29. For example, Rondinelli (1985: 234–235).

30. See Rapley (1996: 37).

31. See World Bank (1988: 25–28); McMichael (1996: 126, 133).

32. A discussion of structural adjustment policies and their effects can be found in Mosley et al. (1991).

33. This is the World Bank definition, in Feeney (1998: 13).

34. *New York Times*, June 17, 1999: C2.

35. There is a vast literature on this aspect of development, of remarkably little interest to most practitioners, for two main reasons. The first is that many of the points made at length by the critics of development are very well known to development practitioners, who live them every day in the field. The second

and more cogent reason is that most critical analyses of development, short of calling for revolution, have remarkably little to say about how change or reform—on whatever scale—is to be brought about. The literature, in other words, is not so much wrong (indeed, it is often extremely perceptive), as it is obvious, and its message is more exhortatory than revelatory.

36. There is a considerable literature criticizing the development industry. See Lappé et al. (1987) for just one example. Some of this literature also looks specifically at the role of anthropology in development. See, for example, Escobar (1995) and Autumn (1996).

chapter 3

PUTTING
ANTHROPOLOGY
TO WORK

ANTHROPOLOGY
AND THE COLONIAL PAST

Anthropology arose—and flourished—during the colonial period. As Europe explored the world beyond the Mediterranean, anthropologists' accounts were added to those of travelers, missionaries, traders, soldiers, and government officials. The first ethnological societies were established in Paris and London in the 1830s and 1840s, and by the late 1870s, anthropology had emerged as a full-fledged discipline.

Anthropology served European expansion well, as the history of the discipline clearly shows.[1] *Applied anthropology*—the use of anthropology outside the boundaries of the discipline itself—was a major aspect of early anthropology.[2] In Great Britain, for example, anthropologists carried out field investigations in far-flung corners of the empire, both to salvage ethnographic data from societies in the midst of major change and also to provide colonial authorities with information and insight as they went about the work of administration. Anthropologists studied such things as land tenure, labor relations, and native legal systems. Some helped train colonial administrators and served as expert witnesses, consultants, and resource persons. By the 1930s, colonial anthropology was well established; many of the classic ethnographies of the discipline were written during this period.[3] Although these were typically set in a timeless ethnographic present, many of them also dealt with culture contact and change.

As we know, anthropology has been heavily critiqued and condemned (both from within and without the discipline) for its activities during the colonial period.[4] But although many anthropologists of the time were indeed involved in aspects of colonial administration, the relationship between anthropologists and administrators was far from simple, and varied considerably from one situation to another. Administrators often ignored what anthropologists had to say, or were at times actually hostile to them.[5]

DEVELOPMENT OF AN APPLIED PERSPECTIVE IN U.S. ANTHROPOLOGY

Applied anthropology in the United States developed in the late 1800s mainly for domestic purposes, centering on Native American populations.[6] World War II—coinciding with the formation of the Society for Applied Anthropology (SfAA) in 1941—ushered in significant new opportunities for the application of anthropology. Ruth Benedict, Margaret Mead, and others produced "culture and personality" studies designed to illuminate the way we, our allies, and our enemies thought and behaved. Other anthropologists became involved in the relocation of the Japanese-American population. Still others provided training and background information for American personnel about to enter unfamiliar areas overseas.

After the war, opportunities continued to grow as the development industry began to take shape. Some of the best writing on the application of anthropology to problems of development and change date from the period of the late 1940s to the early 1960s, when anthropologists were active both domestically and overseas as administrators, consultants, and trainers. Several significant projects in applied anthropology were done during this time, notably the Fox Project in the United States and the Vicos Project in Peru.[7]

At the same time, however, two countervailing influences arose that were to pull anthropologists back into the academy. One was the steady expansion of American universities during the 1950s and 1960s. This provided opportunities for anthropology graduates to choose research and teaching over application and to focus on theory rather than practice.

The second influence was the Vietnam War. Anthropologists largely opposed the war, and many became increasingly reluctant to involve themselves in government-sponsored work. The fact that development aid, as noted in the previous chapter, had became increasingly linked to security issues did nothing to help reverse the trend away from engagement. For many anthropologists, the controversies of the Vietnam era achieved a focus in the intense discussions that surrounded Project Camelot and the Thailand projects (see below).

A decade later, however, things had changed again. The mid- and late 1970s saw the end of academic expansion, coupled with continuing growth in opportunities for anthropologists outside the academy. Legislation such as the National Environmental Policy Act of 1969, the Foreign Assistance Act of 1973, and the Community Development Act of 1974 created a need for studies and reports that anthropologists were ideally suited to provide.

Organizational shifts and realignments within the discipline echoed these changes. In 1978, the SfAA began to publish *Practicing Anthropology*. The Anthropology Documentation Project at the University of Kentucky began collecting applied materials and publishing updated lists of them. Within the American Anthropological Association (AAA) itself, 1984 saw the formation of the National Association for the Practice of Anthropology (NAPA), which over the next decade produced an important series of monographs focused on aspects of application. Academic training for anthropologists also began to change. In the 1970s, only a few programs for applied anthropology existed. By the end of the 1980s, however, dozens of applied training programs had been created, and discussions of course content, internships, and other aspects of training had become a regular feature of SfAA meetings.[8]

Despite all this, application remains stepchild to the more traditional and academic side of the discipline. Applied anthropology still has no unifying theoretical base, and has been largely unsuccessful in asserting its interests and concerns over those of the more traditional mainstream.[9]

With a few notable exceptions, applied anthropologists have remained outside academic anthropology's inner circle, largely unpublished in major journals and book series. Criteria for recruitment, promotion, and tenure inside anthropology departments still tend, by and large, to favor traditionalists, with the result that applied work, for those who are willing to engage in it at all, must of necessity be something of an avocation or a labor of love.

Among traditionalists, debate continues about the precise definition of applied anthropology, its significance for the discipline, and its relation to theory. Some still hold the position that "applied" anthropology is not anthropology at all.[10]

While the academy debated, however, changes had already occurred in the applied arena that began to have profound and long-lasting effects on the discipline. To understand these changes, it is useful to look more closely at how applied anthropology is actually done.

VARIETIES OF ANTHROPOLOGICAL APPLICATION

Today, many anthropologists claim to do applied work, but not all anthropologists apply what they know in the same way. Applied anthropology today falls into three broad categories.

The first of these is the more traditional academic anthropologist, who may, from time to time, participate in applied activities—typically as a short-term consultant or expert witness. For this type of anthropologist, application is interesting and important, but essentially peripheral.

A second type is the applied anthropologist per se. This is typically someone operating from a university base and whose interests center on applied areas. Although this person's teaching, research, and extramural activities reflect these interests, they are carried out from within the context of a university setting.

The third type is the anthropologist practitioner; someone with an advanced degree (M.A. or Ph.D.) in anthropology but with no permanent or secure attachment to an academic institution. Such a person usually works for an outside organization or is self-employed, often as a consultant. Some practitioners have relatively stable and secure jobs, whereas others move from one assignment to the next. Although the application of anthropology is central to their work, none of them have a university home.

These distinctions can be seen in sharper focus below in Table 3.1.

ACADEMIC, APPLIED, AND PRACTICING ANTHROPOLOGY

Although applied anthropology has always counted all three types among its members, it is the appearance of anthropological practice that is of particular interest.

TABLE 3.1 Differences Between Academic, Applied, and Practicing Anthropology

	Place of Employment	Core Activities	Who Judges Results
Academic Anthropologists	Academically employed.	Research; service; grant-writing; publication; teaching. Topics forming the core of one's work are often, although not always, centered on theory.	Inside the academy, evaluations are done by peers, tenure committees, and review boards. Outside the academy, evaluations are done by peer reviewers (for publications or grants) and members of professional bodies.
Applied Anthropologists	Academically employed in most cases; operates as a temporary consultant outside the university at times and in situations of his/her own choosing. The university is used as a base of operations and a refuge.	Similar to academic anthropologists, but with the addition of activities performed on behalf of outside constituencies. These include training, consulting, advocacy, research, and so on.	Results are ultimately judged by one's peers inside the academy. The assessments of outside constituents, although important in many cases, do not usually adversely affect one's career or job security.
Practicing Anthropologists	Self-employed in many cases; employees of agencies and corporations in others.	Activities are widely varied and change according to the assignment. They include research, management, evaluation, training, consulting, advocacy, and so forth.	Employers and clients judge results, usually according to their own standards. The results of evaluation have direct consequences for future jobs or assignments.

ANTHROPOLOGICAL PRACTICE

In 1968 about 75 percent of new anthropology Ph.D.s took academic positions. By 1980, however, one quarter of the membership of the AAA were full-time applied anthropologists, and five years later, there were more anthropologists outside the academy than inside it.[11] In 1986, John van Willigen described the situation this way: "It appears unlikely that the large numbers of anthropologists entering the job market as practicing anthropologists now will take academic jobs in the future. They will not return because there will not be jobs for them, their salary expectations cannot be met, and they just do not want to."[12]

This trend appeared to reach a high point in the mid-1980s, when over 50 percent of anthropology graduates worked outside of academia. Since then, the proportion appears to have stabilized at 30 percent of graduates.[13]

Several things explain the rapid growth of practice. One, already alluded to, was the lack of academic jobs relative to the production of graduates, which meant that the discipline was no longer a closed system, able to fully absorb its own products.

In addition, new fields for anthropology were opening up outside the academy. Public sector programs, backed by legislation, required vast quantities of social data in planning and evaluation. As practitioner networks began to form, more graduates found it easier to find work beyond the confines of the university.

There is now a large and increasingly well-organized practitioner community. The excitement and prospect of nonacademic opportunities have captured the interest and imagination of graduates, and anthropological practice is arguably becoming the most dynamic aspect of the discipline.

Although most published discussion of anthropological practice still occurs within the academy, the academy is no longer able to define and control the culture of practice that is emerging on the outside.[14] Practitioners are increasingly self-organized—through networks, local organizations, and the Internet—in ways that, although not exclusive of the academy, in no way depend on it.

Local practitioner organizations (LPOs) are a particularly important part of this emerging culture of practice. One of the first LPOs, the Society of Professional Anthropologists (SOPA), was founded in 1973 in Tucson. The Washington Association of Practicing Anthropologists (WAPA), followed shortly thereafter.[15] Although LPO membership is typically open to all interested anthropologists, LPOs arose in part because of a feeling that the large, academically dominated national organizations were not responsive enough to issues of practice.[16]

The application of anthropology now looks quite different from the past. Today, the concept of the anthropologist practitioner—a dedicated, full-time professional working outside the university—is well established. Anthropologists are no longer exclusively involved with exotic populations in remote settings; they work within agencies, government bodies, and corporations, both in the United States and abroad, with a range of issues, constituents, and colleagues. Increasingly, such practitioners are full-time staff members within organizations, and have advanced into policymaking roles.

In sum, the growth of practice has produced a large body of nonacademic anthropologists who operate outside the control and purview of the academy. Although a few of these practitioners might be considered in some sense to be failed academics, the vast majority are not. The growth of this community of practitioners has provoked continuing discussion inside and outside the discipline about how anthropology could and should be applied to areas such as health, education, urban planning, social services, the environment, and many others. Practitioners have grown increasingly sophisticated in finding ways to bring anthropology to bear on these and other issues. The task now is to find more effective ways of bringing the world of practice and the world of the academy together, so that each may learn from the other.

Is practice really a different kind of anthropology? In many ways, yes. Practitioners do not merely observe the world, they engage with it as active and committed participants. As participants, they bear the consequences of their actions.[17] They look at things from the inside out, as well as from the outside in.

The world of practice and the world of the academy constitute, in many ways, different cultural worlds. Some of the most salient of these differences are outlined in Figure 3.1.

Practice is not simply another kind of anthropology—it is a catalyst, forcing anthropologists to grow and change, and in the process, rethink both the basis and the purpose of their discipline.

DEVELOPMENT ANTHROPOLOGY TODAY

Within practice, one of the most challenging and exciting fields is that of international development work. Since the 1970s, the number of anthropologists working full-time in the development industry has increased steadily.[18] Within AID, for example, there was only one anthropologist working full-time in 1974. By 1977, there were twenty-two, in

FIGURE 3.1   Some Salient Differences Between Academics and Practitioners

ACADEMIC RESEARCHERS		PRACTITIONERS
Little if any pressure for decisions	⇐ DECISIONS ⇒	Intense external pressures to decide
Few if any timetables, other than the academic year	⇐ TIMETABLES ⇒	Frequent timetables, close deadlines
Collegial and informal relationships. Work is done largely independently	⇐ WORK RELATIONSHIPS ⇒	Hierarchical and formal relationships. Work is usually done with others
Neutrality and objectivity Commitment to truth and discovery	⇐ ENGAGEMENT AND OBJECTIVITY ⇒	Partisan and engaged Commitment is to success
Interest in describing the world. Concerned with explanation (often after the fact)	⇐ THE GOALS OF ACTIVITY ⇒	Interest in changing the world, and concerned with predicting the consequences of choice
Often highly specialized	⇐ DEGREE OF SPECIALIZATION ⇒	Often polyvalent
Levels of analysis and abstraction tend to be either very high or very low	⇐ FOCUS OF ACTIVITY ⇒	Often focused on the mid-level, with an emphasis on implementation
Individuals tend to approach problems from one disciplinary standpoint	⇐ THEORETICAL STANDPOINT ⇒	Attempt to integrate multiple viewpoints
Individuals are largely independent, with little direct or immediate accountability	⇐ ACCOUNTABILITY ⇒	Directly accountable to employers, colleagues, and stakeholders

SOURCES: Adapted from Bernard 1974; Fisher 1988; Barger and Hutton 1980.

1980, thirty-five, and by 1983, over fifty. By the early 1990s, there were sixty-five anthropologists working full-time within AID, many of them in senior positions.[19] Although few held the official title of "anthropologist," many were involved in crucial policy areas, in addition to work in project design and implementation.[20]

What Development Anthropologists Do

Anthropologists working in development perform three closely interconnected roles. They collect and analyze *information*; they help design *plans* and *policies*; and they carry out these plans through *action*.[21]

With respect to *information*, anthropologists design and carry out research on a variety of development-related topics. They develop and test methodologies for improved data collection and assess the results of projects and programs.[22]

FIGURE 3.2   Major Aspects of Development Anthropology

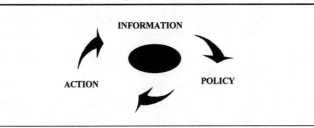

SOURCE: Adapted from van Willigen 1986: 9–10.

Information is directly linked to *policymaking* and *planning*. Anthropologists use information to help them design policies for development work and to plan programs and projects to put policy into effect. Policies for social impact assessment, for resettlement activities, and for the treatment of indigenous peoples are among the key development policies that have been crafted by anthropologists working with AID and the World Bank.

In terms of *action*, anthropologists frequently work as program and project implementers, either alone or as members of multidisciplinary teams. Sometimes, these roles are short-term and temporary, as anthropologists are brought in as consultants at various points in the project cycle.[23] But increasingly, the anthropologist is a full-time member of the project team, involved from start to finish. Indeed, there has been a tendency in recent years to favor anthropologists for the position of group leader or chief of party on the project team because of their broad perspective and their ability to work with a variety of stakeholders.

Anthropology's Contribution to Development

Despite problems with the application of anthropological knowledge and methods to development work (discussed in detail in later chapters), anthropology has had a major impact on development over the past few decades. Anthropology provides, among other things, a clear and keen sense of the real, and can often be crucial for bridging gaps between policies, plans, and ground-level implementation. At the same time, development provides anthropology—and anthropologists—with opportunities to sharpen skills and methods. Good development anthropology must be, above all, good anthropology.[24] A summary of some of the most

MINI-CASE 3.1
DEVELOPMENT ANTHROPOLOGY AT THE WORLD BANK

"Sociological issues," says one observer, "do not naturally fit into the goals and procedures of the World Bank" (Kardam 1993: 1777).

About 70 percent of the World Bank's professional staff are economists (Escobar 1995: 165). Many of the rest are engineers. Horowitz (1996a: 1) says that the ratio of economists to all others at the World Bank is 28 to 1. Robert Chambers (1997: 49) claims that the ratio is somewhere between 20 to 1 and 50 to 1.

Despite the overwhelming preponderance of economists at the World Bank, the number of anthropologists working there has grown steadily in recent years, from twenty-two in 1992 to sixty-four in 1996 (Horowitz 1996a).

During the 1970s, as poverty alleviation began to assume importance, anthropology began to become important at the World Bank. According to Perrett and Lethem (1980), official attention to the "social context" of development projects began in 1972 with a report on the use of anthropology in project operations. The appointment of a full-time sociologist followed soon thereafter.

A focus on poverty meant a focus on the communities of the poor, and how they worked. Anthropologists and sociologists worked mainly in agriculture and rural development projects at first, where perhaps one-third of Bank lending was taking place. The anthropologists and sociologists looked, not at technology and finance, but at human factors and resources, and tried to produce a "fit" between what the projects were attempting to do and what local communities already knew how to do.

Today, the group of anthropologists and sociologists at the World Bank constitute, in Cernea's (1996) estimation, the largest group of social scientists—between fifty and sixty individuals—working on development anywhere in the world.

Social scientists began to advance their agenda within the Bank through informal networks. In the late 1970s, this network surfaced as the "Sociology Group," a voluntary and still informal collection of interested individuals, not exclusively anthropologists or sociologists, who met regularly to discuss, debate, and share information. Kardam (1993: 1779) terms this group "an important vehicle for internal advocacy and change at the Bank." The group used two principal strategies to present its views within the World Bank. The first was persuasion, through discussion and demonstration. The second strategy was the slow and steady transformation of the knowledge held by social scientists about how social factors influenced development outcomes into specific policies and procedures.

(continues)

MINI-CASE 3.1 (continued)

Cernea (1996: 10) summarizes the thrust of this effort: ". . . the socio-logical/anthropological knowledge required for and embodied in social re-search and analysis *is not a luxury or a marginal add-on* to inducing develop-ment, but is as necessary *as the economic analysis is* for designing and ascertaining the feasibility and adequate goal-directedness of development programs" (emphasis in the original).

As Cernea (1991: 21) points out, bringing anthropology and sociology into the World Bank required more than just "inserting" more social knowledge; it involved changing the rules by which the Bank made deci-sions about this kind of knowledge. Policy formulation thus became a key "entry point" for anthropology and sociology.

The following figure illustrates some of the main policy areas—sectoral, cross-sectoral, and general—where anthropology has been influential.

Anthropology and World Bank Policy: Key Areas

- Involuntary resettlement;
  - Indigenous peoples;
  - Nongovernmental organizations;
  - Urban growth;
- Primary education;
- Forestry and reforesta-tion;
- Water resources;
- Poverty alleviation;

This work continues. In March 1996, a Social Development Task Force was set up by President Bill Clinton to recommend ways that the Bank could integrate the social dimensions of development more effectively into its operations.

The picture is not entirely positive, however. The World Bank's policies have been criticized by anthropologists and others outside the agency as inadequate or biased (see Bodley 1988: 406–413, for example, for a cri-tique of Bank policy toward tribal peoples). Other have pointed out that the Bank is still primarily interested in economic growth first and poverty alleviation second. Although it uses social input, it does not accord it pri-macy in its planning. Cernea (1996) characterizes much of Bank thinking as "econocentric," "technocentric," and "commoditocentric." Anthropol-ogy at the Bank, Horowitz (1996a: 4) claims, is "ghettoized"—shunted into peripheral areas, sidelined by the dominant economic paradigm of growth and the operation of a free market.

Clearly, the World Bank has a long way to go in incorporating social is-sues and factors into its operations. Kardam (1993: 1785) comments:

(continues)

Impressive as [these results] may be, the change has been limited, due to the contextual factors and internal counter-resistance as well: limited sensitivity of the Bank to external pressure, resistance stemming from the prevalence of economic paradigms and biases or obsolete procedures. Yet, without the conscious efforts of some staff members, it is very questionable that even these results already achieved could have been attained.

Cernea has observed that one of the main obstacles to getting more anthropology into the development agencies is the generalized ignorance of what social science can do for them, on the part of their current senior staff. He comments: "The magnitude of this obstacle on a global scale is underestimated. This gap [in understanding] persists, and in fact is being recreated with every class graduating from technical colleges, because of the manner in which technical experts are "grown" in the groves of academe" (Cernea 1987: 21).

He also notes that anthropology must, in turn, learn more about the institutional context of the agencies themselves: "Living daily inside an economic tribal culture, I can confirm that anthropology as practice can—indeed must—be strengthened by learning more from economic concepts and by internalizing quantifying methodologies" (Cernea 1996: 24).

SOURCES: Cernea 1987, 1991, 1996; R. Chambers 1997; Escobar 1995; M. Horowitz 1996a; Kardam 1993; Perrett and Lethem 1980; Bodley 1988.

---

important areas in which anthropology has contributed to development work are sketched below.[25]

Research

Anthropologists have generated a great deal of useful research—as well as developing innovative research methodologies—relating to many aspects of development. They have won major research contracts from agencies and foundations for this work, and produced many influential publications. Many of their findings have been turned into important policy recommendations.

Leadership

Anthropologists now play leadership roles in many development projects, often serving as team leaders or chiefs of party. They now work more closely with other specialists on key development issues. For example, problems of poverty alleviation and its relation to long-term environmental sustainability have brought anthropologists, biologists, and ecologists together as collaborators.[26]

Assessment

Because anthropologists have been able to show how some development policies or projects have been detrimental to the lives of supposed beneficiaries, anthropology is increasingly used across the entire cycle of project and program development. Although initially restricted to social impact appraisal and ex post facto evaluation, anthropology is now used with growing frequency at all phases of project development.

Indigenous Knowledge and Local Perspectives

Finally—and perhaps most important—it is slowly becoming accepted that a beneficiary perspective in planning and implementation is not simply useful but essential to development success.[27] Anthropologists have been able to uncover reservoirs of local skill, knowledge, experience, and expertise, and to show policy makers how these resources can be used to shape or reshape the nature of planning and action in the field.

THE DIALECTICS OF APPLICATION

Anthropology's experience with development work has brought several key areas of application into sharp focus. These include *policymaking, brokerage, advocacy,* and *ethics.* Such concerns are not new within anthropology, but in each case, the development experience has added an important dimension to our understanding.

Policy

Development programs and projects do not unfold in a random fashion; they are both created and constrained within a context of rules and

---

MINI-CASE 3.2
ANTHROPOLOGICAL STUDIES OF
DEVELOPMENT PROJECTS

There have been several important comparative studies of development projects, illuminating factors that seem to favor project success. Cernea (1987), for example, presented an analysis of twenty-five large-scale World Bank projects done between 1969 and 1980. Kottak (1985) studied fifty-seven agricultural and rural development World Bank projects. From 1978 to 1984, Development Alternatives, Inc. (DAI) and Research Triangle Institute (RTI) carried out research on twenty-four integrated rural development projects in Asia, Africa, Latin America, and the Caribbean (Honadle and Van Sant 1985).

The Cernea study was based on impact studies that were carried out between 1980 and 1984. Among other things, these studies looked at "sustainability," defined as the maintenance of an acceptable net flow of benefits from the project's investments after its completion. All the projects that were examined had initially been judged successful, with good long-term prospects. Later analysis, however, indicated that although twelve had achieved long-term sustainability, the other twelve had not. Five sets of factors were seen as responsible:

1. Institutional buildup and participation of beneficiaries
2. Technological improvements
3. Socioeconomic compatibility
4. A favorable policy environment
5. Recurrent cost financing or recovery

In his analysis, Cernea stressed institutions as one of the keys to success. He observed (1987: 125) that agencies still prefer to focus on finance rather than on organizing beneficiaries and participants. But projects will fail, he reminds us, unless they create or strengthen local institutions and organizations that will outlast temporary investments.

(continues)

---

guidelines. These rules are embodied in *policy*—frameworks for action and choice, focused on specific goals.[28] Today—and particularly in development work—anthropologists are actively involved with the making of policy.

The policy environment is a special one, very different from the world of the academy. Rather than focusing on theory and long-term research, policy makers address pressing needs of the moment, usually on a short

---

MINI-CASE 3.2 (continued)

Kottak's findings drew attention to the compatibility of projects with their local context. In his study, the thirty projects whose design was compatible with the traditional cultural and socioeconomic context had an estimated economic rate of return (ERR) of 18.3 percent, whereas the twenty-seven projects that were incompatible had an average ERR of only 8.6 percent.

Honadle and Van Sant's conclusions (1985: 5) emphasized the interactive aspects of project development: ". . . program failure is not primarily a result of lack of political will. Instead, it results, at least in part, from wills in conflict and the impact of this conflict on the organization and management of the development process." They identified seven factors that favor project success, five of them "process" factors and two of them substantive or structural factors. Process factors included:

- Collaborative style
  - An emphasis on learning how to make things work instead of relying on predetermined solutions
  - Risk sharing
  - Involvement at multiple levels
- Emphasis on demonstration

Structural factors included:

- Presence of incentives
- The resource base

Success, in the authors' view (1985: 98–99) is owing to a combination of microprocesses, plus "the need to understand the peculiarities of specific circumstances before plunging ahead with broad agendas that may not be appropriate."

SOURCES: Honadle and Van Sant 1985; Cernea 1987; Kottak 1991.

---

deadline. Policy work is anything but value-free and neutral—rather, it is advocacy-based and highly political. And policy—whether good or bad—has consequences, both for those who make it and those who are affected by it.

The policy culture within a development agency will reflect these points, and policy makers will pay most attention to whatever helps them get their job done. This means that information, techniques, or analyses that aid decisionmaking will be favored over theory, thick description, and hypothetical scenarios. Most policy makers don't want more studies or more data beyond what is immediately necessary for their purposes, and they particularly do not want more information if it will challenge what they consider "givens."

The formulation of policy is one thing, but its implementation is quite another. The architect's drawings for a building may be inspiring, but construction itself may prove to be a nightmare. It is here that ideas are put to the test, where plans become practice, and where results—or simply adverse consequences—start to appear.

Part of the reason why policy work is so difficult is the fact that there are many *stakeholders*—groups and individuals with both an interest in outcomes, and the ability to influence them in some way. We will return several times to the topic of stakeholders and their importance in the chapters ahead.

Each group of stakeholders has the potential to either complicate or advance both the process of policy formulation and its later implementation. Anthropologists entering the world of policy must therefore expand their focus from one group to many, and look at how policy dialogues between stakeholders develop and change over time, and how different ways of seeing the world play a role in how policy is developed and shaped.

Years ago, Edward Spicer urged anthropologists to create a comparative ethnography of decisionmaking for policy development, reminding them that an understanding of the way in which ideas are transformed into action was essential for successful participation in that transformation.[29] I'll return to this idea in a later chapter.

Brokerage

The presence of diverse stakeholders often creates the need for what anthropologists term *cultural brokerage*. A typical development project involves a variety of different groups. To work effectively, the anthropologist must manage not only her relationship to all these groups, but also their relationships to each other.[30] This means promoting collaboration and coordination, trading information, sharing resources, engaging in joint planning and action, and reacting quickly to address problems as they arise.

Brokerage, as development anthropologists know well, is not one role, but several. At times, a broker is a *spokesperson* for a group that cannot or will not represent itself. At other times, the broker is a *mediator* between

FIGURE 3.3   Stakeholder Groups in a Typical Project

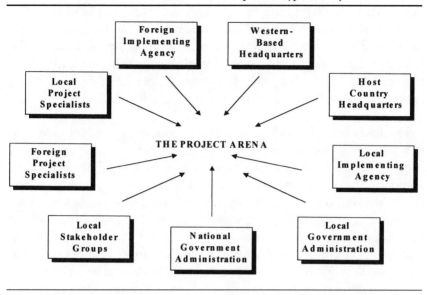

groups that are antagonistic or even hostile. Brokers also serve as *teachers* or *informants*, bringing information back and forth, and sometimes as *catalysts*, making suggestions that eventually produce results.[31] Brokerage is in fact a very complex activity, involving both the mastery and manipulation of symbols, meanings, time, and resources.[32]

It is widely assumed that brokers facilitate the exchange of information, but often, the broker's job is actually to *manage* information. This may involve not telling all that one knows, or telling what one knows in very selective and strategic ways. A broker is a type of interpreter, and as Ambrose Bierce once famously observed, an interpreter is someone who helps two other people understand each other by repeating to each what it would have been to the interpreter's advantage for the other to have said.[33]

As with policy work, brokerage in development makes special demands on anthropologists—demands for which classical theory and ethnography often provide few useful answers.

Advocacy

In the 1960s and 1970s, indigenous movements began to emerge on the development scene, together with such Western-based groups as The

World Council of Indigenous Peoples, Cultural Survival, the International Work Group for Indigenous Affairs, and Survival International.[34]

As development anthropologists became more involved with these groups and movements, *advocacy* became an important addition to the roles they could play in shaping and implementing change. Unlike brokerage, where the anthropologist attempts to be a helpful but relatively neutral go-between, advocacy involves taking sides and making commitments.[35]

The advocacy relationship has three important aspects. First, the anthropologist works for—and furnishes information to—the community itself, rather than working for an outside agency. Second, the topics and agendas to be worked on are determined largely by the community, and not by the anthropologist. Finally, the anthropologist-as-advocate is accountable to the community first and foremost, and only secondarily to professional peers or colleagues.

As advocates, anthropologists can play a number of different roles. They usually work, not as front-line activists, but as researchers, trainers, and resource persons on behalf of less powerful groups. Other roles are sometimes available as historians, lobbyists, expert witnesses, or—in extreme cases—whistleblowers. The overall aim, whatever the advocate's specific role, is the same—to empower the community and help build capacity within it.[36]

Advocacy therefore means subordination of one's own goals to those of the group, working appropriately and efficiently in terms of standards and procedures as defined by the group, and producing results tailored to group needs. Successful advocacy requires a high degree of political sophistication, drawing anthropologists once again into activities and arenas that may fall far outside their training and previous experience.

Ethics

Sooner or later, interactions with stakeholders in a development project will raise questions of *ethics*. As we have seen, the stakeholders in a typical development project include a wide variety of groups, some of which may not even be physically present on the project site. Problems arise when obligations to these different groups conflict, as they inevitably will.

Ethical concerns in applied anthropology are nothing new, of course. The Society for Applied Anthropology issued its first statement on ethics in the 1940s, and since then, several other versions have appeared. The AAA's *Principles of Professional Responsibility* emphasize accountability to six major stakeholder groups: those we study; the public; the discipline; our students and trainees; our employers, clients, and sponsors; and governments. To these groups, we are required to disclose our methods, our goals, and the source of our sponsorship. We must respect the communities we work in. We must not hinder our professional colleagues in their work, at the same time providing open access to our students. We must make our skills and knowledge available to the society at large, and in our work we must render accurate and competent service to those who employ us.[37]

Anthropology's concern with ethics intensified during the 1960s and 1970s. The Vietnam War and its antecedents, especially the well-publicized Project Camelot controversy, raised serious questions within the discipline about the propriety of applied work and the limits of involvement. This debate was at times as much about politics as ethics; as one applied anthropologist observed, "In the radical view, applied anthropology, whatever its expressed purpose, became nothing but a means by which those in power could tighten their grip on the downtrodden."[38]

Development anthropology's ethical dilemmas tend to center—as many ethical dilemmas do—on issues of power and information. What is investigated, whose interests are served, what happens to what we learn, and—most important—what actually happens to *people* as a result of our work, are among the most significant of the ethical minefields that development anthropologists must cross.

Often, we must recommend on the basis of incomplete knowledge. In this respect, anthropologists are little different from most development specialists, but our claims to expertise are often couched in terms of unique in-depth understanding. We may indeed know a great deal about the community in which we once did fieldwork, but how much can we claim to know about a place we have been in for only a few weeks? How much knowledge, in other words, is "enough"?

Development projects are planned and financed by large and powerful agencies that often have explicit political agendas, in addition to whatever socioeconomic concerns they may acknowledge. Projects unfold, often, in poorer countries with no long tradition of political freedom, much less a tradition of unfettered academic enquiry. Certain areas may be out of bounds. In such situations, development anthropologists can face especially difficult choices about where their loyalties and obligations lie.

Much of development anthropology is done under contract, for a spe-

MINI-CASE 3.3   PROJECT CAMELOT, THAILAND, AND COUNTERINSURGENCY RESEARCH

Project Camelot was a social research project begun in 1964 and funded by the U.S. Army. Its goal was to develop "a general systems model which would make it possible to predict and influence politically significant aspects of social change in the developing nations of the world." Specifically, the project sought to develop ways to assess the potential for internal conflict in developing societies and to identify actions that might prevent such conflicts. Originally begun in Latin America, it was intended to include countries in Asia, Africa, and Europe as well. Although anthropological involvement in this project was minimal, the project created a highly publicized controversy, documented by a number of books and articles. Resolutions were passed by professional associations against "clandestine" research and against the use of social science as a counterinsurgency tool. In part because of the stir it raised among social scientists, the project died quickly and without fanfare.

At the same time, however, anthropologists were involved in other activities in Thailand that also would cause controversy and would raise—as Camelot did—fundamental ethical and political questions regarding the appropriateness of certain types of research and how anthropological research ultimately might be used. For some years, anthropologists carried out work among the hill tribes of northern Thailand, work that received substantial funding from the Advanced Research Projects Agency (ARPA) of the U.S. Department of Defense—the same group that later gave us the Internet. As the Vietnam conflict grew, so did ARPA's research funding for northern Thailand. Like Camelot in Latin America, the goal seemed to be the collection of basic cultural and demographic information for counterinsurgency purposes.

The controversy surrounding the Thailand research projects was much more bitter and drawn out than it had been with Camelot, although in time the two events tended to become fused into a single issue. Camelot and Thailand provoked a useful and far-reaching discussion of ethics among anthropologists and forced many field researchers to examine issues regarding the use of data by outsiders, but there is no doubt that the controversy also had a chilling effect on the use of anthropology in international development work for most of the period from the mid-1960s to the mid-1970s, when USAID's New Directions and the World Bank's McNamara Doctrine presented new opportunities.

SOURCES: Sjoberg 1967; Jones 1971; Beals 1969; Belshaw 1976; I. Horowitz 1965, 1967; Watkins 1992; Wax 1978; Wolf and Jorgenson 1970.

cific client who is only one of a number of stakeholders. Often, the nature of the problem that the anthropologist is to work on—and often, the shape of the expected solution—have been defined in advance by the client. Issues that lie outside the client's interests—or that might possibly be detrimental to those interests—are in effect, ignored.

Development anthropologists quickly learn that they, like other specialists, are paid to do the client's bidding. Although paid specialists are allowed to complain a great deal, and sometimes are allowed to persuade those in power to see things differently, one basic rule remains: If we cannot persuade them, then we either fall into line or get out.

Finally, anthropologists must decide how much to tell of what they know, and to whom. This has been called the "dirty hands—guilty knowledge" problem.[39] Waste, fraud, corruption, incompetence, and inattention are not necessarily more widespread within the development industry than elsewhere, but they are certainly present. Anthropologists, like others, have had to carefully consider whether to tell everything they know (and to whom?) about how development projects actually get done. Speaking truth to power is a fine idea in principle, but will it dry up future jobs? Worse, will it erode popular support for development overall?

There is little consensus at present within the discipline with regard to these and other questions. Again, the demands of development work have challenged anthropologists in multiple ways, forcing them to extend their own capabilities at the same time as their beliefs and principles are being tested.

SUMMARY
OF CHAPTER 3

Chapter 3 has examined how anthropology has been applied to contemporary social problems. Applied anthropology has been a feature of the discipline from colonial times, and today it is a vital and growing part of the discipline.

Anthropological practitioners who do not have a university affiliation are the fastest-growing category of applied anthropologist, and many of them are involved in international development. Within the development industry, they work in a number of different areas, collecting information, formulating policy, and designing and managing projects in the field.

Anthropologists have had a major impact on key aspects of development work, despite a variety of problems. At the same time, the nature and scope of development work has challenged practitioners and their discipline in a number of ways. Despite these successes, development anthropology—and applied anthropology in all forms—still retains an ambivalent and second-class relationship to its parent discipline.

ENDNOTES

1. See for example van Willigen (1986), R. Chambers (1985), Grillo and Rew (1985), Ervin (2000).

2. Pitt-Rivers is said to have coined the term in the 1880s. A. R. Radcliffe-Brown used it in the 1920s, as did Bronislaw Malinowski, who called for the establishment of "practical anthropology" to study how societies under colonial rule were changing.

3. See Gardner and Lewis (1996: 29), Naylor (1996: 10), and Grillo and Rew (1985: 10) for discussions of this period. Forde (1953) provides a concise account of anthropology in British colonial Africa.

4. See Gough (1968), Hymes, ed., 1972, Asad (1973), and so on for more details.

5. See Naylor (1996: 10); Gardner and Lewis (1996: 33).

6. See van Willigen (1986) for a detailed discussion of the early development of applied anthropology in the United States.

7. The Fox Project took place among the Mesquakie Indians from 1948 to 1959. Rubenstein (1986) provides a discussion and background citations concerning the project. Vicos, also known as the Cornell-Peru Project, was begun in 1949 by Allan Holmberg, and lasted until the mid-1960s. Doughty (1987) and Mangin (1979) provide accounts of this project.

8. Trotter (1988) provides an excellent introduction to the structure, content, and philosophy of these applied training programs. In 1989, the SfAA issued a *Guide to Training Programs in Applied Anthropology* (Hyland and Kirkpatrick 1989) listing nearly thirty such programs in the United States. In Britain, events took a similar course, but later. Grillo and Rew (1985) provide a useful summary of these developments. In 1977, the Royal Anthropological Institute set up a Development Anthropology Committee. In 1985, the Applied Anthropology Group was formed, later to become GAPP (the Group of Anthropology in Policy and Practice). By 1983, GAPP had 150 members. Like their American colleagues, British applied anthropologists are increasingly influential within their discipline, often from positions outside the academy.

Shore and Wright (1996) give a useful review of the current status of applied anthropology in Britain.

9. See Partridge (1985: 139, 141).

10. Interestingly, this position is echoed in some quarters in France. See Nolan (1998).

11. Bodley (1994: 352); E. Chambers (1985: 215).

12. van Willigen (1986: 34).

13. Fiske and Chambers (1996: 4–5).

14. See Fiske and Chambers (1996: 8).

15. SOPA's founding has been described by Bainton (1979). Bennett (1988) produced a NAPA Bulletin detailing the growth of LPOs. Fiske and Chambers (1996) provide additional information about LPOs.

16. E. Chambers (1985: 215).

17. See Partridge (1985: 144) on the same point.

18. Hoben (1982) and Pillsbury (1986) provide a comprehensive overview of the growth of development anthropology.

19. See Weaver (1985); Grimm (1998).

20. See Ferguson (1997) for the history of anthropology's involvement with development.

21. van Willigen (1984: 278).

22. Several anthropological studies of development projects (Uphoff 1985; Kottak 1991; Cernea 1987) have made major contributions to our understanding of the ways in which social factors affect project success or failure.

23. See Wilson (1998) for a discussion of anthropologists as consultants.

24. Hoben (1986: 194). See also Horowitz (1998a: 1).

25. See Horowitz (1994: 5–8) for an excellent discussion of some of these points.

26. Horowitz (1996b: 336) comments: "Today it is not uncommon for an anthropologist to lead a team composed of economists and other technical specialists, because not only is cultural expertise desired, but it is increasingly recognized that anthropologists, by virtue of the holistic focus of their discipline, are often best able to integrate the various specialist reports into a coherent set of recommendations for action."

27. See Cernea (1991: xii) and Green (1987: 24).

28. van Willigen (1986: 9, 143).

29. Spicer (1976: 129–132).

30. Gow (1991: 11).

31. See E. Chambers (1985: 30–32) for more discussion of some of these.

32. There is a fascinating literature on this in both political anthropology and symbolic interactionists within sociology. See, for example, Bailey (1969, 1983, 1988, 1991) and Goffman (1969) for an introduction.

33. In Bierce (1958: 69).

34. See Bodley (1994: 377) for a discussion of these.

35. See van Willigen (1986: 118) for more discussion of advocacy.

36. "The aim of the expert," say Schensul and Schensul, "must be to increase the capability of client group members to speak for themselves in political, planning and service areas" (in Grillo and Rew 1985: 25).

37. From Kemper and Royce (1997: 479–480).

38. Angrosino (1976: 3–4).

39. See Fetterman (1983).

PART TWO

---

development projects
examined

IN PART ONE, "ANTHROPOLOGY AND DEVELOPMENT," we
looked at two things: how international development grew into a major
worldwide industry and how, at the same time, anthropology developed
its capacity for applied work, particularly within the development industry itself.

Part Two, "Development Projects Examined," looks at how development is done in the field, particularly at how anthropology is used in this
effort. Chapter 4, "The Nature of Development Projects," describes what
development projects are and how they are used by agencies to implement change in the field. Chapter 5, "Information in Project Development," looks at the role of data in the process of project development.
Chapter 6, "Framing Projects," looks at how projects are actually designed and focuses on the important initial decisions that will "frame"
the undertaking. Chapter 7, "Managing Projects," discusses some of the
key tasks involved in project implementation. Chapter 8, "Assessing
Projects," concludes the examination of projects by looking at how they
are reviewed and judged.

chapter 4

THE NATURE OF DEVELOPMENT PROJECTS

A *project* is essentially a management system for creating change, a mechanism for turning ideas into outcomes. Projects are how policies and programs are actually implemented. A *policy* is a broad statement of principles to guide action. It sets forth an overall goal or direction, describes in general terms what should be done, and offers some guidelines for getting there. A *program* is based on a policy. It takes the goals and guidelines and begins to operationalize them in terms of sets of activities and priorities that guide the allocation of resources. Policies and programs are essentially plans, or statements of intent. A project, however, puts these plans into action in a particular place and at a particular time

CHARACTERISTICS OF PROJECTS

Most development assistance is channeled through projects. From a donor's point of view, projects are an efficient and effective way to organize resources and focus effort. Projects promote accountability, set boundaries, and establish rules and procedures. In short, projects give people a measure of control—or at least the illusion of control—over events.

FIGURE 4.1   Policies, Programs, and Projects

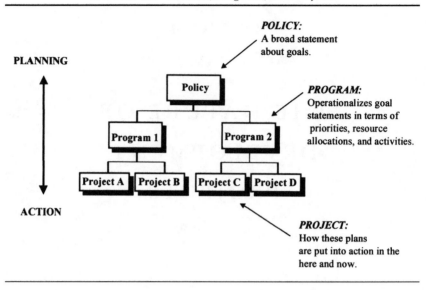

Although projects are favored by donors, they are not without problems.[1] Their temporary and limited nature may encourage temporary and
piecemeal solutions. Because projects are time-consuming and labor-
intensive, there is a tendency to take shortcuts. The project is sometimes
made bigger, to lower overhead costs. All too often, projects are planned
with incomplete information, or using simplified models or assumptions
that do not really reflect the local context.

Projects have certain special characteristics. They are *limited* in scope,
space, and time, and they are often *experimental,* designed to test new approaches or concepts. They are *developmental* in the sense that they are
intended to set in motion a chain of events that will continue after the
project has ended. They are also *value-laden;* that is, projects represent
choices made by planners and other stakeholders about alternative visions of the future and acceptable ways of getting there. Finally, projects
are *collaborative;* requiring different groups of people—often with different viewpoints—to work together.

Although projects can be a very effective way to reach development
goals, they are notoriously difficult to plan and implement. In part, this is
because projects bring groups and organizations together that may not
share the same values, needs, perceptions, assumptions, and goals. Differences among participants therefore characterize the context of any proj-

ect. These participants enter the project arena with different worldviews, different concerns, and different expectations, all of which become immediately important the moment they begin to interact. Successful projects create synergy between them and create outcomes that no one group could achieve by itself.

As one observer comments, development projects begin as *plans,* but quickly turn into *contexts.*[2] Project development, like life itself, is about coming to terms with the different ways of seeing the world that exist within this context. In this sense, a project is an extended negotiation between different groups of social actors. The anthropologist's role here is twofold: to uncover differences and similarities between stakeholders and to help find ways to use this diversity to forge common purposes.

THE STRUCTURE AND
LIFE CYCLE OF PROJECTS

Project Operations

All projects, whatever their nature, have a similar set of procedures or operations that guide their development.

Framing.   The initial phase of project development is where the design is laid out, through a set of *framing decisions* that determine the project's key characteristics.

Framing decisions include decisions about the specific *goals and objectives* to be achieved, the *strategies* for doing this, and the *procedures* by which the project will be carried out. Such decisions must take into account a wide variety of factors and variables, including who the stakeholders are at various levels, what other projects are currently being planned or implemented, and how development criteria are prioritized. Information about the local environment and the stakeholders groups operating in this environment is crucial to successful design.

Once the basic framing decisions have been taken, other aspects of design can be completed. The *resources* needed to achieve project objectives must be specified, for example. The *activities* that will form the core of implementation need to be spelled out. The *responsibility* for these—including personnel, structures, and procedures—needs to be assigned. And *timetables* for execution, however tentative they might be at this stage, need to be drawn up.

Management.   Project management is the *implementation* phase of the project, where the various activities are carried out and monitored. During this phase, there will almost certainly be adjustments to the design, as more information from the project environment comes in and as the project team and local participants gain more experience with the project and how it works.

Assessment.   As the project begins to show results, judgments need to be made, both about the results and about the ways in which they were achieved. The *monitoring and evaluation* function thus provides judgments both about the operation of the project and about project outcomes. Through assessment, planners seek to understand what lessons have been learned from this project that can be applied to future efforts.

Project Elements

All projects are composed of four basic elements or building blocks.

Resources.   Resources are the tangible and intangible assets that support the activities of the project. Resources include materials, personnel, information, money, equipment, and time. Some projects require few resources; others need extensive support. Money and equipment are often less important for project success than less tangible resources such as commitment, goodwill, or reliable information.

Activities.   Activities are the tasks and operations undertaken by the project. Project activities depend on project resources being available and being coordinated properly. Again, some projects consist of numerous complex activities, whereas other projects consist of fewer, simpler ones. For the more complex activities, a high degree of technical or managerial skill may be required.

Strategies.   A project's strategy is the plan or approach used to justify, shape, and coordinate various activities of the project. Since there are usually several different ways to reach any given goal or objective, the choice of strategy is quite important. Inappropriate strategies will waste project resources, and may not fit with the routines, preferences, and capabilities of various project stakeholders.

FIGURE 4.2   Basic Project Elements

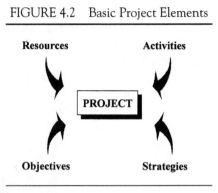

Objectives.   These are the specific outcomes, goals, purposes, or aims de-sired by the project. Objectives are the concrete end points toward which resources, activities, and strategies are focused. The objectives chosen for a project must be consonant with the resources available and the strategies employed. But more important, objectives must be realistic and relevant to the concerns of stakeholders.

Agency Project Cycles

The elements and operations sketched above are combined in the *project development cycle*, from the point at which project planning first begins until the day that the final evaluation report is submitted. Although each development agency will have a slightly different way of doing this—and each will have different sets of policies and procedures to guide project development—the project development cycle is similar for most organizations. Mini-Case 4.1, "The World Bank Project Cycle," presents the developmental sequence for a large multilateral agency. It is at the identification, preparation, and appraisal stages of the project cy-cle that detailed contextual information is of crucial importance.

Although the project cycle—whether of the World Bank or any other agency—appears simple in outline, an agency's design and approval process can be extremely complex and time-consuming. Once a project is approved, teams must be recruited, information collected, and materi-als and equipment procured. Local populations must be consulted, local politicians brought on board, and requisite signatures ad approvals ob-tained. For a typical World Bank or AID project, all this may take sev-eral years before implementation actually begins.

MINI-CASE 4.1　　THE WORLD BANK PROJECT CYCLE

The World Bank's project development cycle divides framing, managing, and assessing projects into six stages: identification; preparation; appraisal; negotiation and presentation; implementation and supervision; and evaluation. The Bank typically will approve hundreds of projects in any given year, but only those that meet stringent requirements will complete the cycle.

Identification

Project ideas can arise from several different sources: Bank missions, other UN agencies, private sponsors, and so on. Eventually, however, the project must be formally proposed by the host country government. At this stage of the cycle, planners are primarily interested in basic questions such as: Who will benefit from the project? Will outcomes justify the costs? What different scenarios might there be for achieving comparable results? The idea for the project must also compete with other potential projects.

The World Bank Project Cycle

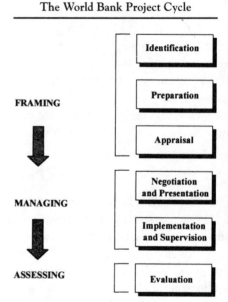

Preparation

If the decision to continue is made, then background work begins. Typically, such preparation work is carried out by the host country itself, with Bank supervision. "Preparation" essentially refers to the preparation of a detailed project proposal that covers all the major aspects of the undertaking, including technical, financial, economic, social, and managerial considerations. The feasibility of the project is tested during this phase, and if things are satisfactory, then a tentative timetable for action is drawn up.

(continues)

MINI-CASE 4.1 (continued)

Appraisal

At this stage, the project faces its most important test—World Bank appraisal. A World Bank team carefully reviews the work of the host country borrower, focusing particularly on four areas: the project's technical aspects; the organizational requirements and performance levels needed to achieve success; the economic impacts, benefits, and rates of return; and the financial viability of the undertaking.

Negotiation and Presentation

The World Bank presents its findings. If these are generally positive, then the Bank and the borrower begin to negotiate whatever issues or details remain before launching the project. In some cases, the negotiations result in considerable reworking of the project proposal; in others, they focus mainly on routine matters. Once negotiations are concluded, the project is formally presented to the Bank's executive directors for approval.

Implementation and Supervision

After approval, funding is released to begin the project. The borrower is generally responsible for doing the work of implementation, and will typically issue bids for goods and services, including development consultants, experts, and managers of various kinds. Funds are typically disbursed in stages, with the World Bank keeping a close eye on how things are developing. Borrowers must, as a rule, conform to the Bank's extensive set of rules regarding procurement, accounting, and reporting.

Evaluation

Evaluation is carried out by an independent World Bank unit that reports to the executive directors. Evaluations typically look at how the actual implementation of the project compares with the original proposal, what results are achieved, and what might be done in the future to improve similar projects.

SOURCE: World Bank Information Briefs #A.04.4.94.

APPROACHES TO
PROJECT PLANNING

The framing decisions that set a project in motion will occur within an overall approach to planning and design. Project planners do not simply make choices about the project itself; they also choose, at many points, how to plan.

Two quite different approaches or planning styles exist, one directive, and the other interactive. No project is ever developed using only one or the other of these, but at the extremes, they are distinct in terms of assumptions, priorities, and procedures, and they carry important consequences for the project. *Directive planning*, power-based and relatively rigid, stands in contrast to *interactive planning*, which is information-based and more flexible. These and other differences between the two approaches are shown in Figure 4.3

Directive Planning

Directive planning is sometimes called blueprint planning. Detailed plans are drawn up in advance, and implementation occurs in a linear, sequential fashion. Project decisions during design and implementation are relatively "pure" and can be made in terms of a few controllable variables, usually of a quantitative nature.

Building a house is an example of this approach: Working from blueprints, materials can be ordered in advance, tasks laid out sequentially, and timetables made for completion of the steps of phases in construction. The initial plan serves as an accurate picture of the final product. In this sense, most of the planning work takes place at the "front end."

Directive planning assumes that the problem to be addressed is understood, that planners already know how to deal with it, that most of the important variables in planning are known and quantifiable, and that other participants share the same perceptions and values as the planners. It also assumes a relatively stable environment from start to finish.

The directive approach to planning is somewhat akin to driving a train down a track. Any difficulties encountered are assumed to be easily remedied through minor adjustments of a technical nature. Once the project is under way, major changes are discouraged, and indeed, such changes are usually quite difficult to make. Minor errors will not normally disrupt the plan, but major errors will often derail the project altogether.

FIGURE 4.3   Directive and Interactive Planning: Main Distinctions

DIRECTIVE PLANNING		INTERACTIVE PLANNING
The environment is assumed to be known and predictable, and largely controllable.	**HOW PLANNING TAKES PLACE** ⇐ ⇒	The environment is not completely understood, is dynamic, or is not entirely controllable.
Detailed knowledge of techniques, outcomes and contingencies is assumed to exist at the start of the project. Little new or additional learning is seen as required to make the project work. The knowledge framework is imposed on the local environment.	**THE ROLE OF THE LOCAL CONTEXT** ⇐ ⇒	Incomplete knowledge is assumed, and one of the project's goals is to discover what to do in the environment. New learning is seen as essential to success. Meaning is developed within the local context, not imposed from outside.
Overall strategies and objectives (together with resources, activities and timetables) are spelled out in advance. Design decisions are largely final; few modifications of the project are possible at later stages.	**THE ROLE OF EXISTING KNOWLEDGE** ⇐ ⇒	Objectives and strategies emerge from on-site investigation. Resources, activities and timetables are adjusted as experience is gained. Design decisions are experimental and dynamic. Modification occurs frequently as learning takes place.

Interactive Planning

Interactive planning—also known as learning-process planning—relies heavily on information and learning.[3] Interactive planning is based on the premise of uncertainty: the likelihood that conditions, problems, and solutions are *not* completely known at the outset. Knowledge must be obtained as the project proceeds, and appropriate modifications made on the basis of this learning. A linear sequence is no longer assumed. With interactive planning, project decisions are often "impure" and made in terms of shifting and often qualitative factors. Interactive planning requires an interaction between designers and the project environment—human and physical—during the project cycle, and a structure that will permit the reassessment and adjustment of plans previously made.[4] Implementation often becomes creative and experimental, requiring innovative management approaches.

In this sense, interactive planning is rather like a sailboat race. The goal may be clear, but the wind and currents are constantly shifting, and the boat's crew will work constantly to trim the ship in response. As new information becomes available, the project responds to it.

These two approaches contrast most sharply, perhaps, in terms of how they respond to error. Mistakes in directive planning are often assumed to reflect poor preparation or poor implementation. In interactive planning, however, errors are essential to the process of learning; they point the way to places where project modification is necessary.

Which Approach Works Best in Project Development?

Most development projects are planned using some combination of these two approaches. Even the most straightforward construction project, for example, will incorporate some element of feedback and modification, just as an open-ended community development project needs some advance structure and planning. Project designers must therefore choose how structured—or how flexible—they will be in their planning.

As we will see in the next chapter, project design must integrate a number of different elements to be successful. The local environment—particularly the participant groups—must be integrated with the project agency so that they work together. The concept or idea that forms the basis for the project must be compatible with both the agency and the participants. The delivery structure for the project must fit with local capabilities. Finally, the outcomes of the project must be relevant to local needs.

With these things in mind, planners can make decisions about how directive or how interactive the project should be. Figure 4.4 sets out some of the questions that must be asked in this respect

Some project situations make the choice of approach relatively easy. Disaster relief, humanitarian assistance, or emergency evacuations will, by and large, be projects undertaken in a highly directive manner. There is either no time for more sophisticated planning or no need. Vaccination projects in the face of an epidemic, on the other hand, will almost certainly incorporate some knowledge of the local environment and of stakeholder groups, but the technical requirements of the project will probably determine its major outlines.

Most projects, however, present planners with important choices, even when they appear relatively simple on the surface. Building a dam, for example, might be seen as a relatively straightforward "blueprint" project, to be carried out in a highly directive manner. But the resettlement activities that must accompany the dam are far from simple, and require planners to develop a highly sophisticated understanding of—and interaction with—local stakeholders.[5]

FIGURE 4.4   Choosing the Appropriate Approach

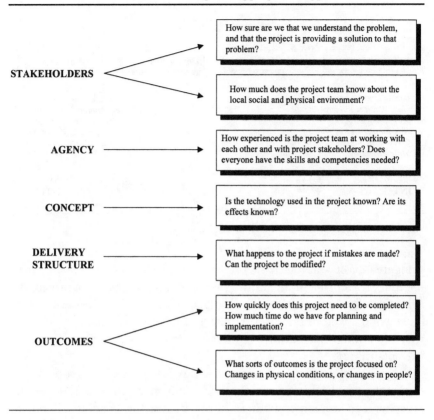

Indeed, most projects will depend for their success, in one way or another, on the extent to which they mesh with local arrangements. For this reason, it is usually highly desirable to incorporate as much interactivity as possible into the process of project development.

Types of Projects

How rigidly a project is planned is also a function of what type of project it is. Although each project is unique in many ways, projects are designed, in an important sense, to generate useful learning about what works and what does not. Successful projects—or successful project elements—are often transferred from one situation to another. As learning proceeds, some aspects of project development become less interactive and more formulaic.

FIGURE 4.5   A Range of Project Types

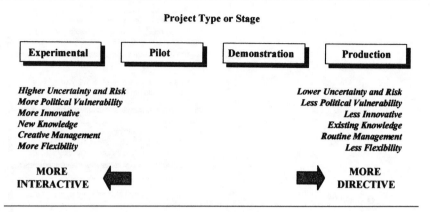

SOURCE: Adapted from Rondinelli 1983: 90.

Figure 4.5 sets out four basic project types. As we move from an experimental project to a production-type project, more aspects of project development become routine. The danger, of course, is that routines that
have worked well in one context may not work well in another. For this
reason, planners must always be alert to ways in which context interacts
with planning

Experimental projects contain many unknowns, including the definition of the problem, its possible solution, and appropriate techniques and
procedures to use. Experimental projects must achieve a close alignment
with the local context, so they are often planned in an interactive way,
with significant time devoted to research, feasibility studies, and discussion.

Pilot projects are designed to test the appropriateness of something
that has worked elsewhere (or that has worked on the drawing board).
Attention therefore concentrates on developing effective methods of
implementation, transfer, and dissemination. Planners look at the local
context mainly in terms of its fit or lack of fit with the existing model.
Where discrepancies or problem areas are noted, the project is modified
accordingly. There is still a high degree of interactivity with the project
environment.

A *demonstration* project, on the other hand, is designed primarily to in-
duce acceptance of a tested approach, technique, or procedure by local
populations. Attention focuses here on the replicability and suitability of
the project in one or several areas. The emphasis has begun to shift more

toward directiveness; the concept or technique driving the project is assumed to be a solution. If it does not work in the demonstration environments, then planners will look more closely at why, but often, they will do this only after major problems begin to appear.

Finally, a *production* or *replication* project is one where efforts are being made to diffuse project benefits as widely as possible, across a range of situations. Attention centers on the delivery systems for doing this and the arrangements for generating project benefits on a large scale. At this point, most of the bugs have been worked out of the system. Although planners are interested in why projects fail at this point, they will be inclined to seek answers in the implementation arrangements, not in terms of the project concept itself.[6]

PROJECT DEVELOPMENT
AS AN EMERGENT PROBLEM

The directive approach is seductive. It presents the image of a controlled and logical approach, likely to be particularly attractive to risk-averse funders.[7]

But the typical development project, however certain its technology or cost-benefit calculations might be, unfolds within a context of greater or lesser uncertainty. The social or physical environment may be unfamiliar; the project's technology may be untried; members of the project team may be newcomers to the area. The project is a developing drama, played out against a background of diverse and shifting concerns, where the learning curve is particularly steep.

A willingness to embrace and learn from error becomes particularly important in these situations. Directive projects are at a disadvantage here; not only is there a reluctance to admit error, there is often an inability to sense when an error has occurred, at least until it is too late.[8]

Interactive planning, on the other hand, is better able to accommodate error—indeed, the approach relies on errors to indicate the correct path. Mistakes in project work hardly ever happen randomly or for no reason; they arise out of interactions with the project environment that can teach planners, if they so choose, a great deal about how that environment is put together. Errors help reveal planners' and stakeholders' assumptions and blind spots.

Unlike technical problems, which simply require the application of a formula or technique, project development is an *emergent problem*, one that requires learning new things and new ways of thinking about those things, and to adjust our strategy as we learn. Count von Moltke, the Prussian field marshal, put it this way: "Strategy is a system of makeshifts. It is bringing knowledge to bear on practical life, the further elaboration of an original guiding idea under constantly changing circumstances."[9]

Unfortunately, many project planners fail to follow this advice. Under the multiple pressures of time, money, and bureaucratic expediency, planners often bring a ready-made template into the project environment, but then neglect to adapt it to local circumstances. This directive approach, of course, considerably simplifies the process of project development, but it also rules out alternative approaches and makes it difficult to either learn from the environment or to modify the project, as time goes on.[10]

Project Development as Reflective Practice

Most projects, to be successful, will have to conform to local norms and standards.[11] But which ones?

Local norms are hardly even uniform or homogeneous, and so project development becomes a process of negotiation within and among multiple groups.[12] Involved are relationships of exchange and barter, as well as instances of coercion, deceit, manipulation, cooptation, and other even less savory forms of interaction. No wonder, then, that the project development cycle is so often characterized by stress, emotion, and uncertainty.

The process of project design is therefore one of adaptive change, where issues and opportunities arise as the project proceeds. Many problems that turn out to be crucial for project success may not even be visible at the initial stages.[13] Eventually, the project is either made compatible with the core requirements of the context in which it exists, or it is marginalized or otherwise rendered neutral.

Project development is a good example of what Donald Schön has termed "reflective practice"—a process of gradual, interactive problem solving, where techniques are applied, the results are assessed, and the learning gained is applied to subsequent actions.[14] Schön says: "The enquirer's relation to this situation is transactional. He shapes the situation, but in conversation with it, so that his own models and appreciations are also shaped by the situation. The phenomena that he seeks to understand are partly of his own making; he is in the situation that he seeks to understand."[15]

The task in project development is not simply to figure out how to solve a particular problem. It is to discover in the first place what the relevant problem is and how it should be approached, *before* designing an intervention. In this sense, project development resembles intelligence gathering rather than research. Planners will never have complete information at the outset, but they will need to act. Decisions will therefore be made quickly and incrementally, even as new information and new learning appears.[16]

ANTHROPOLOGY AND PROJECT DEVELOPMENT

Development projects are a form of cross-cultural drama; a play in which many of the actors do not really know their lines very well at first. Although there is a script, there are also departures from that script, and success requires the actors to come to terms with each other, to make necessary and appropriate adjustments to the script, and to eventually produce a coherent and satisfying show.[17]

Anthropology, with its emphasis on discovery rather than prescription, is an ideal catalyst in this process of creative meaning-making. Its qualitative approach breaks down barriers between different stakeholders in a project, illuminates areas of relevance, and helps people talk and plan meaningfully across differences that would otherwise divide them.

At the *framing* stage of project development, anthropology helps identify problems, problem structures, and stakeholder groups. Once groups have been identified, anthropology provides tools for understanding their characteristics, needs, and capabilities. Finally, anthropology can help match these characteristics to their counterparts within the development agencies involved in project development. From this, appropriate and realistic project arrangements can be designed and negotiated.

At the *management* stage of a project, learning and negotiation become even more important. Anthropology helps to illuminate and guide relationships between stakeholders as project activities unfold. Anthropology also helps these groups deal with unexpected developments, new information, or changes in the surrounding context of the project.

Finally, at the *assessment* stage, anthropology helps stakeholders understand outcomes in terms that make sense to everyone. If the project is successful, anthropology can be used to help ensure that benefits continue and that arrangements are sustained over time. Should the project fail or produce negative outcomes, anthropology can often help pinpoint causes, helping stakeholders design appropriate modifications.

Successful project development requires stakeholders to do two main things: to learn as they go, both about their surroundings and about each other; and to manage their interactions successfully. Anthropologists play important roles by collecting and analyzing information and by serving as brokers or facilitators between and among groups. Our inductive, qualitative, and holistic approach generates the kinds of understanding that both complements and considerably enhances more structured and quantitative approaches. Rather than seeing the project as a series of discrete things, anthropologists will look at it as a developing system, and pay particular attention to the relationships between the various parts, levels, and components.

Are Anthropologists "Experts"?

The anthropologist's role in project development is quite different from that of other specialists. Because so much project work involves uncertainty, and because so much is often at stake, agencies tend to seek out "experts." When one is working on a deadline, there is enormous pressure to turn to people who claim to already know the answers, rather than to spend time trying to determine what the appropriate questions are and how to answer them.

Expertise in project development may be a necessary condition for success, but it is hardly a sufficient one. Although anthropologists are indeed a kind of expert, their expertise lies primarily in techniques of discovery and interpretation, not in the provision of ready-made certainty. In this respect they are very different from some of the other experts involved in development.

Our willingness to accept the truth that emerges from field investigation is probably one of our greatest assets, as well as being a potential source of irritation to other project specialists. As the "uncomfortable science," anthropology tends to bring a certain quality of disassurance to development work, uncovering and challenging misconceptions and unexamined assumptions.[18] Table 4.1 sets out some of the major differences between anthropologists and other development "experts."

Project Development in Context

Although each project is unique, all successful projects must fit with their surrounding context. Technical, financial, and managerial issues

TABLE 4.1 Experts and Others

Technical Expert	Anthropologist
Usually deals with things. Outcomes are expressed as facts and expert opinions.	Usually deals with people. Outcomes center on cultural meanings and interpretations.
The expert "owns" the domain. He or she is expert because of their mastery of subject matter. The expertise is located in the person of the expert.	Expertise is located in the project context itself. The anthropologist possesses certain skills, but is primarily a conduit or an interpreter for meanings from this context.
Knowledge is bounded by disciplines and subject areas. Facts are "objective" and neutral, "out there" in the world, in pre-set categories.	Knowledge is a social construct, and not always conventionally bounded. The process of generating knowledge and meaning is a dialogue.
The expert is presumed to know, and must claim to know, regardless of any uncertainties.	The anthropologist is also presumed to know, but is not the only person to have relevant knowledge. Uncertainties can be a source of learning for all stakeholders.
The expert keeps a certain distance from the "client," and maintains the expert's role.	The anthropologist must enter into the client's thoughts and feelings.
The expert looks for respect and status from the client.	The anthropologist looks for openness and a real connection with the client.

SOURCE: Adapted from Schön 1983: 42.

are clearly important, but it is the context surrounding these that will ultimately determine how well techniques, money, and management work. Successful projects create outcomes, choices, and opportunities that people value, by processes that they understand and can influence. Successful projects, in other words, must make sense within the surrounding context. The context of a project has three main aspects:

- The *inner environment* is the part of the project that can be ordered and regulated by project authorities. Typically, this would include all internal operations of the project planning or implementation unit.
- The *proximate environment* exists outside the project unit itself, but in close contact with it. This environment has an important influence on the project, but is, in turn, influenced by it. This en-

FIGURE 4.6   The Project Context

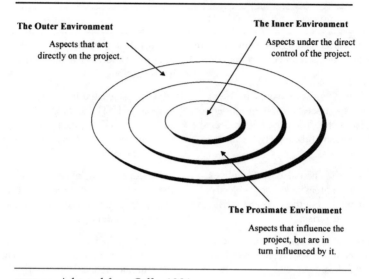

The Outer Environment

Aspects that act
directly on the project.

The Inner Environment

Aspects under the direct
control of the project.

The Proximate Environment

Aspects that influence the
project, but are in
turn influenced by it.

SOURCE: Adapted from Siffin 1981.

vironment includes project beneficiaries, participants and stakeholders, local authorities, donors, and other groups.
- The *outer environment* also affects the project, but is not significantly subject to project influence or control. The outer environment includes such things as the national economy, the political
and legal system, the climate, topography, natural resources of the
area, and so forth.[19]

Making sure that the project fits with its context requires not only
considerable prior understanding of the project context, but continued
learning throughout the life of the project. Mini-Case 4.2, "The Case of
the Arabic Typewriters," illustrates how different aspects of context interacted over time in an urban development project in Tunisia.

Context-based projects will therefore encourage the identification of
relevant stakeholder groups before crucial framing decisions are taken.
They will seek to involve the stakeholders in significant aspects of planning, implementation, and assessment. Project design will be as flexible
as possible, so that the project can respond to new information, and
there will be well-designed systems for monitoring and evaluation to
capture this information. Finally, planners will treat the project experi-

MINI-CASE 4.2
THE CASE OF THE ARABIC TYPEWRITERS

In the early 1980s, I managed an urban upgrading project in a slum neighborhood of Tunis. All three aspects of the project context were important to the way the project developed, but they were important in different ways.

The *inner environment* of the project consisted of the project team and its office in the community of Mellassine. As the project director, I and my Tunisian counterpart had a great deal of control over the team and what it did; we could hire staff, assign tasks, set deadlines, purchase equipment, and modify the project as events unfolded.

Aspects of Context in the Tunis Project

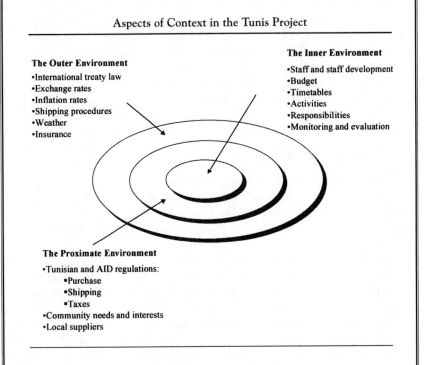

The Inner Environment
•Staff and staff development
•Budget
•Timetables
•Activities
•Responsibilities
•Monitoring and evaluation

The Outer Environment
•International treaty law
•Exchange rates
•Inflation rates
•Shipping procedures
•Weather
•Insurance

The Proximate Environment
•Tunisian and AID regulations:
　•Purchase
　•Shipping
　•Taxes
•Community needs and interests
•Local suppliers

To do these things successfully, however, required all of us to learn a great deal about each other and our capabilities. For my part, I needed to learn—and quickly—how to adapt my management style to the cultural and bureaucratic requirements of a Tunisian office. My Tunisian counter-

(continues)

part and coworkers, in turn, needed to become comfortable with an American in their midst. Because the project was funded in large part by an American agency, they needed to learn about, and adapt to, some variations in reporting and procedures.

Beyond the walls of the project headquarters lay the *proximate environment,* consisting of various government offices, AID's Tunis headquarters, and the different community groups who were project beneficiaries. Here, we had much less control but a measure of influence. To coordinate activities between the different groups, we needed first to learn a great deal about them and then to persuade them to collaborate with us and with each other. This aspect of project development was never-ending; as each phase of implementation unfolded, new issues, problems, and opportunities emerged. Our ability to keep the project moving forward depended on the skill with which our project team was able to ensure that each group's interests were—to the extent possible—being met.

Finally, of course, the *outer environment* had a major influence on our project. As a bilateral aid project, we were subject to a plethora of Tunisian and American laws, treaties, and conventions, none of which we could influence in the slightest. We were also at the mercy of various macroeconomic conditions, such as rates of exchange and inflation. Here again, our ability to develop the project successfully required us to learn about these aspects of the outer environment and to make sure that project arrangements reflected them.

The interactions between these different levels went on throughout the project. One simple example—the case of the Arabic typewriters—will perhaps suffice to impart both the complexity and the flavor of this unique choreography.

Early in the project, my staff and I decided, on the basis of a preliminary needs assessment, that training for small business owners in the project area would be a major project component. Our goal was to produce training materials in Arabic that met needs articulated by local artisans.

To do this, we needed staff and equipment. A draftsman was assigned from municipal headquarters, together with several trainers. Now we needed several Arabic typewriters to help us produce written materials, and it was at this point that our project began to head into uncharted waters.

First, we needed to consult with our project staff about the technical specifications of the typewriters—size, cost, typefaces, and so forth. Then we needed to obtain approval from municipal authorities for their purchase. This could not be done, however, without pro forma invoices from local vendors. These were duly obtained and presented.

(continues)

MINI-CASE 4.2   (continued)

At this point, USAID entered the picture. The typewriters in question, we were informed, could not be bought with AID funds, since they had not been produced in approved countries. Approved countries, it eventually turned out, meant the United States. My accountant Toufik turned to me when he received this news. "I wasn't aware," he said, "that you used Arabic typewriters in America."

After a fairly lengthy search, we found that IBM did indeed make Arabic typewriters, but that they needed to be ordered from their headquarters in France. Invoices were once again procured, only to be refused by AID's controller. "It's not an American-made IBM," we were told, "but a French one. And besides, we think the motors are actually made in Mexico."

At this point, I sought advice from my firm's headquarters in Washington. "Ask the AID director in Tunis for a waiver," they said. "He can waive anything he wants to. *If* he wants to."

Glimpsing light at the end of the tunnel, I met several times with the director, finally obtaining the prized waiver for the purchase of three Arabic typewriters from IBM in France. I bought a round of Turkish coffee for the project staff to celebrate our victory.

More AID regulations were to come, however. The typewriters needed to be properly insured, by policies and companies acceptable to AID. They needed to be shipped to Tunisia from France on American flag carriers, but since an American ship could not be located, the director again signed a waiver.

Finally, there remained the small problem of import authorizations. Toufik and I went to the main customs office. "Of course, duty will have to be paid," said the *Chef de Douane* behind the desk.

"It's a bilateral aid project," I pointed out. "Exempt. Duty-free."

"Says who?"

"It's in the project document."

He raised his eyebrows. "Bring it."

The document was brought. "It's not in Arabic," said the man.

"Silly me," I said, fixing a smile on my face. "Be right back."

Several days later we were back. The man behind the desk peered suspiciously at the papers. "*Our* ministry didn't sign this," he said at last.

"The Ministry of the Interior did," I replied. "They approve all the foreign aid."

He sniffed. "They don't control customs, monsieur. Get a letter from them." I sighed.

(continues)

Several weeks later, we returned with the letter. "We need a bill of lading," the *Chef* said.

I turned to Toufik. "Call Paris," I said. "Tell them to ship."

Our story reached its climax one chilly winter afternoon, two weeks later. As we all sat huddled around the space heater in our project office sipping tea, Toufik appeared in the doorway, his face carefully composed.

"I have news," he announced in a quiet voice. "The shipping agent just called. Our typewriters left Marseilles two days ago on a freighter."

A cheer went up.

Toufik raised his hand. "*Lekin ha'ja uxra.* There's one other thing. The ship sank this afternoon off the coast of Algeria, in a freak snowstorm." He paused. "The crew were saved, *alhamdullilahi*, but all the cargo went to the bottom."

Although to say that we were stunned by the news would be an enormous understatement, we at least knew now what we had to do next. We repeated the entire process, and this time, the fates were kind. Waivers were signed, approvals were forthcoming, and the Mediterranean remained calm. Eighteen months after our project team had first decided that Arabic typewriters would be needed, they arrived. We unpacked them and set them up, and then went home for the day.

That was not quite the end of the story, of course. The next morning, I found our project secretary, Najoua, sitting at her desk reading a *roman policier*. "Why aren't you working?" I said, indicating the new typewriters. "I would think you'd be dying to try them."

She shook her head. "That's not in my job description," she said, folding her arms. "If you want me to type in Arabic, you'll have to give me a raise."

Behind her, Toufik shrugged and raised his eyes to heaven, the ghost of a smile on his lips.

*   *   *

The saga of the typewriters illustrates quite well, I think, the interplay between personalities, policies, and forces of nature in determining when and how projects develop through time. Decisions made within the inner environment of the project were modified by forces in the proximate environment, and these, in turn, were acted upon by aspects of the outer environment in unpredictable ways

Changing the context means changing the forces and thereby altering what happens and why. Projects, however carefully they are planned, are bundles of small stories, each of them as complex in its way as that of the typewriters.

ence as an opportunity to acquire both new learning about the environment and new insight into how to apply their skills and experience most effectively within that environment.

⟶ ⟶ ⟶

SUMMARY OF CHAPTER 4

Chapter 4 has looked at development projects; the primary way in which development assistance finds its way to the grass roots. Projects are a bureaucratically convenient way of organizing resources and effort, and are shaped according to strategies and goals that must be decided very early in the process of project development.

The chapter looked at several contrasting approaches to project planning. Directive approaches rely mainly on assumptions of certainty regarding the environment in which the project will operate. Interactive planning, on the other hand, makes learning about the project environment part of the planning process itself. Since most development projects operate across a cultural interface—or across several—interactive approaches usually work best.

The context or environment within which a project operates will have three main parts or aspects: an inner environment under the direct control of the project itself; a proximate environment with which the project interacts and that includes beneficiaries and other outside stakeholders; and an outer environment that, although acting on the project, is largely outside its influence.

Anthropologists contribute in many ways to the development of projects, but two of their key roles are as providers of information about project context and as brokers between various groups operating in that context. The broker's role is complex but crucial in situations where groups do not share common perceptions, values, or visions of the future.

ENDNOTES

1. The role of projects—and their pros and cons—in development work has been discussed by numerous authors, including Honadle and Rosengard (1983), Conlin (1985: 76), Gow (1991), Uphoff (1990), and Rondinelli (1992: 529).

2. Pigg (1997: 270).

3. See Korten (1980); Korten and Klaus (1984) for more details of this approach to planning.

4. See Honadle and Van Sant (1985: 92). Brinkerhoff and Ingle (1987: 9) call this approach "structured flexibility."

5. See, for example, Cernea and Guggenheim (1993) and Cernea and Mc-Dowell (2000). Earlier, an entire issue of *Practicing Anthropology* (vol. 12, no. 3, 1990) was devoted to dams and resettlement.

6. From Rondinelli (1983).

7. Rondinelli (1985: 235).

8. Gow (1991).

9. Dörner (1996: 97–98).

10. Gow (1991: 3).

11. See Epstein and Ahmed (1984: 50).

12. See, for example, Partridge (1979: 26; 1985); Honadle and Van Sant (1985: 117).

13. Rondinelli (1983: 14–15).

14. Schön (1983: 40).

15. Schön (1983: 150–151)

16. Moris and Copestake (1993: 63–64).

17. Koenig (1988: 345–364) provides a nice example of how different partners in AID-financed development projects interacted to uncover the project's meaning.

18. Firth, in Grillo and Rew (1985: 23).

19. Siffin (1981); Honadle and Cooper (1989: 1531).

chapter 5

INFORMATION IN PROJECT DEVELOPMENT

PROJECT LEVELS

Planners use information throughout the project cycle to integrate five different project levels. These include the *stakeholders* involved in the project, the *agency* responsible for project implementation, the project's central *concept* or *idea*, the project's *structure*, and the hoped-for *changes* or *outcomes*.

Stakeholders

As we've seen, stakeholders are groups and organizations at the local level with both an interest in what happens in a project and some measure of influence over these outcomes. Stakeholder groups have specific structural and cultural characteristics, skills and capabilities, and agendas. Stakeholders also have history.[1] Since stakeholders can either lend or withhold support, their interests and needs are of primary importance.

The Agency

The local project team that controls project resources and is responsible for implementation is almost always linked to one or more development agencies, local or international, whose interests they represent. Like local stakeholders, the agency has a culture and structure, and these affect project outcomes.[2]

The Concept or Idea

Every project will have a concept or idea at its core. Often, this is an innovation or new technology to be tried out as part of the project, perhaps a machine, or a new variety of seed. Alternatively, the concept may be a strategy, an approach to doing the project, or a methodology.

The Project Structure

As discussed in Chapter 4, a project is composed of arrangements that link resources, activities, strategies, and objectives. These must be compatible with the needs and capabilities of both the stakeholders and the implementers. They must also be appropriate for the particular idea or concept that is being attempted.

The Changes or Outcomes

Finally, all projects aim for specific outcomes. These must be relevant to the needs of both stakeholders and the implementing agencies, and must be realistic in terms of the concepts and structures employed.

INTEGRATING PROJECT LEVELS

Integrating different project levels is somewhat akin to building a house. Without a proper foundation, a house will not stand. But the foundation is merely the substructure for other elements, equally important to what the house will eventually become. Foundations support walls, windows, and ultimately, the roof.

In like manner, successful projects achieve a fit between the needs, characteristics, constraints, and capabilities that exist at each of the five levels outlined above. A project is not an abstraction but is anchored in the socioeconomic environment of its stakeholders, with whatever constraints and potentials this includes. The implementing agency, in like manner, will have certain characteristics that will both limit and enhance its possibilities. Only through interactions between the agency and the stakeholders will the idea or concept that forms the core of the project emerge. This concept will, in turn, contain its own inherent re-

FIGURE 5.1   Integration of Project Levels

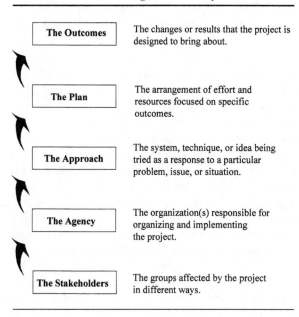

| The Outcomes | The changes or results that the project is designed to bring about. |

| The Plan | The arrangement of effort and resources focused on specific outcomes. |

| The Approach | The system, technique, or idea being tried as a response to a particular problem, issue, or situation. |

| The Agency | The organization(s) responsible for organizing and implementing the project. |

| The Stakeholders | The groups affected by the project in different ways. |

quirements. The requirements will be addressed—well or badly—by the structure and operation of the project design. Finally, the combination of stakeholders, agency, concept, and project will be focused on a set of outcomes that will be either feasible and appropriate or not.

Information is needed about each of the five levels for purposes of planning, management, and assessment. Without a basic understanding of the stakeholder community, the project agency, and the nature of the change(s) proposed, little understanding will be gained of either the process of project implementation or the outcomes of the completed project. Failure to comprehend how these levels are constituted—and how they may interact—will have negative consequences for any project. Mini-Case 5.1, "Trees in Haiti," discusses a successful forestry project where levels were successfully integrated.

Here and in the chapters to follow, I will look in detail at each of these levels. The rest of this chapter will focus primarily on *stakeholders*, first by looking at who they are and why they are important, then examining some of the ways anthropologists can develop their understanding of these groups. The ideas and concepts that underlie projects, together with delivery systems for translating these ideas into action, are exam-

---

MINI-CASE 5.1   TREES IN HAITI:
THE AGROFORESTRY OUTREACH PROJECT

Trees in Haiti could be considered an endangered species. Centuries of woodcutting combined with steady population growth and a rising market for charcoal have denuded vast areas of the Haitian countryside. Reforestation projects, by and large, have been unsuccessful, and indeed, Murray speaks of a "generalized hostility" to tree projects.

The problem, as Murray saw it, was both simple and daunting: "to instill in cash-needy, defiant peasant charcoal makers a love, honor, and respect for newly planted trees." Partly because of his earlier work on Haitian land tenure, Murray was called in by USAID to take on this task, and given substantial ($4 million) funding to work with. He comments: "My elation at commanding resources to implement anthropological ideas was dampened by the nervousness of knowing exactly who would be targeted for flak and ridicule if these ideas bombed out, as most tended to do in the Haiti of Duvalier."

Convinced that systems of land tenure, livestock rearing, and growing crops were not in themselves fundamentally incompatible with trees, an innovative system for providing peasants with lightweight, fast-growing seedlings was devised. A second innovation was to mix trees and crops on the same land, coupled with the message to peasants that these were their own trees, not the state's, and that the project expected people to harvest nuts, fruit, or wood and sell them, just as they would any other crop. "Haitian peasants are inveterate and aggressive cash-croppers; many of the crops and livestock that they produce are destined for immediate consignment to local markets. For the first time in their lives, they were hearing a concrete proposal to make the wood tree itself one more marketable crop in their inventory."

The project needed to convince peasants that trees would mature quickly; that they could be grown in combination with crops; and that the peasants themselves would own the trees. The third item was the most crucial, in the sense that if the Haitian government were to manage the project, it would almost certainly fail.

There was strong pressure from American officials within the local USAID mission, however, to continue to invest the Haitian bureaucracy with project authority, in the name of "institution-building." "Having equated the term 'institution' with 'government bureaucracy,' and having defined their own career success in terms, not of village-level resource flows, but of voluminous and timely bureaucracy-to-bureaucracy cash transfers, such officials were in effect marshaling U.S. resources into the service of extrac-

(continues)

MINI-CASE 5.1 (continued)

tive ministries with unparalleled track resources of squandering and/or pilfering expatriate donor funds."

Instead, the project succeeded in setting up a U.S.-based NGO as the main management authority, which then linked with local Haitian NGOs. These local NGOs provided support, technical advice, and most important, village organizers who were responsible for spearheading community efforts.

The project lasted from 1981 to 1985. Initially predicting that 3 million trees might be planted, the project had planted 20 million trees by the end of its fourth year. Although tree harvesting for charcoal was taking place, it was also clear that peasants were "banking" their trees as well, and leaving them in place.

As a result of project success, some perceptions have changed. Local NGOs, for example, have come to see that an ecology/conservation approach to trees is probably less effective than considering trees as the peasants do—as a cash crop. Murray noted ". . . by nudging these [Private Voluntary Organization] PVOs away from ethereal visions of the functions of trees, the [Agroforestry Outreach Project] AOP has brought them into closer dynamic touch with, and made them more responsive to, the economic interests of their peasant clientele."

USAID's operations have also changed somewhat. They are more willing to work with local private institutions, but for bureaucratic reasons, need a larger "umbrella" institution as their main recipient of funds. By the mid-1980s, nearly 60 percent of USAID/Haiti's funding was going to nongovernmental bodies.

The success of the project is owing in large part to anthropology. Murray comments: "We are dealing, not with an ongoing project affected by anthropological input, but with a project whose very existence was rooted in anthropological research and whose very character was determined by ongoing anthropological direction and anthropologically informed managerial prodding."

Anthropology was particularly significant in these ways:

- Detailed ethnographic knowledge of the Haitian context was used to frame the project. This included knowledge of peasant social and economic systems, horticulture, land tenure, and marketing systems.
- Anthropological methods were used during the design phases. Interviewing and participant observation were employed to determine the feasibility of various project options, to elicit folk tax-

(continues)

MINI-CASE 5.1   (continued)

onomies of trees, and to investigate institutional performance. Knowledge of Haitian Creole was used to design relevant baseline data collection systems.

• Anthropological theory also helped shape the project. The project used what anthropologists know about the evolutionary shift from hunting and gathering to domestication to recast trees as a cropping and harvesting issue rather than a conservation issue.

In essence, the project based itself on what Haitian peasants already knew and did. The real changes brought about by the project were at the level of the change agents and the development agencies themselves. Project designers—most of whom were anthropologists—gained new insight into how the dynamic of local systems could be harnessed for change.USAID, however reluctantly, was led to reconsider its modalities of development assistance.

SOURCE: Murray 1987.

---

ined in Chapter 6. Aspects of agency operation, including organizational culture, are covered in Chapter 7. Finally, project goals and outcomes will be discussed in Chapter 8.

IDENTIFYING PROJECT STAKEHOLDERS

What Are Stakeholders?

As we have seen, stakeholders are groups and organizations having an interest in the project and its outcomes. Stakeholder groups are the bedrock of all projects, and without detailed knowledge of these groups, success is unlikely. Although some stakeholders may be physically distant from the project site, I am primarily concerned with local stakeholders—community groups found within the project area itself, whose members are likely project beneficiaries.

However composed, stakeholders share three important characteristics: they have *interests* in the project, *resources* that they can make available to help with project development, and *power* to advance or impede the process. If stakeholders feel that their interests are being taken account of, they will be likely to support the project. If they feel their interests are ignored or threatened, they may withhold support or actively oppose a project. Since stakeholders' beliefs, values, and preferences will have a marked effect on project outcomes—and hence, on project success—an important part of project development involves identifying who the stakeholders are and what they are like.

Stakeholder groups may have a geographical basis or they may coalesce around a particular field of activity or interest. They may be people who have access (or lack of access) to certain goods or services. They may be determined by various other characteristics, such as age, class, sex, wealth, or education. Finally, stakeholders can be at-risk groups of various kinds. Mini-Case 5.2, "Stakeholders in Mellassine," outlines the range of stakeholders involved in the Tunis urban upgrading project, and some of the more important roles they played.

Local stakeholder communities will have well-established systems for managing their lives. These systems, although not immutable, will be highly resistant to change from the outside. When local systems interact with outside ones—such as those represented by an implementing agency—it is not always possible to predict in advance where the incompatibilities may lie, and more important, how they will be resolved in practice. It is therefore very important to have an in-depth understanding of local communities and how they work at the earliest stages of project development, before project goals and procedures are decided.

Who Are Stakeholders?

Anthropologists can play a critical role in developing planners' understanding of local stakeholders. Local stakeholders are hardly ever one group of people, but several, with multiple and sometimes conflicting interests, and it is a mistake for planners to assume uniformity.[3]

Once relevant groups have been identified, a variety of important things must be learned from these groups, including the ways in which they make decisions, the values that guide their choices, and the resources they employ to meet their ends. If there are important symbolic aspects to decisionmaking and choice, these, too, should be learned about, before key framing decisions are made.

Table 5.1 presents a simple framework for preliminary stakeholder analysis, focused on some of the most important things planners will need to know at an early stage of project development. This will also

MINI-CASE 5.2 STAKEHOLDERS IN MELLASSINE

From 1979 to 1982, I was the director of the Mellassine Integrated Improvement Project for the Urban Poor (IIPUP), an urban upgrading project in one of the peripheral slum communities of Tunis. At the time, I was a socioeconomic planner with the Washington-based firm of PADCO (Planning and Development Collaborative), which had a long-term contract with AID to deliver technical assistance and other support services to a variety of urban projects around the world. The story of how this project developed and what outcomes it achieved would fill a book, but of particular interest and importance was the variety of different stakeholders who emerged as design and implementation proceeded.

The diagram below sets out the main stakeholders.

Relationships Between Stakeholders

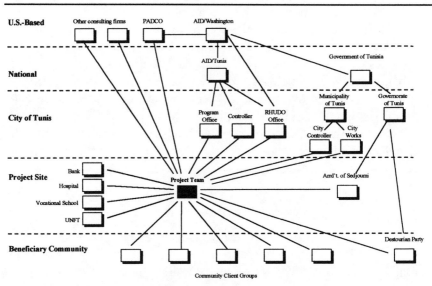

The principal roles each of these stakeholders played in the project appear in the table below.

Each stakeholder had a different interest in the project; each had a different influence on it. The major government donors (Tunisian and American) assumed that because they had provided money, they therefore had a high degree of control over implementation, but this proved to be not quite the case. Other stakeholders, some with very little visible power, were nonetheless able to influence the project, using a variety of strategies. In this respect, the Mellassine IIPUP project was not at all unusual.

(continues)

MINI-CASE 5.2 (continued)	
Principal *Stakeholders*	*Stakeholder Roles and/or Interests*
AID/Washington	AID provided the funding for the project, through a bilateral agreement with the Tunisian Ministry of Foreign Affairs.
Tunisian Ministry of Foreign Affairs	The Government of Tunisia formally approved the project. Subsequent changes in the project had to be approved by this ministry
AID/Tunis	AID/Tunis was responsible for project implementation.
Program Office	Within AID/Tunis, the Program Office was in principle responsible for project implementation. In reality, they shared this responsibility with the RHUDO office (see below).
Controller's Office	The AID/Tunis Controller's office was responsible for budget supervision and for disbursement or reimbursement of project funds to Tunisian entities.
RHUDO Office	AID's Regional Housing and Urban Development Office occupied a special niche. Although nominally under the control of the AID/Tunis mission director, RHUDO's funding came directly from Washington, which effectively removed them from AID/Tunis control. Relationships therefore had to be negotiated on a day-to-day basis between these two parts of the AID/Tunis Mission.
PADCO	**The Washington-based Planning and Development Collaborative International (PADCO) had the implementation contract for the project through AID/ Washington. They provided project management services and logistic support.**
Other Consulting Firms	Project funding included amounts for U.S. technical assistance from other firms, as needed.
Project Team	The team assembled on the project site included myself and over twenty Tunisians (secretaries, clerks, counterparts, drivers, technicians, janitors, and so forth).
Municipality of Tunis	The Municipality of Tunis was the principal Tunisian implementation organization. The mayor's office oversaw in principle all project operations.
City Works Office	The City Works Office was responsible for all major construction and upgrading projects in the city of Tunis, and had day-to-day responsibility for project operations.
City Controller's Office	The City Controller's Office approved all budget requests from the project.
Governorate of Tunis	The governor's office controlled the region in which the project took place, and had to approve major aspects of the project.
Destourian Party	The ruling political party was the main organizing entity within the governorate, and served as the official voice of the local residents.
Participating Agencies	The project was composed of several different elements: small business loans, social services, vocational training, and so on. Each required the participation of a local organization.
Local Banks	Several local banks helped the project to administer the small business loans.
Social Affairs Office	This government agency supplied social workers to the project.
Local Hospital	The local hospital provided health education specialists to the project.
National Union of Tunisian Women	This government agency ran a vocational training school for young women.

(continues)

MINI-CASE 5.2   (continued)

My role as an anthropologist who also happened to be the project's director was to find ways to mediate between the various stakeholders, who spanned several continents, spoke three different languages (French, English, and Arabic), and operated using several different legal, fiscal, and administrative systems.

In some cases, my role centered on bringing different groups of stakeholders together and helping them negotiate mutually acceptable arrangements for project implementation. In other cases, however, brokerage involved explaining one group's way of thinking to another, as when AID's procurement regulations ran up against the (literally) Byzantine system used by the City of Tunis (compare with Mini-Case 4.2). The resulting project—which was ultimately successful—did not represent a triumph of one of these cultural systems over the other, so much as the slow and often painful crafting of a "project culture," within which rules, categories, and procedures were developed that differed at points from those operating elsewhere in different systems.

---

help planners understand what they need to tell different stakeholder groups about the project, and may provide some initial clues to how these groups might be able to interact with the project in constructive ways later on.

Not all stakeholders, of course, will be equally committed to the project. This type of preliminary analysis will therefore be useful in arranging different groups along a rough continuum of support. One way of doing this is presented in Figure 5.2. Even a simple analysis of this type, if done early, can help planners avoid designing projects for which there is weak or nonexistent local support

But stakeholder groups may not be obvious to planners at first. Sometimes important groups are simply not identified. Sometimes groups are identified but mislabeled. And sometimes, various subgroups (often with conflicting needs) are identified as a single group.

Mini-Case 5.3, "Who Lives Here?" discusses how domain analysis was used to help planners identify different stakeholder groups in an agricultural project in rural Senegal, and then to understand some of the keys to eliciting participation from these groups.

TABLE 5.1   A Matrix for Initial Stakeholder Analysis

Who are the different groups?	Stakeholder groups can include local organizations, communities, businesses, interest groups, individuals, officials, institutions, and so on.
What power and influence do they have?	Stakeholders have varied and multiple interests. They may be beneficiaries, gatekeepers, informants, controllers, funders, legislators, subscribers, employers, and so on.
What do they want or need from the project?	Similarly, they may have very different needs and expectations of the project. Some groups would like change; others would like to maintain aspects of the status quo. Some would like economic benefits, whereas others may be more interested in the acquisition of new skills, enhanced responsibilities, or more power.
What can they contribute to the project?	Stakeholders have resources that can be made available to the project. These might include knowledge, skills, money, participation, materials, political support, or advice.
What more do we need to know about them?	Working effectively with stakeholders will require project planners to learn more about them, including their composition, size, history, personalities, leadership structure, rules, preferences, linkages, position on other issues.

FIGURE 5.2   A Range of Project Stakeholders

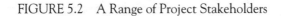

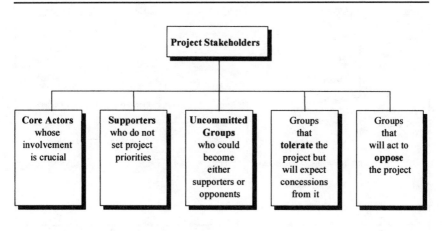

source: Adapted from Ilchman and Uphoff 1969 (in Staudt 1991: 66).

MINI-CASE 5.3
WHO LIVES HERE? STAKEHOLDERS IN SENEGAL

Here is an example of a relatively simple domain analysis, based on some project design work I did in Senegal in the late 1970s when I was part of a USAID team designing an agriculture project in a rural Senegalese village.

The technical requirements of the project called for heavy labor inputs at various periods. The engineers and agronomists assumed that all able-bodied villagers would participate, and they were puzzled by village leaders' hesitant reactions to their proposals. We realized that before we could discuss participation with residents, we needed to understand more about how the community was structured.

Numbers alone were not sufficient; the project team needed some insight into what the numbers represented. In a series of joint sessions involving villagers and project technicians, we were able to "map" two significant cultural domains that would greatly affect who would participate in the project and when. These maps shed considerable light on two seemingly simple questions: Who lives here? and How does time work here?

The results were surprising to the project technicians. Our analysis showed that this seemingly homogeneous village was in fact made up of several different groups, not all of whom would either benefit from or participate in the project. The "map" (below) of the kinds of people inhabiting the world of the Senegalese villagers shows both the groups and the organizing principles used to create those groups.

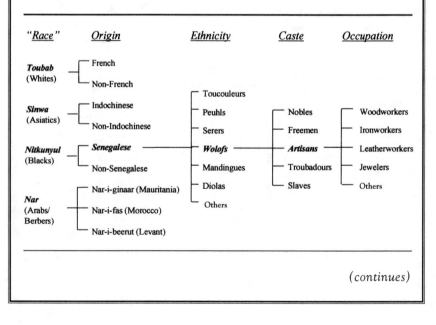

"Race"	_Origin_	_Ethnicity_	_Caste_	_Occupation_
Toubab (Whites)	⌈ French ⌊ Non-French			
Sinwa (Asiatics)	⌈ Indochinese ⌊ Non-Indochinese	⌈ Toucouleurs ├ Peuhls ├ Serers	⌈ Nobles ├ Freemen	⌈ Woodworkers ├ Ironworkers
Nitkunyul (Blacks)	⌈ _Senegalese_ ⌊ Non-Senegalese	_Wolofs_ ── ── ── _Artisans_ ├ Mandingues ├ Diolas	├ _Artisans_ ├ Troubadours ⌊ Slaves	── Leatherworkers ├ Jewelers ⌊ Others
Nar (Arabs/ Berbers)	⌈ Nar-i-ginaar (Mauritania) ├ Nar-i-fas (Morocco) ⌊ Nar-i-beerut (Levant)	⌊ Others		

(continues)

MINI-CASE 5.3 (continued)

As one might expect, this village-centered view of the world was quite different from that of the foreign "experts" who were designing the project.

Wolof villagers had relatively few categories for non-Africans (although, interestingly, they distinguished between three different types of Arab/Berber groups). Villagers had relatively simple, broad categories for outsiders (for example, whites, Asians, and Arab/Berbers), but elaborate and specific categories for local residents, who distinguish between ethnic group, caste, and within caste groups by occupation.

The values and expectations attached to the various categories, which do not appear above, were strikingly different. Project planners were unaware, for example, of the caste system within Wolof society, the existence of a slave group, and of the complex rules that govern relationships between castes, slaves, freemen, and nobles, and between members of different ethnic groups. These relationships had clear implications for both who participated in the proposed project and who was likely to benefit from its results. None of this, needless to say, would have necessarily emerged from a Western-style household survey.

In a similar way, mapping *time* yielded other important insights. Although the villagers used the same daily, weekly, and yearly calendars as the technicians, the divisions held quite different meanings for them. Irrigation schedules had to be adjusted, for example, to daily prayer times, daily siesta times, and extended prayers each Friday at the mosque. The lunar month of Ramadan placed other restrictions on village labor. Finally, twilight, or *timis,* when witches were said to appear, would find no villagers in the fields.

Thus, the temporal divisions recognized and used by villagers were linked to cultural patterns that would greatly affect what work could be done at different times of the day, week, or year. Discovering these patterns meant that they could be incorporated into the project design at an early stage.

If we had simply labeled community residents in terms of some set of outside—albeit more familiar—categories, we would have missed the more significant distinctions made by the residents themselves. Local distinctions often provide important clues to key aspects of values, structures, and preferences.

This is not to say that local categories and values do not pose problems in themselves for project development. In the case above, the discovery by the project team of a caste of slaves raised important questions in their minds regarding who would do most of the work on the project and who would derive the most benefit. Ultimately, these issues had to be negotiated with community residents, and the resulting compromises were highly instructive for everyone.

The roles played by stakeholders—and the interactions between them—can be managed constructively, providing that sufficient information is available at an early enough stage in project development. Failure to understand stakeholders, their needs and potentials, and to plan for their involvement in the project will almost inevitably create problems and surprises later on.

LEARNING ABOUT STAKEHOLDER COMMUNITIES

Because stakeholder support is so critical to project success, systematic investigations should take place early in the project cycle to build up an accurate and detailed picture of what key stakeholder communities are like. Anthropological skills are well suited to these initial explorations, particularly when they are used to establish the parameters of investigation, establish significant cultural domains, and identify and define locally relevant categories, values, and issues.

Basic Questions

What one learns—and how one learns—from a community depends in large part on what one already knows. If secondary data are available for the project area, then it should be used, provided that it is relevant and trustworthy. Often, however, these data are either missing or flawed in some respect.

Whether or not good secondary data exist, planners should have an overall framework, however broad, to help guide and structure their investigations. There is no fixed model for this, but Table 5.2 provides a basic outline that is useful across a range of situations.

Having an initial framework helps planners in several ways. First, it pinpoints areas in which information is lacking. Second, it guides the collection of new information. Finally, as the framework develops, it helps planners answer key design questions. Systematic data collection will help identify likely areas of concern to community residents, the types of solutions they would prefer, and the kinds of strategies they believe would be most effective and appropriate for reaching those solutions. More important, however, looking systematically at stakeholder communities will also help identify important differences *within* these groups.

TABLE 5.2 Some Principal Components of Community Studies

Aspects	Examples of Information Needed
People	Who lives in the area? What is their structure and composition? What divisions exist? What is the basic profile in terms of things like health, education, employment, income, and so forth? What is the pattern of leadership? What aspects of their belief system, values, and practices seem important? Do some groups have more power or influence than others?
Environment	Where are the physical and social boundaries of the community? What aspects of climate, topography, natural resources, or seasonal variations seem important? What outstanding natural features mark the area? How is environment connected with livelihood?
Infrastructure	What institutions, organizations, facilities, or services exist? What is their relationship to local populations, now and in the past? What is likely to change in the future?
Resources	What important assets does this community possess, or have access to? These might include financial resources, intellectual resources, human resources, informational resources, and so on. How are these assets held and managed? What rules govern their use?
Modes of Livelihood	What are the principal bases of the economy? How are people organized for work? How are they connected and/or differentiated? Are there extremes of wealth and poverty? What are current economic trends? How are resources and benefits distributed? How is time patterned?
Issues and Concerns	What things have engaged the time, thought, and energy of people here? What are people's main concerns or issues? How do they see these issues? Are there differences of opinion regarding these? What sorts of options are seen as acceptable or workable for dealing with them?
Principal Constraints	What factors or conditions lying largely outside the control or prediction of the community are important for understanding what is happening inside the community itself? How do people see these things? Have they changed over time?

Collecting Information

Although planners rely heavily on good data for decisionmaking, they often have no clear idea what constitutes "good" data in the first place.[4] Although many people believe that quantitative data are better than qualitative data, numbers alone will not help if what's being counted has no relevance to what one really needs to know. Data have little inherent value or meaning, in other words, unless they are connected to a context. At this point, the data become *information*.

If I am told, for example, that the temperature on the project site to-day is "30," I have a piece of data. But that datum is relatively useless un-less I also know something about the context surrounding it. If "30" is a Fahrenheit number, then I will need to put on a warm coat to go outside. If the number is Celsius, I can wear short sleeves. If I am in the north-eastern United States in January, 30 degrees Fahrenheit will not be un-usual, but if the month is August, something odd has happened to the weather. If I am in Australia or Argentina, however, the situation would be reversed. A temperature just below freezing will be entirely appropri-ate for the start of the Winter Olympics, but not for the start of the La-bor Day weekend.

Although project specialists often assume that they already hold the knowledge necessary to make a project work, anthropologists take a somewhat different approach. While not challenging what project spe-cialists know, anthropologists can bring valuable additional insight to bear. They seek relevant knowledge within the stakeholder communities, using a variety of methods, many of them qualitative and open-ended. This approach serves as a useful counterweight to preconceived notions.

All knowledge—including what project specialists know—is embed-ded in a cultural context, and carries with it a set of associated values, as-sumptions, and biases. Specialists often know a great deal about very spe-cific topics, but have much less understanding about how these topics are connected, in space and through time, with other systems. Local stake-holders, on the other hand, may know much less than specialists do about specific things, but they may have a much better idea about how their environment works as a totality.[5] Unfortunately, indigenous knowl-edge is often either ignored or downplayed by project planners.[6]

These different spheres of knowledge do not conflict, but rather com-plement and enhance each other. Indigenous knowledge can be usefully combined with what planners know—or are able to learn—to produce a clearer picture of the situation. Indigenous knowledge, embedded as it is in a local cultural system, is more than mere data—it includes ideas about what things are in the world and how they are linked together, along with notions of the appropriate way to learn about and use these things. Local knowledge, in other words, cannot simply be "plugged into" planning.[7]

Counting to One

It is always tempting to start data collection with a survey. Surveys are a time-honored way to collect data in a systematic and controlled way.

They can be very useful in project development, particularly in terms of creating a data series over time to measure specific changes. Surveys can also help identify and describe subgroups within a population.

But surveys also have important disadvantages in project work. One problem is that of misplaced concreteness, coupled with premature closure. In our rush to acquire understanding, we often pick what we hope is a central or key variable, and build data collection around this.[8] Another problem is that Western-style surveys usually contain a number of embedded assumptions about people that are hardly ever true of people elsewhere.

But the most basic problem with surveys is that, to design and use one properly, you need to know what information you are looking for and how it manifests itself in the local context. As one investigator points out: "To identify something, the observer must know what qualifies as that thing, or that kind of thing. This entails counting to one."[9]

In the cross-cultural environment of a typical project, counting to one—that is, deciding what to count, why, and how—must necessarily precede any attempt at analysis and eventual understanding. If you're in a strange country and you notice someone winking at you from across the room, you can certainly count the winks, but how do you know what they mean? Cleveland comments: "It is only when goals are subjectively defined, either arbitrarily by an individual or group, or interactively through social negotiation between individuals and groups with different values, that one can begin to subjectively measure with empirical data the extent to which a certain process or structure conserves natural resources, promotes social equity, or is economically rational."[10]

Survey designers in cross-cultural situations need to understand what things, *in this specific context,* are worth counting, and on what basis. Outsiders to a culture cannot simply impose categories and meanings on a situation without losing much of what is significant in it to the people concerned. What is significant cannot, in most cases, be determined by a quick site visit alone. Mini-Case 5.4, "Rural Development Tourism," outlines some of the pitfalls involved in such site visits.

What to count is a harder question to answer than it might seem at first. Most data-collection techniques assume that the units to be looked at, questioned, counted, or measured are known and essentially self-evident. But this is rarely the case in an other-cultural environment. Even very basic units, such as households, vary across cultures to a significant degree.

For example, conventional Western thinking assumes that each person belongs to a single domestic group—a "household"—and that this

MINI-CASE 5.4   RURAL DEVELOPMENT TOURISM

Site visits are a common way for project planners to collect information. Unlike surveys, site visits can be done at relatively little expense and do not require elaborate preparations. But they can turn into what Robert Chambers (1980) has termed "development tourism," containing a host of biases:

- Spatial bias. Information-gathering visits are concentrated on easy-to-reach areas, almost always on good roads (and hence more developed).
- Project bias. Ongoing, "successful" projects tend to be visited frequently. This is the problem of what Chambers (1993: 115) has called "shining islands of salvation"—projects that are exhibited as showcase pieces and receive special support and attention. Project failures, or areas previously bypassed, tend to be ignored.
- Person bias. Visitors tend to meet the better-off people who already have access to services and benefits. Other things being equal, these people tend to be adult males in their prime, who are more powerful, better educated, and more articulate than others in the community.
- Dry season bias. Visits tend to occur when travel is easy, weather is better, and disease and hunger are less prevalent.
- Protocol bias. Everyone is very polite during a visit. Awkward questions are not asked and replies are usually predictable and courteous. Bad news is seldom exchanged.
- Professional bias. Visitors, however ignorant they may be of local conditions, are almost always seen—and treated—as experts. Solutions are almost always expected to flow from experts to locals, not the other way around.

Because of these biases, planners often do not see major problems in a community, such as structured poverty. What information they do collect is usually incomplete and faulty. Little rapport with locals has been achieved; attention has focused on things rather than relationships; and the area has been seen at only one short point in time. The "experts" who make such visits learn little, and instead tend to reinforce their preconceptions.

I was an unwitting and somewhat unwilling participant in an episode of rural development tourism in the late 1970s when I was working as the anthropologist member of a project design team in Senegal's Ferlo region. Because I was one of the few members of the team who spoke French as well

(continues)

MINI-CASE 5.4 (continued)

as several local languages, I frequently accompanied other specialists as they collected their data.

One day, I found myself with a livestock economist. "Need to find some herders," he said. "Gotta do a local needs analysis, talk to a few of 'em."

"No problem," I said, putting the Range Rover in gear.

We crisscrossed the bush, finally spotting the dust cloud that meant herds clustered around a water point. We parked the Range Rover at the edge of the herd. Some 500 head of cattle and two dozen herders stood and watched us approach. The economist waved at the tallest man. "You," he said. "Need you to answer some questions."

Anticipating Miss Piggy by several years, the tall herder pointed to himself and opened his eyes wide. "*Moi?*"

Without preamble, the economist plunged ahead. "Want you to tell me what your basic needs are." He looked up, notebook in hand, pencil poised. "Anytime you're ready."

The herder turned to me, his face a mixture of alarm and amusement. He spoke in Wolof. "What does this *toubab* want?"

"It's all right. He just wants to ask questions. About your basic needs."

"My *what?*"

"Wait." The economist was waving his hand. "Wait. I need your basic needs *in priority*. Put 'em in priority, OK?"

Everyone had gathered around now, their faces expectant, their eyes gleaming with curiosity and excitement. This was better than a film. What would happen next?

Finally the herder spoke. He turned to the man. "You come from America," he said. "I hear that in America, there are many, many good things." He spread his hands. "I think you should bring one of each of those good things here. When we have seen everything that there is, *then* we will tell you what our needs are."

He smiled. "In priority, of course."

*   *   *

How can these biases be overcome? Chambers offers these suggestions:

- Seek out specific groups—women, nonusers, and people untouched by services. Include these groups in your meetings and discussions.
- Look for key indicators of poverty in a group: housing, tangible assets, birth weights, wages, and so on.

(continues)

MINI-CASE 5.4   (continued)

- Go beyond routine contacts: Seek information from a variety of different groups and individuals with different viewpoints.
- Ask open-ended questions and listen carefully to the answers.
- Visit during the off-season and stick around for a while.
- Drop in at odd times and try to dispense with ceremony. Try to become unimportant.
- Get off the main roads and do some walking.
- Take your time.
- Use multiple approaches to data gathering.

SOURCES: R. Chambers 1985, 1993; Moris and Copestake 1993; Nolan 1997; Ryan 1981.

---

can be located on a map as part of a larger unit called a "community." But we also know from experience that in many societies, the household as an enumeration unit may not be the same as the household as a social or economic unit.[11]

Attempts to impose externally-defined constructs on local contexts are likely to result in misleading or unintelligible data. Anthropologists wisely assume very little about the interconnections between individuals, whether grouped in "households" or not; instead, they attempt, through participant observation, to discover these.[12] Households, like "farms" or "villages," are cultural constructs, whose shape, function, and meaning are tied to the local context.

The question of "what shall we count?" is therefore several somewhat more complex questions:

- What things are available for counting?
- How many different kinds of things are there?
- What accounts for the "different-ness" of these various things?
- What do these things mean to local stakeholders?
- What do we need to know about these things for our purposes?

Using domain analysis and other qualitative research techniques, anthropologists can help uncover the characteristics of the sociocultural world of the project environment, as seen by its inhabitants. By discovering through qualitative approaches how members of a group categorize and define their experience, we can eventually learn what quantitative variables are worth looking at, what they mean, and how to count them.

I learned this the hard way as a budding fieldworker. Mini-Case 5.5, "The Bassari Village Census," discusses what went wrong with my attempt to impose outside categories on a West African village.

MINI-CASE 5.5   THE BASSARI VILLAGE CENSUS

Early in my fieldwork in West Africa, I wanted to do a census survey of the people in the Bassari village where I lived, to gather what I thought was simple, basic demographic information relating to sex, age, occupation, and so on. I had done similar surveys in the United States and in Great Britain, and felt confident that this would be a simple matter. I had a number of fairly simple questions I needed answers to, and I hoped that my survey's results would provide a useful database for further investigation.

As the survey proceeded, however, I became painfully aware that my survey questions, based on what I had assumed were relevant categories, were causing problems for my respondents. Instead of being the straightforward exercise I assumed it would be, my survey provoked confusion, contradiction, and occasional distress among my respondents. As I investigated the sources of error and confusion, I began to learn important things about both the structure of Bassari village society and about the values that villagers held.

Many of my questions either could not be answered in the form in which they appeared or they referred to things that made no sense. Rather than being a tool for discovery about the environment, my survey was proving to be an obstacle to understanding. Had I persisted with my original survey, the data would have been misleading and essentially worthless. Thanks to the patience of both my field assistants and the villagers, I was eventually able to "count to one"—in other words, to understand what the relevant cultural categories were and how to frame questions about them. Some of the more important modifications that I made to my original survey appear on the following page.

(continues)

MINI-CASE 5.5   *(continued)*

The Bassari Village Census

Original Questions	*What I Learned as I Began to Carry Out the Survey*	*How I Changed the Questions*
Name	Bassaris have several names: a child's name, a birth-order name, and an initiation name. Different names are appropriate for different situations or encounters. A respondent might give any of these names if questioned.	Initiation name Birth-order name Other names
Age	Most older Bassari do not know their age, except in terms of age-grades, which span six years.	Age-grade name
Family Name	The Bassari have eight matrilineal groupings. Each lineage has certain ritual rights and duties.	Lineage name
Parents' Names	I omitted this question when I learned that the villagers whose parents were dead would sometimes become distressed if asked to say their names.	Omitted
Village of Residence	The Bassari have a word for "village" but it also means country or nation. Instead, the Bassari group themselves in terms of their allegiance to a chief, or in terms of ritual obligations or membership in agricultural work groups. I eventually used "neighborhood," denoting households that exchanged agricultural labor with each other.	Neighborhood of residence
Occupation	Everyone in the village is a farmer, but there are a number of spare-time specialist occupations, such as palm-wine tapping, pottery, ironsmithing, curing, and clairvoyance.	Omitted
Wife's Name	Bassari society is characterized by polygyny, a high rate of divorce, and the levirate, where a widow can be inherited by her dead husband's brother.	Wife's name Previous wives Number of present wives
Children's Names	Because they are matrilineal, children take the mother's lineage name, not the father's. Paternity is not of great importance to villagers, and there is even a category of child "of the village," meaning that its father is unknown or unacknowledged.	Birth-order names Other names Parents' names

TABLE 5.3 Javanese Indicators of Prosperity

Indicator	Low Prosperity	Medium Prosperity	High Prosperity
House	Bamboo	Combination	Brick/plaster/teak
Rooms	1–2 small rooms	—	Many large rooms
Floor	Dirt	Bricks covered with cement	Polished cement blocks
Lighting	Small oil lamps	Hanging kerosene lamps	Home generator
Transportation	None	Bicycle; draft cart	Motorized vehicle

SOURCES: Adapted from Honadle 1982; Soetoro 1979.

Measures and Proxies

Even when one has decided what one wishes to know, measures may not be intuitively obvious. If direct measures are not possible, then *proxy measures* must be found. Here again, these cannot be simply transferred from one cultural setting to another; they must be situated within the local scene, if they are to have meaning and relevance. Just as the employee turnover rate may be an indirect but accurate indicator of a troubled workplace in the United States, so the price of work elephants in a local market in Southeast Asia may be an indicator of the extent of illegal logging going on in the area, and the number of village houses with tin roofs may indicate just how lucrative the illegal logging is.[13]

The measurement of prosperity or poverty is particularly important in many projects. Even in very poor nations, there are significant gradations in poverty. Understanding these, and how they are manifest, is essential for designing appropriate interventions. Locally defined indicators of wealth and poverty must be found, ranked, and measured. Once investigators understand local ranking systems, they can construct indices of wealth. In Java, for example, investigators found a number of specific local indicators of poverty. Table 5.3 sets out some of these by way of illustration.

Rapid Assessment

Rapid assessment procedures (RAP) are frequently used to begin the process of learning about the project environment. Rapid assessment can provide project planners with quick and useful answers to a variety of important questions at the outset of the project development cycle, and can pinpoint areas for further, more structured investigation.

RAP emerged in the 1970s as a broad term encompassing a variety of approaches with a common aim: to shorten the time necessary for understanding the local project context and at the same time transcending some of the limitations and biases of more traditional data collection methods. RAP is particularly useful, of course, when the project environment is unfamiliar. Two seminal conferences established the framework for RAP: one at the University of Sussex in 1978, the other at Khon Kaen University in 1985. Since then, an extensive literature has emerged.[14]

RAP is not one technique but many. It is a team-based approach to information gathering; semi-structured, multidisciplinary, open-ended, and highly flexible. RAP has several distinctive characteristics that distinguish it from other data-gathering approaches. It is *rapid* (to provide timely information to decision makers), *eclectic* (combining different methodologies), and *holistic* (covering many aspects of community life). It is *interactive* (emphasizing dialogue between outsiders and locals); *evolutionary* (goals and methods develop as learning proceeds), and *indigenous* (meaning that predetermined questionnaires are replaced by approaches and techniques developed for the local environment).[15]

Rapid assessment can quickly help planners make framing decisions for the project. Describing a farming system in overall terms, for example, will help planners determine where in that system the project might intervene. Drawing up a profile of different farming villages can help planners choose the best locations for project activities. Within the selected communities, an overview of the demographic and socioeconomic structures there will guide decisions about who project beneficiaries should be. Mapping out a calendar of major yearly events (including weather patterns) will enable people to schedule project activities at the appropriate times.[16] RAP is also useful when dealing with rapidly developing problems, such as famines or epidemics, where traditional investigative procedures might take too long.

RAP uses available information wherever possible, obtained from local inhabitants through a process of two-way dialogue. Indicators and measures are developed that accurately portray local realities and that are recognized as valid by local people. As new information emerges, working hypotheses may be discarded in favor of new ones, and investigations may change course somewhat. Multiple methods are used in the investigation—an approached termed *triangulation*—to provide a more holistic picture.

TABLE 5.4 Common Methods Used in Rapid Assessment

• Examination of records	• Nonintrusive methods
• Direct observation	• Participant observation
• Confidential interviews	• Daily activity analyses
• Key informants	• Case studies
• Delphi method	• Social network analysis
• Identifying key indicators	• Surveys
• Group interviews	• Key informant interviews
• Individual interviews	• Life histories
• Workshops and focus groups	• Advisory groups/task forces
• Aerial surveys	• Community meetings
• Group and individual rankings	• Area tours

RAP explicitly locates data within their local context, and focuses, furthermore, on internal variations in data, not just overall averages and patterns. The use of triangulation not only provides a better picture of the situation, but it encourages project specialists to talk to each other across their disciplines and to locals. Some of the methods commonly used in RAP are listed in Table 5.4

Although RAP is designed primarily to benefit the project team by providing it with better information, a variation, termed participatory rural appraisal (PRA), places somewhat more emphasis on the empowerment of local communities.[17] PRA empowers stakeholders primarily by giving them a say in what information is collected and how, and what is done with it. It also attempts to alter the working relationships between outside specialists and locals in fundamental and lasting ways. In PRA, outsiders facilitate but do not dominate; methods are open and flexible; and the process of learning is characterized by partnership and sharing of information.[18]

Unlike RAP, which is often characterized as quick and dirty, PRA requires investigators to spend significant amounts of time in the field and tends to result in richer, more textured data. Its success depends on the quality of the relationships that investigators are able to establish with local people. Indigenous knowledge forms the foundation for this approach; locals are no longer simply informants, but leaders and teachers, helping investigators to understand their world.

RAP and PRA are not distinct approaches, but variations on a single set of themes: locally grounded information, progressive learning, multiple data-collection methods, and the primacy of local people as experts. These approaches do not replace other discovery methods and do not resolve all questions and issues. Rapid assessment is not an end in itself, but rather the beginning of a dialogue between planners and stakeholders, as a means to promote mutual learning. Nor are they foolproof. Even approaches that emphasize local participation may still ignore issues of gender, power, and process.[19] In some cases, participatory approaches may raise local expectations unrealistically, or distort the dialogue between locals and outside investigators.[20]

MANAGING INFORMATION GATHERING

Whatever the approach used, it should be clear by now that information gathering is a crucial part of project development. The need for information is greatest at the beginning of the project cycle—precisely the point in time at which planners and stakeholders know the least about each other.

Under pressure to get things moving, planners sometimes conclude that they can rely on what they already know to develop the project, rather than trying to extend the boundaries of their understanding. There is a well-known tendency for experts to assume that if they do not know something, it is either because they feel that it is not worth knowing (otherwise there would already be data available for them to look at); or that they can simply guess at its significance without doing any real investigation.

Alternatively, of course, the temptation may be to collect more information than is really necessary. This does not guarantee a better project, and indeed, the amount of time and energy needed to collect information may seriously hamper other necessary activities. Data aren't free— their collection and analysis takes up time and uses scarce resources, one of which may be administrative capacity itself.[21]

To avoid either of these extremes, project planners must make the best use of the data that they already have; make clear decisions about what additional data they require; and gather this additional data in the most effective and efficient way possible. All information for project development represents a compromise between what is desirable and what is possible under the circumstances. Collecting information is costly and time-consuming, so requirements should be kept realistic.

Two useful principles of information collection are *optimal ignorance* and *appropriate imprecision*.[22] Optimal ignorance asks: What facts are *not* worth knowing? Appropriate imprecision asks: What level of *accuracy* will suffice for decisionmaking? Using these two guidelines, information collection procedures can be devised that are economical yet useful.

In a low-income urban redevelopment project in Sri Lanka that I was involved in during the 1980s, for example, it was necessary to know something about the composition of the communities to be served and their income levels. Our community surveys asked people their names (from which their ethnic background could generally be derived) and noted key local indicators of wealth. These included the type of roof on the house, the presence of bicycles or motorbikes, and the type of furniture in the house. The degree of religious organization in the community was estimated by a quick visual survey that counted the number of mosques, churches, Buddhist or Hindu temples, and religious schools in the area. Although these data were by no means comprehensive and were hardly methodologically sophisticated or elegant, they were sufficient to allow project planners to make important framing decisions about how to meet community needs effectively, and where to site proposed services and activities.

Looked at in this way, information collection and analysis is more like intelligence gathering than rigorous research. Project personnel often need to take decisions on the basis of what they know *now*, and later, as other aspects of the situation reveal themselves, they modify these decisions. For this strategy to work, however, it is necessary to know what is significant, and why.[23] This argues, once again, for a flexible, interactive style of project development.

SUMMARY OF CHAPTER 5

This chapter examined how information is used in the development of projects, as a way of fitting them to their context. The chapter began by outlining and describing five levels of a project, each of which must be integrated with the others for the project to be successful.

The key to project success lies primarily—although not exclusively—with the first of these levels, the project stakeholders, and the rest of Chapter 5 dealt mainly with aspects of this group.

Various approaches to collecting information about stakeholders were discussed, in particular the value of rapid assessment procedures, or RAP, as an effective way of beginning to identify salient aspects of the stakeholder community. The chapter concluded with a discussion of some of the important aspects of the management of information gathering.

ENDNOTES

1. Vol. 26, no. 9 (1998) of *World Development*, edited by Peter Castro, presents a series of discussions and analyses of how stakeholders' past history with development projects had an influence on current project plans and outcomes.

2. Klitgaard (1997), for example, describes how institutional failures can act to doom otherwise well-designed programs for poverty alleviation. Grindle (1997), on the other hand, provides material on how organizational features help public agencies in developing countries perform well.

3. Kottak (1991: 431).

4. Gow (1994: 5).

5. DeWalt (1994).

6. Grenier (1998: 46–51).

7. Gardner and Lewis (1996: 120).

8. See Dörner (1996: 186–188). Focusing on just one thing, or a small number of things, saves us time, analytical work, and relieves us of the burden of collecting so much information. Of course, it may also help us avoid the issue of learning about—and coming to terms with—the local culture altogether.

9. Kirk and Miller (1986: 9).

10. Cleveland (2000: 271).

11. Wilk and Miller (1997: 64).

12. Turton (1988: 133).

13. Honadle (1982: 635–637).

14. Sondeo, rapid rural reconnaissance, and farming systems research are some of the other names applied to rapid assessment. Approaches and techniques are discussed in numerous publications including Simmonds (1985), DeWalt (1985), Khon Kaen (1987), and Beebe (1995; 2001). A French version, called ECRIS (Enquête Collective Rapide d'Identification des Conflits et des Groupes Stratégiques), is outlined in Bierschenk and Olivier de Sardan (1997). Anthropological applications of RRA include Scrimshaw and Hurtado (1987), Scrimshaw and Gleason (1992), and Bentley et al. (1988).

15. Molnar (1991: 11–23); see also Moris and Copestake (1993: 39).

16. This example is more fully discussed in Moris (1981b: 38).

17. Robert Chambers (1994a, 1994b) has been one of the main proponents of this approach.

18. Robert Chambers (1997: 104–5).

19. Grenier (1998: 43–45). Despite its promise, participatory approaches can become "bureaucratized" in the view of some observers (Labrecque 2000: 217, for example), and may even work against peasant mobilization.

20. Bierschenk and Olivier de Sardan (1997: 240) point out: "In Africa, where the 'development rent' (that is, foreign aid) is now a structural part of the economy of many villages and has become integrated in peasant strategies . . . any inquiry is seen, by the villagers, as the putative beginning of an aid flow, and people are trying to play to the research team the fairy tale of a united and dynamic village, the needs of which are exactly what one thinks the foreigners are ready to offer."

21. R. Chambers (1993: 17).

22. See R. Chambers (1985: 403).

23. See, for example, Moris and Copestake (1993: 63).

chapter 6

FRAMING PROJECTS

As I noted in Chapter 4, all projects start with a set of what can be called *framing decisions*—design choices that will provide the project's essential structure. The most important framing decisions are concerned with project *purposes*, project *strategies*, project *sustainability*, and project *learning*. Although changes in the project will still be possible later on, they will occur within this initial framework.

PROJECT PURPOSES

The first and most important framing decision concerns the purpose of the project. This involves choosing the problem, issue, or opportunity on which the project will focus, and at the same time specifying the type and magnitude of outcomes desired.

Typically, this is where initial community studies are done, using rapid assessment techniques or some other methodology. At this point, the capabilities and priorities of the implementing agency begin to encounter the realities of the surrounding environment. As information is collected and analyzed, salient issues will emerge that help further define the overall shape of the project. Eventually, broad goals are narrowed, and transformed into specific objectives to guide further planning.

What Needs to Be Done?

Projects begin, therefore, with the identification of something that needs to be done. The focus for a project can come from many different direc-

FIGURE 6.1   Where Project Ideas Come From

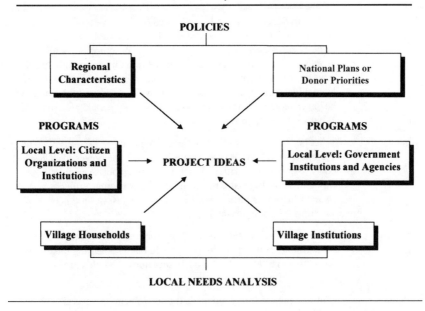

tions. It can be identified by the project team through investigation, or it can be identified by stakeholders. Alternatively, it can simply be handed down from donors or government ministries, as a result of previous plans, studies, or programs.

Choosing Between Different Options

At the outset, planners have multiple options. But since a project must quickly define its focus, these options need to be ranked or otherwise sorted in terms of some clear *criteria*. Although criteria may come from the implementing agency, the information needed to make decisions based on criteria will come mainly from the project environment. Some of the criteria most often used in choosing a project are outlined in Table 6.1.

Tracing Problem Structures

Choosing a focus for the project is only the beginning. The issue, problem, or opportunity that forms the focus now needs to be analyzed and understood before appropriate responses can be drawn up. Planners use a

TABLE 6.1 Criteria for Choosing Strategy Options

Relevance	Is the problem or issue to be addressed by the project of significant concern to stakeholders? Is it of equal or comparable concern to the implementing agency? How urgent, severe, or important is this problem compared with others? Will solving this problem help solve others? Whose opinions will planners take into consideration here? How widespread is the problem? How widespread will the solutions be? Is coverage an important issue? How many people are affected? What would happen if people did nothing?
Change	What happens if the project succeeds? Who wins? Who loses? Who gets more, and less? Which groups are they? The powerful? The poor? Women? Minorities? What downstream outcomes might one expect from a successful resolution to this particular problem or issue? What other issues might be affected by work on this one? Will solutions be lasting or temporary?
Learning	If the project addresses this issue or problem, what is the potential for learning? Is it high or low? If people learn something this time, does this have "spin-offs" to other situations? Can this project be replicated elsewhere, or extended?
Process	How complex is the problem? Is it one problem, or several? Which problems could be best addressed, given the available skills and resources? Is anyone else doing work in this area? If so, how are this agency's efforts going to fit in? Are required inputs available locally? Will they be available after the end of the project? Can planners actually control what happens here? Do people have enough time to effect change?
Level of Effort	How manageable is this particular issue? Is it within the scope of agency abilities? Is there a fair chance that they can actually do something about the problem with the resources and skills at their command? Which problems are of the greatest concern to the community? How effectively can the community participate in planning and implementation? Will participation increase local capacities?

variety of tools and techniques to help them do these things, including *force-field analysis* and *branching-tree diagrams*.[1] Both of these help planners develop a more precise understanding of how a problem is structured. Both require a prior understanding of context. By understanding a problem's structure, they can begin to see possible solutions to that problem.

Force-Field Analysis.   Force-field analysis, developed by the psychologist Kurt Lewin, is useful for understanding why a given situation is the way

FIGURE 6.2   A Simple Force-Field Analysis

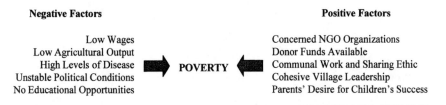

Negative Factors		Positive Factors
Low Wages		Concerned NGO Organizations
Low Agricultural Output		Donor Funds Available
High Levels of Disease	**POVERTY**	Communal Work and Sharing Ethic
Unstable Political Conditions		Cohesive Village Leadership
No Educational Opportunities		Parents' Desire for Children's Success

it is. Lewin pointed out that any situation at a given point in time is the result of a complex set of forces, some acting to maintain the situation and some acting to change it. It follows that if the balance of forces is changed, the situation itself may change. By understanding the nature of these forces, in other words, planners can also understand how to change them.

To describe the nature of these forces, it will usually be necessary to work with local stakeholders to understand how they see the problem or issue, the surrounding context, and the likely leverage points. I can illustrate this with a simple example. Imagine examining "poverty," defined as low per-capita income, in a rural village. A simple force-field analysis (see Figure 6.2), based on preliminary investigation, might turn up the following factors "for" and "against" poverty.

In this example, the force-field analysis draws attention to a range of influences, positive and negative, that affect poverty. Typically, project planners look at the various forces they've listed, and ask whether any of the positive or negative influences can be altered in any way or whether new positive forces can be introduced.

Branching-Tree Diagrams.   The branching-tree technique takes this one step further, and looks at the cause-effect relationships between various factors operating to produce a situation. As before, planners begin with the statement of the problem issue—in this case, poverty. They then work backward, asking, "What causes this?"

Our earlier example now becomes somewhat more complex, but at the same time more understandable in terms of linkages.

In our example, several conditions appear to combine to produce poverty: low wages, low agricultural output, high levels of disease, and unstable political conditions (see Figure 6.3). For each condition, planners then ask, "Why is that?" In this way, they construct a multilevel analysis of the problem focus.

FIGURE 6.3   A Branching-Tree Analysis

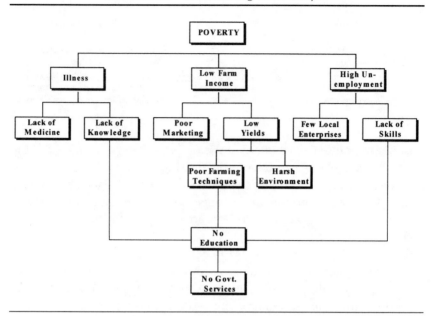

As the analysis proceeds, planners begin to understand how a problem is structured. This in turn gives them important clues as to what project objectives could or should be. They continue to add levels until they are satisfied that they have outlined as much of the causal chain as possible.

A branching-tree analysis demands skill, competence, and patience. A tree diagram should not be based on guesses, but on understanding. As with the force field, detailed contextual information is necessary to outline the problem structure. When used successfully, it can clarify problem definition and help identify feasible solutions. A branching tree can not only summarize what is known, but can help to structure further enquiry.

Choosing an Intervention Point

Both the force-field and the branching-tree exercises help planners identify likely *intervention points*, and thus project objectives. Planners will be drawn to aspects of a problem that they can actually do something about, and where results will, if successful, have positive impacts on other parts of the problem structure. These must be linked to agency capabilities and priorities.

The examples presented here, of course, are relatively simple. Real-life situations are usually more complex; the causal chains and the positive and negative forces may not be entirely clear, or they may be so elaborate that designers make mistakes in mapping them.

PROJECT STRATEGIES

Once the project's goals and objectives have been outlined, appropriate *strategies* for attaining objectives must be crafted. The term "strategy" denotes the broad method or approach to be used in producing the desired outcomes. At this stage of project development, planners need to quickly generate a set of alternative strategy options, and from these, to select what will work best.

In the above example, if the overall goal is to reduce poverty, there seem to be several points in the structure where intervention might be possible. The problems of bad weather, lack of civil authority, or weapons may go beyond the project organization's mandate and capability. At other points, solutions may be available. Several of the salient factors in the situation seem connected to the *lack of education*. Schooling, then, may be a possible project strategy.

It will not, of course, be the only strategy available. Since a given objective can often be reached in several quite different ways, the choice of strategy becomes an important framing decision. Some options may be culturally unacceptable—to either implementers or stakeholders. Others may be impractical, expensive, or risky.[2] But some options will appear well suited to the project context, workable, and straightforward.

As with other aspects of project development, the analysis of strategy options cannot be done effectively without detailed contextual information. The criteria used to evaluate strategy options may be straightforward, but these criteria will still need, as before, to be defined and interpreted within a local context. In this process, anthropological input can make an enormous difference to the degree to which strategy options fit with the context in which they are to operate.

Strategy options can be tested in various ways. Two things are of most concern to designers as they make decisions about strategy: What *resource demands* will this strategy make on the project?; How will this strategy fit with the various levels of project *context*?

TABLE 6.2 Common Aspects of Strategy Options

Criterion	Local Aspects
Startup and Recurrent Costs	All project strategies will require both startup costs and recurrent costs. If the startup costs will be borne by the project, how will recurrent costs be provided? What local resources are available for this, and what is the likelihood that they will be forthcoming? Are these resources controlled by specific groups? What are the implications for project sustainability?
Time and Resources Needed	Strategies may require continual commitments of time, energy, space, or equipment. If so, are these inputs present in the project environment, and are they likely to be available when needed? If labor is needed, for example, who will provide this, and on what basis?
Spread and Equity Issues	The project may not benefit everyone to the same extent. If so, who specifically will benefit, and who will not? How many people will benefit? What are the implications, now and in the long term, of how benefits will accrue?
Management Inputs Needed	If the project strategy requires a level of management or supervision, does the local beneficiary community possess the skills and willingness to provide this? If not, where will the necessary management expertise come from?
Levels of Risk or Uncertainty	All projects carry a certain amount of risk. What are the risks here, as perceived by local stakeholders, and what importance do those risks assume in the local context? What happens if the project fails?
Effectiveness	"Effectiveness" refers to the extent to which a strategy actually works, to deliver what it was intended to. How is effectiveness defined locally? Do stakeholders have different expectations from planners in this respect?
Side Effects	Project strategies may have side effects. Sometimes these are known in advance; sometimes they are unanticipated. If known side effects appear, what would be their impact on stakeholders? How do stakeholders view the likelihood of such side effects, and how do they view their consequences? In the case of unanticipated side effects, what systems are in place to signal their appearance?

Resource Requirements

All strategies demand *resources*, and resources, by definition, are scarce. Planners therefore need to assess the resource demands that a particular strategy or approach will make on both the stakeholders and the implementing agency. Although the resources of the agency are presumably known, the resources available in, and required from, local stakeholder communities may not be.

Some resources—for example, money, people, and equipment—are obvious. Others—such as time, knowledge, goodwill, or expertise—are less easily defined but no less important for project success. It makes sense, therefore, to identify in advance all the important resources that a strategy is likely to require, to attempt to specify the magnitude of need for each resource, and to determine, to the extent possible, whether that needed resource is actually available to the project. Table 6.3 presents a simple checklist for resources.

Fitting Strategy Options to Context

Chapter 5 addressed the three basic aspects of context: the *inner environment* of the project itself, where planners have a high degree of control or influence; the *proximate environment,* which includes local stakeholder groups; and the *outer environment,* where planners have little if any control.

Strategy options can be weighed against each aspect of context, using a variety of tools that model aspects of the project. These models serve as mini-scenarios, allowing designers and participants to rehearse the way arrangements will work, to detect and examine flaws, and—where necessary—to go back to the field for more information.

The Inner Environment: Drafting a Logical Framework

One way to model a project is to view it as a linked chain of cause-and-effect relationships. Project resources are used to carry out sets of activities, which in turn are expected to produce direct outcomes. These, in turn, eventually lead to longer-term results. Suppose, for example, that we followed up on the results of our earlier force-field and branching-tree analyses, and set out to design an education project. What would the cause-effect relationships look like?

Figure 6.4 sets out the logic chain for a school project that was intended to raise incomes. The provision of textbooks makes classes possible. Classroom instruction makes it possible for beneficiaries to obtain better jobs. This leads to more income, more savings, and consequently, more investment. More investment eventually produces a stronger national economy, which in turn promotes political stability in the region.

TABLE 6.3   Project Resources

Resource	Local Factors
Money	Will financial contributions be needed from local stakeholders to start or maintain the project? What is a reasonable level of contribution to expect? What segments of the stakeholder population can afford to contribute? Can contributions be sustained?
Time	Are stakeholders required to devote time to the project? How much time is required? What are the patterns of activity within stakeholder groups, and how will the project's demands fit in with these? Which groups will not be able to devote time to project activities?
Labor	If labor inputs are required from stakeholders, what is the nature of these? Who in the stakeholder community is able and willing to supply the necessary labor? Are there aspects of social structure that preclude certain groups from participating?
Equipment and Facilities	Does the project require certain facilities or equipment (such as tools, space, storage) from stakeholders? Are such things available locally? Are there conditions attached to their use? Are these things owned or controlled by specific subgroups within the stakeholder community?
Skill	The project may require highly specific sets of skills. Are these skills available locally? Who possesses these skills? How are such skills related to leadership, influence, and other aspects of social structures?
Knowledge	The project may require local knowledge. What is the nature of this knowledge, and is it available from stakeholder groups? Can the project's needs for knowledge be fitted together with local knowledge systems, or will some form of "translation" be required? How accurate or reliable is this knowledge? Is there disagreement about this knowledge with stakeholder groups? Do different groups of stakeholders possess different types of knowledge?
Enthusiasm	All projects require commitment and energy to carry them forward. If these things are required from local stakeholders, how will they be obtained? What aspects of the project are most appealing to them, and how can these be highlighted? What subgroups among stakeholders are particularly interested in the project, and why? Does this pose problems for other groups?
Legitimacy	Does the project require approval or sanction from leaders within the stakeholder community? If so, how can this be obtained? Are there trade-offs for this approval? What consequences might these have for project implementation and sustainability?

FIGURE 6.4   An Example of a Project Logic Chain

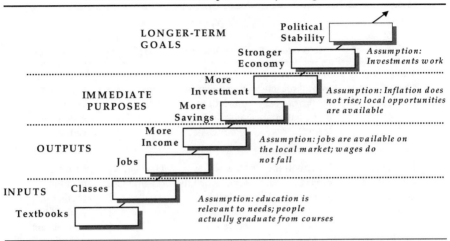

This chain of logic is often expressed in a more formal and comprehensive way, through a *logical framework*. The logical framework helps planners to visualize project components and the relationships between them, to define target indicators and measures, and to list the main assumptions on which the logic of the strategy depends.

FIGURE 6.5   The Logic of the Framework

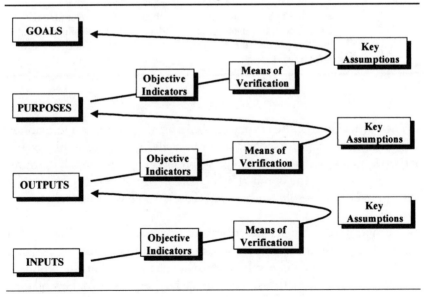

TABLE 6.4   The Layout of a Logical Framework

Project Component	Narrative Summary	Objectively Verifiable Indicators	Means of Verification	Important Assumptions
Long-Term Goal(s)	What's the overall reason for the project at the national level?	What will signal that the project has contributed to wider goals?	How will we obtain these data?	What helps determine whether objectives contribute to long-term goals?
Project Purpose (Short-Term Objectives)	What will the project accomplish if it's done properly?	How will we know when the project is over? When it is successful?	How will we obtain these data?	What helps determine whether outputs result in the achievement of immediate project objectives?
Outputs	What kind of immediate results will we get from proper use of the inputs?	How will we know when results appear?	How will we obtain these data?	What helps determine the magnitude and quality of outputs?
Inputs	What activities and resources have to be put into this project for it to work?	How are we going to measure these inputs?	How will we obtain these data?	What helps determine the availability and effectiveness of inputs?

The vertical axis of the framework links *inputs* (resources and planned activities) with *outputs* (specific and relatively immediate results of the activities). Outputs are then linked to project *purposes* (middle-term results that flow from the outputs), which are in turn connected to broader *goals* (longer-term results with wider value). Table 6.4 presents the full framework.

The narrative summary describes the project's linkages. Managerial control is greatest at the point where inputs are turned into outputs, and project planners should be able to virtually guarantee that the promised outputs will result from the inputs provided. As events move beyond outputs to purposes and then to goals, various external conditions (expressed in the assumptions column) come more into play, and direct control over results lessens.

The logic of the framework says, in effect, "if *these* inputs, indicated and measured in *this* way, are provided, and if *these* assumptions hold true, then *these* outputs will result." The horizontal axis makes explicit the conditions under which linkages will occur and how they will appear; it lists *indicators*, means of *verification*, and important *assumptions*. Indicators should be objective, specific signs that indicate progress in the project. Multiple indicators may often be necessary. The means of verification refers to the methods by which these indicators will be identified and measured. Finally, key assumptions are the important conditions lying largely outside the control of the project itself, but that nevertheless have an important effect on what happens. Key assumptions should be monitored as the project goes along, to see if there are changes.

The logical framework is primarily useful for making sure that the project is internally coherent. It forces planners to be clear about what goes into a project, what is expected to come out, and why. It helps planners see and understand the interrelationships between inputs and outputs, between outputs and results in the short and long term. It specifies how planners and others will know when predicted results have been obtained and it identifies the kinds of information that will be needed to track these. Finally, it makes key assumptions explicit.

The Proximate Environment: Mapping the Delivery System

As a way of assessing strategy options, planners often find it useful to design an *access structure* showing how project services will be delivered. Whereas the logical framework focused mainly on the internal aspects of the project, the access structure examines the project's relationship with its stakeholders in the proximate environment.

An access structure contains three basic elements: a *gate;* a *line;* and a *counter.* The gate separates eligible beneficiaries from the ineligibles. The line arranges beneficiaries in order of priority. The counter organizes the allocation of various goods and services to beneficiaries. Since each project strategy will have a different set of outputs, a different set of procedures, and often a different set of beneficiaries, outlining the access structure helps planners match services with needs. These can be represented in a simple diagram.

FIGURE 6.6   A Basic Access Structure

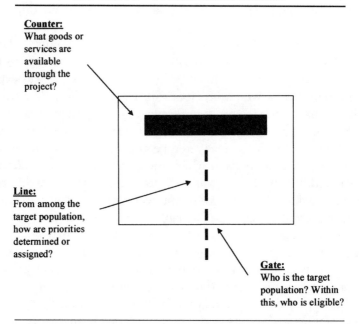

Counter:
What goods or
services are
available
through the
project?

Line:
From among the
target population,
how are priorities
determined or
assigned?

Gate:
Who is the target
population? Within
this, who is eligible?

Here again, detailed prior knowledge of stakeholder communities is necessary to ensure the operation of the delivery system. Once target populations have been identified, they must be differentiated to determine eligibility and order of priority. Project services or outputs, in turn, must be carefully tailored to the needs and preferences of designated beneficiaries.

Mapping out the project's access structure will help ensure that the right people are served; that the services provided under the project are relevant to their needs; and that an efficient and effective system of delivery is in place. It will also help planners understand what sorts of information beneficiaries might need to obtain and make use of project benefits, and, as the project unfolds, what sorts of information they themselves will need to determine whether the services provided are appropriate.

The access structure also alerts planners to potential problems and how they might need to be resolved during implementation. Sometimes, for example, clients or beneficiaries have difficulty getting connected to the system. Sometimes the system is badly organized, slow, or corrupt. Sometimes the services provided do not meet beneficiary needs. Beneficiary reactions to a badly designed access system can range from ignoring or bypassing it to attacking or subverting it.

The Outer Environment:
Outlining a System Matrix

Finally, planners need to know how the proposed project strategy will connect to its outer environment, that area of context over which project personnel have little or no control. Here, a *system matrix* may prove useful.[3]

Like the logical framework, the system matrix has two axes. The vertical axis outlines the main elements of the project. These include its *purpose* (the basic intention of the project); *inputs* (who or what comes into the project's system); *outputs* (who or what is produced by the system); *sequence* (the steps by which inputs are transformed into outputs); *environment* (the outer context—legal, administrative, financial, and so forth—within which the system operates); *physical components* (for example, equipment or space); *personnel*; and *information*.

The horizontal axis has five dimensions: *narrative* (a description of each project element); *rate* (the measure of performance of the system); *controls* (aspects of monitoring and regulation); *interfaces* (the connections between this system and others); and *targets* (anticipated changes in the state of the system).

Although not all cells in the system matrix necessarily need to be filled in for a particular project, the matrix improves project design by helping planners understand connections between the project and the surrounding environment that supports it. Used in tandem with a logical framework, it uncovers some of the main assumptions necessary for project success.

Here, for example, is a system matrix for the fictitious education project (see Table 6.5).

Looking at the matrix, it is immediately obvious that several external relationships are crucial to project success. One point of vulnerability clearly resides in the *input* column, where adequate numbers of entering students depends, among other things, on the rate of graduation from primary school, the ability to pay school fees, and the available numbers of females. Another key interface involves *output*: without adequate university placements, and without jobs for graduates, even the most successful students will ultimately fail to achieve their goals, no matter how good the school has been. At other points, too, key relationships appear:

TABLE 6.5 A System Matrix for a School Project

	Narrative	Rate	Control	Interface	Targets
Purpose	Educates students	Maintain enrollments; increase enrollment of females	School board, national laws, teachers' union	Other secondary schools competing for budget, staff, and students	Stable enrollments and staff; adequate budget, acceptable graduation rates
Input	Secondary students	200 entering students each year	Available places; recruitment; competitiveness; ability to pay school fees	Village households; regional primary schools	Increased enrollments, especially of at-risk groups
Output	High school graduates	150 graduates each year	Examinations; fee payments	Jobs; university places; social services	Increase quality; increase job placement rate; increase university admissions; decrease completion time
Sequence	Four years, grades 9–12	Average time to completion: 4.5 years	Various review cycles	—	Streamlined procedures; fewer failures or holdbacks
Environment	Rural region; isolated, poor and sparsely settled	Regional five-year development plans; in-migration; population growth; local industrial development	National Assembly; Ministry of Planning; private industry; international aid donors	Regional capital; departmental capital; Regional Assembly; governor's office	Sustainable financial base; economic growth
Physical	Buildings and equipment	Regional budget; project budget	Local school administration; local project management	Regional government	Completion of five-year plan for education
Personnel	Teachers; staff; support personnel	Recruit adequate numbers of teachers to meet demand	Teacher certification; collective bargaining agreements	Teachers' Colleges; Peace Corps; other specialized agencies	Increase quality and skills
Information	School records; course syllabi and descriptions; databases; budgets	Information needs through the student cycle	Review and audit procedures	Primary schools; universities and industries.	Improved records; easier collection and analysis

For example, the number of instructors graduating from teachers' colleges will have a marked effect on the project, as will the availability of continued funding through national and regional government structures.

Here, as with other aspects of project design, the need is for detailed, accurate, context-based information, of both a qualitative and quantitative nature.

PROJECT SUSTAINABILITY

Assuming that a project can be made compatible with the various aspects of its environment, what will guarantee its long-term survival? Although projects themselves are designed to be temporary, their outcomes should not be. *Sustainability* depends, ultimately, on the degree to which the project is compatible with its surroundings. Projects that are too much at odds with established cultural systems are likely to find themselves under assault in one way or another.

Internally, good project design is crucial. This includes clear, realistic, and measurable goals, and arrangements for achieving these that lie within the capacities of both the implementing organization and the various stakeholders. Financially, the project needs to be economically sound, with affordable operating costs, a secure and stable source of inputs, and—if a product is involved—outlets that are reliable.

The active involvement of major stakeholders is also required. If local stakeholders will be responsible for long-term management and maintenance, then adequate training and support must be provided during implementation. These and other aspects of stakeholder participation in project design and implementation will be discussed in more detail later in this chapter.

Externally, the project needs to fit with its surrounding policy environment. Any necessary policy changes needed to promote the project's long-term viability should be negotiated and settled before implementation is begun.

Most of the key sustainability issues, as one might expect, involve stakeholders in one way or another. Although these issues will be somewhat different for each project, some of the most important ones are outlined in Table 6.6.[4]

Since stakeholder involvement is so crucial to project success and sustainability, it will be useful to look at this aspect of project development in more detail.

TABLE 6.6   Key Aspects of Sustainability

Transfer	If activities will be "handed over," will there be a plan in place for doing this? Have counterparts been designated? Is there a timetable for handover? Is additional training needed to ensure smooth handover? Is there a contingency plan in place?
Resource Flows	What resources will be required to fund long-term benefit flows? What will be the source of needed external resources? How much of the needed financial and administrative inputs are available locally?
Management Capacity	Will organizational capacities be sufficient to maintain essential systems to continue benefits? If not, how will they be improved? What aspects of service will be run locally? Who will control this?
Maintenance	How will the project be maintained? Will people be trained to do this? Will there be resources to support needed maintenance?

LOCAL PARTICIPATION

How local stakeholders should be involved in the project constitutes one of the most important framing decisions planners have to make. Creating the conditions under which communities can actually influence development outcomes is both a challenge and a major opportunity.[5]

Participation is essentially a relationship between the project team and stakeholders. This relationship may be weak or strong, permanent or temporary. It may touch all aspects of the project or only a few. In some projects, participation is primarily defined in terms of the contributions that local people make to project implementation, in time, labor, knowledge, or other forms of support. In other projects, however, participation means involvement in decisionmaking, having control over resources, and perhaps even having veto powers over major aspects of the undertaking. In these cases, participation is a way to empower local stakeholder groups and to build their skills and capacities.[6]

Stakeholder participation makes sense for several reasons. Stakeholders, for example, often have skills and knowledge that are useful for project development. Stakeholder involvement may significantly lower project costs and ensure a better distribution of benefits. Increasing stakeholder capabilities through participation can help ensure long-term project sustainability.[7]

Participation can only be successful, however, if it is carefully planned. At the framing stage, planners must therefore address three questions concerning participation. What kinds of *activities* will stakeholders participate in? What *kinds of people* will participate? How much *power* will they have?

Activities

Some forms of stakeholder involvement are clearly not participation in any real sense. "Informing" the local population is not the same thing as participation. "Consultation" with locals, where already-made plans are outlined and perhaps discussed, is hardly better. Even continuous consultation, where some local residents are involved in an advisory capacity, may amount to little more than tokenism and rubber-stamping.

True power-sharing, in contrast, usually involves some form of partnership, substantial representation on decisionmaking groups, delegated authority, or outright citizen control of some or all aspects of the project.

During implementation itself, stakeholders can be involved in a wide range of project activities. They can help plan the project, participate in implementation and project assessment, and—if the project is successful—continue to manage it later on. Table 6.7 outlines some examples of how stakeholders can be involved.

People

How these activities will be done is closely connected to the question of who will do them. Here again, planners need to understand how local stakeholder communities are structured to avoid organizing participation in inappropriate ways.

If the project elects to work through local leaders, for example, then it becomes important to know who the local leaders are and what leadership actually consists of in the stakeholder community. This can become a complicated question, often requiring detailed ethnographic knowledge of social structures and processes. Mini-Case 6.1, "Bassari Leadership Structures," outlines how influence is configured and determined in a West African society, and illustrates how complex the issue of leadership can become.

TABLE 6.7   Types of Stakeholder Involvement

Type of Involvement	Examples
Broad Authority Stakeholders make the essential framing decisions that shape the project, and control the project as it unfolds.	Governing boards; local project authorities
Limited Authority Stakeholders make decisions about some, but not all, aspects of the project.	Committees
Design Stakeholders do part or all of the project design work, based on overall specifications.	Local contracting groups
Management Stakeholders are responsible for the running and maintenance of part or all of the finished project.	Project officials and employees
Labor Stakeholders do some or all of the on-site work.	Laborers and artisans during construction; staff once construction is complete
Advice Stakeholders offer recommendations and criticisms of plans and policies at various stages of the project cycle.	User or beneficiary associations; local consultative committees

Power

How people participate is fundamentally a question of how much *power* they have to determine the shape and operation of the project. Power forms a continuum, of course, and control may vary at different points in the project development cycle. Three basic degrees of power that structure most arrangements:

- Voice: The least powerful option, *voice* gives locals the opportunity to discuss, question, and recommend plans and goals set by others. Such recommendations may or may not be taken account of by agency officials.
- Vote: Here, locals are given a formal say in the planning and operation of the project. *Voting* can take many forms: Locals may be

represented on committees, for example, where they form a majority of stakeholders. Or they may be given token representation on a few bodies, where their votes alone cannot determine the outcome.

- Veto: This option gives locals an absolute right of refusal. *Veto* power may not extend to all aspects of the project, and it may not involve all members of the local community. But it does give elements of that community the ability to stop or at least delay important parts of the project.

Obstacles to Participation

Deciding on the nature and type of stakeholder participation will require planners to take into account three aspects of the project environment: existing rules and policies; the nature of the stakeholder community; and the nature of the project. Each aspect may pose obstacles.

Existing Rules and Policies.   Host country or donor policies may obstruct participation. Political or administrative structures may constrain it; highly centralized agencies find it difficult to work directly with the people. Cumbersome financial procedures are another obstacle. Requirements that all aspects of the project be preplanned—the blueprint approach to project development—may also make participation difficult. Finally, technicians or bureaucrats who consider themselves experts who do not need to consult with local people constitute a particularly formidable obstacle.

The Nature of the Stakeholder Community.   The nature of the community itself will also influence what form of participation is possible. There may be no real community organization at the start of the project. The community may be riven by factions, divided by lines of class, ethnicity, politics, or religion, uninterested in the project, or hostile to it. Conversely, several competing organizations may exist that fight with each other for control of the project.

Some communities that are not internally divided may nevertheless not be particularly cohesive or homogeneous. Residents may therefore find it difficult to define the common interests that are necessary for collective action. Many urban communities, for example, are not particularly stable, and transients may be unwilling to invest their time and energy in long-term projects.

MINI-CASE 6.1   BASSARI LEADERSHIP STRUCTURES

Bassari society is organized along lines of sex, age, lineage, and residence. For each organizing dimension, a leadership structure exists, having overlapping but often quite distinct roles. Men and women are arranged in parallel and complementary age-grades. Overall leadership is in the hands of elders and a set of age-grade leaders within each age-grade. Generations are connected through a complex set of ritual and agricultural exchanges that follow a six-year cycle. Men and women possess different, yet complementary, bodies of ritual knowledge. They also assume different yet complementary agricultural duties and separate ownership of key crops. In addition, lineages control different aspects of ritual life and are responsible for important shrines. Geographically, Bassari farmers are linked in patterns of neighborhood labor exchange, with individual household heads as leaders. Villages are likewise linked in reciprocal labor and ritual patterns.

Village leadership is typically weak within this structure. Although French colonial administration is generally characterized as "direct," meaning that local leaders were replaced by French-style officials, the French in Bassari country actually created "traditional" leaders, giving them the title of *chef coutumier*, and investing them with significant decisionmaking power. These "customary chiefs" were responsible for tax collection, the organization of conscript labor, and local law enforcement. With independence this system disappeared, with nothing to replace it. Today, Bassari village chiefs have little real power, and function mainly to collect taxes and communicate information from the central government.

Finally, individual Bassari also hold leadership positions by virtue of special skills they may have, either learned—as in the case of ironsmithing—or innate—as in the case of clairvoyants. Thus, there is not one dimension to leadership in Bassari society, but many, and these cannot be effectively understood without an understanding of how the society as a whole is put together.

Because "leadership" in Bassari society is highly diffused and specific, multiple groups and individuals are involved in even the most basic decisions. Decisions about whether to begin cash-cropping rice, for example (which actually occurred during the 1970s and 1980s in some Bassari villages), would involve not only village chiefs, but also age-grade leaders (since age-grades provided much agricultural labor to village households),

(continues)

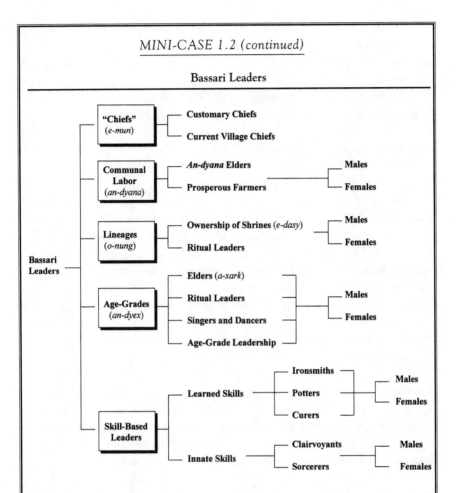

MINI-CASE 1.2 (continued)

Bassari Leaders

an-dyana leaders (who arranged communal labor schedules), elders of both sexes (since males and females control different crops), and ritual leaders of various kinds (since they control the forces that ultimately make the crops grow). No one person or group, in other words, has the authority to make these kinds of decisions, even if they appear to affect only individual farmers or households.

SOURCE: Nolan 1986.

Traditional styles of leadership and decision will of course influence patterns of participation. Vested interests may capture the project; community leaders may be incompetent or corrupt; and self-styled representatives may not speak for groups such as women, the old, the young, and the poor.

The community may be largely unskilled, and hence unable to participate in certain ways. Lack of basic numeracy and literacy, for example, will make it difficult for community residents to do certain jobs. In other communities, specific job-related skills may be lacking—for example, bookkeeping, data processing, construction, or management.

The Nature of the Project.   Certain features of the project may impede participation. Complex procedures, high technology, high standards, capital-intensive procedures, and unfamiliar materials may make participation difficult. Although some projects are merely complex, others are actually dangerous. Large construction projects, for example, frequently result in injury and sometimes death.

The timing of project inputs, the location of project activities, and the daily schedules involved may conflict with local arrangements, and thus preclude the participation of important groups of stakeholders.

Some projects, such as electric and water hookups, home improvement loans, or educational programs, affect only individual families. In cases such as these, little or no support may be required from the community as a whole. Instead, support rests on families or individuals. Other projects, however, touch everyone, and require group support—the siting and construction of community facilities, access roads, reblocking and demolition, planning sewer and drainage lines, and so forth.

Implications for Project Design.   As I have emphasized, designing participation into a project requires planners to have—or to develop—an in-depth understanding of the stakeholder community. At a minimum, planners must understand how stakeholders are socially, politically, and economically organized. They must be familiar with the skills, knowledge, and technology possessed by different groups of stakeholders, with patterns and forms of decisionmaking, and with local value systems. Finally, they must understand how all of these things combine to produce patterns of leadership, resource allocation, and intergroup cooperation.

Participation demands a degree of decentralization, flexibility, and autonomy on the part of the agency. This means that where possible, interactive rather than directive planning styles should be emphasized, and decisions should be made as close to the ground as possible. Participation may also require incentives to keep people involved.

Finally, participation must actually work—and be seen to work—to be effective. The implication of this is that initial efforts should concentrate on relatively simple, short-term, highly visible activities, so that residents can quickly judge the value of participation.

PREDICTING
PROJECT IMPACT

Once the main framing decisions have been taken, projects usually undergo some form of *appraisal* process. This is done along several key dimensions, which appear in Table 6.8.

Although all of these are important, it is *sociocultural appraisal* that holds the most interest—and promise—for development anthropologists.

Sociocultural Appraisal

Sociocultural appraisal (sometimes called *social impact analysis*) has been a feature of AID and World Bank projects since the mid-1970s, and is now common practice in many, if not most, development agencies.[8]

Sociocultural appraisal provides a major opportunity for anthropologists to ensure that issues of context are properly addressed in project designs. Such appraisals bring the skills and knowledge of the anthropologist to the fore, and allow these to be combined with those of other project specialists to produce insights and understandings that no one discipline could achieve on its own. Sociocultural appraisal is also, of course, an occasion for in-depth interaction between those who design the project and those who stand to benefit from it.

Sociocultural appraisals pay particular attention to the differential impact that projects may have on specific groups, such as women, children, farmers, or the unemployed. An effective sociocultural appraisal can help promote the commitment and participation of these and other stakeholders, minimize negative effects, and ensure sustainability.

Although methodologies vary from one agency to another, a typical sociocultural appraisal will look at three related things: *appropriateness; impact;* and *spread.*

Appropriateness involves assessing whether the project as framed will work among the stakeholder groups involved. Who has an interest in this project, and who does not? What local talents can be used in project design, implementation, and maintenance? What is the social profile of participants? How will participants communicate with themselves and with others regarding the project?

TABLE 6.8   Other Forms of Project Appraisal

Environmental	How will the project affect the physical milieu? Projects that alter the way in which local resources are used (for example, water, forest products, land), or that change local practices (such as fishing, farming, hunting) will almost certainly require close examination. Projects involving industrial production, mining, or other activities that generate toxic waste products will also necessitate an environmental impact study. Fragile ecosystems (wetlands, swamps, savanna, alpine areas, reefs, and so on) need special attention. The scope of the assessment should include people, plants, animals, air, and water. An adequate assessment of the environmental aspects of a proposed project should enable planners and other stakeholders to see clearly the costs and benefits, now and in the future, of the various options under consideration. Special attention should be paid to delayed consequences and to effects occurring outside the immediate project area (for example, downwind or downstream). The assessment should be able to point to alternative designs or design modifications that will substantially reduce negative outcomes. Finally, the assessment should be able to be used to design a monitoring and evaluation component capable of tracking effects as the project proceeds.
Economic/ Financial	What are the monetary costs and benefits of this project, and who will bear them? Is the project commercially viable? Sustainable? What will be the broader effects of the project on the economy of the community, the region, and the nation? Financial appraisal typically includes an analysis of the expected income and expenditure, as well as an examination of where benefits are likely to appear, for whom, and for how long. An economic appraisal, on the other hand, looks at the likely impact of the project on the larger regional or national economy. Cost-benefit ratios and internal rates of return are usually a central component in financial and economic analysis.
Technical	What are the technical requirements of the project, and are these affordable, reliable, reasonable, and manageable? Where do technical inputs come from, and is this source assured and reliable? What are the costs of project technology, both in terms of initial outlay and of recurrent costs, and how will these be borne? What skills are required to manage the technology, and are these present? If not, who will do this?
Organizational	How will the project affect—or be affected by—the groups and organizations that will carry it out? What is the quality of management required? What skills and talents are needed, and which are actually available? An institutional appraisal looks at the management implications of a project by examining the capacities of the various organizations charged with project implementation and maintenance. This involves looking at a host of variables, including policy, skill and experience levels, incentives, and the demands that other concurrent activities will place on agencies and organizations. Specific aspects of an institutional appraisal would usually include attention to financial management capabilities (including the ability to absorb and deploy foreign aid disbursements), the ability to use outside technical assistance if required, and the ability to adequately monitor and evaluate the project, once it is under way.

Impact refers to how the project will affect stakeholder groups. Who will benefit and who will not? What will change, and what will not? What effect will this project have on their economic status? On their social organization, pattern of livelihood, and institutions? Investigators also look at how changes in one aspect of community life may provoke changes in other aspects. Who is likely to be affected, and how? What is the likely magnitude of the changes that will occur?

Questions of *spread* are concerned with how widely the benefits of the project are likely to extend beyond the immediate project area. How will timing affect project outcomes? How can the magnitude of changes be controlled? How can the project be modified if necessary?

Project Modification and Redesign

The emphasis in appraisal is the assessment of the likely future consequences of the project, in particular, on its long-term sustainability. Good appraisals can uncover and pinpoint specific aspects of project design that can be corrected before implementation begins. A few projects will have major adverse effects, high costs, or other unacceptable features, and these will be discarded. Other projects, however, will have undesirable aspects that might be changed by altering the design. In some cases, the changes may be evident and straightforward. In others, further analysis and design will be necessary.[9]

The identification of strong and weak aspects of local implementing organizations, for example, can help planners modify and, if necessary, simplify the project in key respects. An institutional appraisal can also be used to craft a training plan to address specific weaknesses, as well as a localization or handover plan for transferring management responsibilities to local stakeholder groups.

Environmental assessment needs to be done early enough in the project cycle to permit modification of the design, if required. Properly identifying environmental problems at an early stage may save considerable money in remediation costs later on, and may actually increase benefits substantially, for example, through energy savings or the costs of cleanup. It is important to involve stakeholders at all stages of an environmental assessment, both to determine its scope and methodology and to discuss its implications for the project.

MINI-CASE 6.2
SOCIAL FEASIBILITY IN NORTH CAMEROON

In 1976, Allan Hoben conducted a social feasibility analysis for the USAID mission in Cameroon. Partly as a result of his findings, USAID decided not to fund the proposed project, which centered on rural development and resettlement. Hoben's descriptions (1986) of his involvement with this proj-

(continues)

MINI-CASE 6.2 (continued)

ect and how he conducted the feasibility analysis are interesting in their own right, but what is particularly relevant for development anthropologists conducting similar analyses in the field are his remarks on how anthropologists and others can ensure that their findings are taken seriously.

Hoben asks, "Do development agencies ever take the advice of consulting anthropologists?" and answers with a "resounding 'sometimes'." For advice to be taken seriously, he advises anthropologists to analyze and understand the decisionmaking context in which they are operating: to look, in other words, at agency culture and structure in much the same way that they look at beneficiaries.

The goal of such analysis, Hoben writes, is to understand the options available to the agency as it develops a project; how the agency sees the choices that will have to be made; how the agency sees the beneficiaries and what assumptions it makes about them; and what kinds of information would be most useful to agency staffers as they move ahead.

When looking at a donor agency, Hoben recommends focusing on a set of key questions.

A. What are the main economic and political functions of the agency, and how do these generate pressures on the agency?
B. Are there differences between headquarters and the field office in terms of how these pressures operate?
C. What are current agency policies and procedures relating to the specific job you are being asked to do?
D. Who are the key decision makers in the agency, and what frameworks are they using to decide things?
E. What processes are used to make decisions about project development, and where is the agency right now with respect to these?
F. Who in the agency is likely to be an ally and supporter when you make your recommendations?

He continues with a set of recommendations for how findings should be presented:

1. Findings should be discussed beforehand with key individuals. No one should be surprised at the last minute.
2. Identify the key assumptions that underlie the project, and then show how your findings relate to these assumptions.

(continues)

MINI-CASE 6.2 (continued)

3. Relate your recommendations to previous experience, here or else-where, if possible. Avoid unsupported theoretical arguments.
4. If you raise a problem, try to put forward a solution to that problem.
5. Write succinctly and concisely, and summarize your findings and rec-ommendations at the outset. This may be all that some people read.

Hoben's final point echoes Robert Chambers's notion of "appropriate imprecision." More data, Hoben says, would probably not have been either useful or necessary. ". . . a longer study could have established the social, economic, and environmental costs of resettlement schemes more pre-cisely, but it would not have affected AID's decision to reject the project" (1986: 192–193).

SOURCE: Hoben 1986.

SUMMARY OF CHAPTER 6

Chapter 6 has looked at the process of project design—the "framing de-cisions" that will determine the project's character.

Framing decisions center on two fundamental aspects of project devel-opment—deciding what the problem is that will be addressed by the project and deciding what approach or strategy to use to address it. Sev-eral techniques for making these decisions were discussed and illustrated.

Choosing project strategy is another key framing decision. Again, sev-eral tools and techniques were discussed, in particular those that help to fit the project to its environment.

The logical framework, for example, was presented as a way to address the inner environment of the project. The access structure, on the other hand, connects project arrangements to the proximate environment of the project, by making explicit how stakeholder communities will be served, what benefits will be available, and who will be eligible for benefits. Finally, the system matrix is one way to map the linkages and relationships that exist—or that should exist—between the project and aspects of its external environment.

Other key framing decisions were discussed, in particular issues of project sustainability and the participation of stakeholders in planning, implementation, and assessment. All of these are matters that can be addressed at an early stage of design. The chapter concluded with a discussion of impact assessment, in particular its sociocultural aspects.

ENDNOTES

1. See Delp (1977) for an overview of some of the most useful of these.

2. In the early 1990s, I worked with a group of Russian factory managers on strategic planning exercises. "Imagine a village," I said, "far out in the *taiga*. You want to raise the average family income in that village by 50 percent. What are your options?" Suggestions were quickly forthcoming. "Build a factory," said one man. "Give people government cash grants," said another. "No, a school, to teach skills." "Reorganize the *kholkoz*." Eventually everyone had contributed except one older man, who sat frowning in the corner. "*Nu*, Vasili, what's your suggestion, eh? You haven't said a word." He waved his hand disgustedly. "Too complicated," he said. "It would be easier just to shoot the rich."

3. Delp (1977:67)

4. See Honadle and Van Sant (1985: 109–110) and Grenier (1998) for more discussion of sustainability issues.

5. Winthrop (1998: 8).

6. See Oakley (1991: 17–18).

7. Although we tend to assume that participation is an axiomatic principle of "correct" development, this may not necessarily be the case. Stone (1989) provides a detailed example of participation from Nepal. In it, she also raises questions about the extent to which an emphasis on local self-reliance and participation can be seen as the imposition of Western cultural values.

8. AID's version of social impact analysis is called "social soundness," and was developed by anthropologists in the 1970s. See, for example, Cochrane (1971, 1976) and Cochrane and Noronha (1973) for accounts by one of the anthropologists who was central to this effort. Aside from these specific approaches, specially tailored for the needs of individual agencies, there is an extensive literature on broader aspects of social impact analysis. See, for example, Halstead et al. (1984), Finsterbusch (1980), Carley and Bustelo (1984), Branch et al. (1984), Roche (1999), and Goldman (2000).

9. Typically, there will be disagreement between project specialists about the extent of change necessary in a project's design and about the procedures for making those changes (compare with Conlin 1985: 80).

chapter 7

MANAGING PROJECTS

MANAGEMENT NEEDS
IN PROJECT DEVELOPMENT

Project hardware includes not only tangible things like equipment, money, and buildings, but also the hard-wired aspects of organization such as deadlines, targets, and procedures. *Project software,* on the other hand, refers to the local systems within which the hardware exists and must function. All too often, planners concentrate on the hardware and neglect the software. But a project is a cross-cultural joint venture, pulling together a variety of cultural styles, structures, procedures, and assumptions.

Project management is essentially about making project hardware and project software work together. Anthropologists are increasingly involved in project management, primarily because of their skill in doing this. Project managers—whether they are anthropologists or not—work in an environment that contains multiple interest groups and differing value systems.

Although many management tasks are routine, four in particular demand cross-cultural skills and understanding: analyzing *organizational culture;* promoting effective *decisionmaking; negotiation and conflict resolution;* and enhancing *technical assistance and counterpart relationships.*

The following sections will examine these one by one.

173

ORGANIZATIONAL CULTURE

Culture and Management Style

Management practices are not universal. Typically, a development project will bring multiple cultural systems into close and sustained contact with one another. Clashes of management style are almost inevitable.

Even the simplest project will have one or more international organizations working with one or more host country organizations and a range of stakeholder groups. The possibilities for conflict and misunderstanding are not only numerous, but often significant. Problems tend to center around different ideas of what to do and how to do it, based on sets of deeply held but usually tacit *core values*.

Although each society has many values that make up its culture, core values seem particularly important in helping to organize that culture's worldview. Although these may not be shared by everyone, they are *core* in two important senses: they are held by large numbers of people in a society and they are seen as significant, even by people who do not share them, for structuring interactions and responses.

The operation of an American workplace, for example, reflects some of the core values of wider U.S. culture. These values are normative, in the sense that they are not always adhered to in practice, but tend, in most organizations, to shape how people think, interact, and react. Some of these are set out in Table 7.1.

Many Americans consider workplace values such as these to be nearly universal, or at least, to be the desired standard across the world. In reality, they are hardly ever found in quite the same way in cross-cultural situations. Americans working on development projects overseas have reported a host of management-related issues, which appear—in the American view—to contribute to project failure or inefficiency. Interestingly, many of these violate one or more of the American core values mentioned below.

Hiring and firing, for example, may be done on the basis of patronage or connections, rather than on merit. The public goods of the organization may be used or diverted by private individuals for their own ends. Maintenance of essential equipment or buildings may be neglected, and the technical requirements of machinery may be ignored or violated. What should be "rational" and "objective" decisions may be politicized and personalized. Top managers may refuse to delegate, with the result that although subordinates in an organization are idle, those at the top

TABLE 7.1   Some Core Values of an American Workplace

Organization	Typically, an American firm will be formally organized into some sort of hierarchy. Different parts of the organization will be specialized, and each part will have both a specific set of roles and a defined relationship to the other parts of the organization.
Interaction	Interactions that emphasize directness, informality, and decisiveness, coupled with a reliance on the written word as the final expression of a business relationship. Many relationships are also characterized by impartiality and a concern for fairness, which can often override personal friendships.
Decision Processes	A rational and directive decisionmaking ethos, based largely on rules, policies, and empirical data ("facts and figures"), and weighted toward either/or thinking. Meetings as a frequent method of conducting business. Although they take different forms, almost all meetings have as their purpose making decisions in a relatively specific, overt way.
Performance Standards	Performance standards and judgments based on values such as efficiency, competition, punctuality, competitiveness, individual initiative, hard work, risk, and so forth.

are continually overloaded. Schedules and commitments may be shifting and uncertain, resulting in a lack of continuity.

Americans often consider these issues to be deviations from the normal functioning of the system. They may not be. In some cases, the problems *are* the system. Table 7.2 presents some of the dimensions along which culture influences management style.

Components of Organizational Culture

These variations in workstyle apply not only to individuals, but also to groups, in which case we may speak of *organizational culture*. There are usually multiple organizational cultures operating in the project arena. The implementing agency may have a culture very different from the host country administration; foreign specialists may differ significantly from local counterparts in the way they work; and stakeholder groups may present diverse profiles.

TABLE 7.2 Some Cultural Contrasts in Organizational Operation

Culture A	Managerial Task or Function	Culture B
The situation can and should be changed.	Defining Problems	The situation cannot be changed or should be accepted as is.
Look for new and different ways to do things.	Defining Options	Base future choices on past traditions and precedents.
Use individual decisionmaking.	Making Decisions	Use group decisionmaking.
Responsibility is individualized; delegation comes from the top.	Carrying Out Decisions	Responsibility is shared; all levels participate and reach consensus.
People can influence the future.	Planning and Scheduling	People cannot change the future.
You get what you bargain for.	Negotiation	You get what you need.
You are rewarded for results.	Rewards and Recognition	You are rewarded for effort.
You identify with the project or the company.	Group Identification	You identify with your family or kinship group.
The best-qualified person should be hired.	Hiring	Family, group, and friendship obligations should take precedence.
People can be removed if they do not perform.	Firing	Removing people causes distress and loss of face and is rarely done.
Anyone can rise up through the ranks.	Promotion and Advancement	Advancement is reserved mainly for people with the right background and connections.
Openness and freedom of expression are encouraged.	Communication	Opinions conform to the ideas of the leadership.
Directness and honesty are emphasized in feedback.	Feedback	Keeping interpersonal relations smooth and harmonious is important.

SOURCES: Adapted from Adler 1986: 14–15; Harris and Moran 1991: 79–80; Austin 1990: 355.

This picture is made even more complicated since foreign donor agencies may not have one organizational culture, but several. The headquarters culture of an agency, for example, may be very different from the culture of a specific overseas branch of the same organization. In some cases, elements of different cultures are combined within a single office.

Agencies often have broad orientations that determine how they operate. Some agencies have a task orientation, where results are valued above all else. Others have a hierarchical or bureaucratic orientation, where rules and roles predominate and where it is less important to be right than it is not to be wrong in terms of protocol or procedures. Some agencies are fiefdoms, under the control of a strong central personality. Others are collegia, stressing equality and consensus.[1]

So, for example, in the Tunisian project I managed in the early 1980s (outlined in Mini-Case 5.2), the consulting firm that held the major contract for the project was clearly a collegium with a task orientation. Within the organization, individuals were expected to work collaboratively and constructively with each other, and to get the work done quickly and professionally. AID, the U.S. government bilateral, funded the project, and it was clearly a bureaucracy where staffers were concerned about following rules. The various Tunisian organizations were a mixture of bureaucracies and fiefdoms. Managing the relationships between all of these was a full-time job.

These organizational cultures provide the institutional framework—and many of the limits—within which the project will succeed or fail. Although organizational cultures are infinitely variable, they are not chaotic, and one can begin to build an understanding of their character in terms of a few key variables, such as structures, purposes, procedures, and personalities. These are set out in more detail in Table 7.3.

When different organizations collaborate, the project becomes an arena within which different views of the world compete and interact. Successful projects are ones in which these cross-cultural contacts result in synergistic and creative outcomes, going beyond what the individual organizations could achieve by acting alone.

All too often, however, organizations fall into an adversary relationship and attempt to impose their view on their partner. Projects implemented under these conditions are likely to have significant problems, and may not be sustainable in the long run. Mini-Case 7.1, "Cattle, Culture and Confusion," outlines one such project in Senegal.

TABLE 7.3   Some Key Variables in Organizational Culture

	Structures
Roles and Responsibilities	How is the organization formally structured in terms of jobs and titles? What responsibilities and expectations go with these titles?
Leadership	Who's in charge? How far does that person's authority extend? Are there other, more informal, leaders who don't appear on the organization charts? What authority or responsibility do formal and informal leaders have? How does someone get to be a leader in this group?
Alignments	Inside every organization there are less formal groupings. Do these correspond to the organization's official structure, or are they different? Are there factions or subgroups within the larger group? What roles do these groupings play within the organization? Are they supportive or antagonistic?
	Purposes
Goals	What overall goals and outcomes is this group seeking? What outcomes do they seek to avoid? Who has decided these things? What strategies are they using to accomplish these ends? How successful are they?
Performance Standards	How does this organization judge whether it is doing its job properly? What standards does the group have in common for the performance of its assigned tasks? Is there disagreement over these standards? Are these standards specific to this group? Who sets these standards?
Motivators	What is it that excites people in this organization? What turns them off? What do people feel they are getting out of working for the organization? Do they want things that they are not getting?
	Procedures
Communication	How are messages passed along in the organization? Are communications formal, informal, or both? Is there a grapevine that provides an alternative to established channels?
Decisionmaking	Who makes decisions in the organization, and what are the factors or values that influence these decisions? What are the established ways decisions are made, and how long does this usually take? Are decisions accepted by others, or are they resisted or subverted?
Control and Feedback	How does the organization police and regulate itself? What sets of rules are in force, and how are they applied? How are people given information about their performance within this organization? Is this done publicly and formally, or informally?
Participation	How are people involved with each other in this organization? Who is involved in the major decisions that are taken? Who joins in discussions? Who is generally excluded from things?
Resolving Conflict	How does the organization handle disputes? Do people have established ways of doing this, or does every dispute get settled informally or in an ad hoc manner? Are these disputes resolved, or do they continue to be a problem?

(continues)

TABLE 7.3 *(continued)*

Personalities	
Background	Do the group members have common or diverse backgrounds? What things do they have in common? What things differentiate them? How important do these seem to be? What are the factions, jealousies, and rivalries between people?
Patterns of Participation	How do members of the group seem to work together? What do they do as a group, and as individuals? Do they cooperate well, or are there difficulties?
Discourse	How do members of the group talk to each other? What languages, methods, or modes do they seem to prefer? Do they engage in code-switching or other distinctive behavior when they communicate? Are they high or low context?
Leadership Styles	What styles of leadership seem to be favored by the people in the group? What are the expectations of a leader? What are the values that people associate with good leaders? With bad?
Attitudes, Perceptions, and Expectations	What seems to matter most to the people in the group? What are their dominant views on life? Are there specific issues that mean a great deal to them?

DECISIONMAKING

During the course of a project, planners must make hundreds or even thousands of decisions. Many of these are made under conditions of uncertainty and ambiguity, where opinions as to the proper course of action differ and where the difference between right and wrong choices is not immediately apparent. Because so many choices need to be made so quickly, project personnel learn to pay particular attention to *key decisions*. Earlier, we identified some of these key decisions in the chapter on framing projects.

These and other key project decisions share a number of common characteristics. For one thing, significant resources are involved. Since these could always be used in other ways, decisions that commit important resources are key decisions. Decisions that are irrevocable or difficult to change are also key decisions. Decisions that involve choosing between a variety of different options, where different subjective opinions are involved rather than some universal standards, are also key decisions. Decisions that then "lock in" other, later decisions are clearly key decisions.

MINI-CASE 7.1   CATTLE, CULTURE, AND CONFUSION: THE SODESP LIVESTOCK PROJECT

Anthropologists working in development are well aware of the necessity of performing a social soundness analysis on the local project beneficiaries, but we have paid remarkably little attention to the culture of the implementers. I am as guilty of this as anyone, as this case study will show.

The SODESP livestock project in Senegal, analyzed by Boyle (1984), was one I worked on in its early stages as a member of the USAID design team. The project was approved and begun, but eventually USAID withdrew funding. Although our team looked in some detail at both the culture of the local herders who would be project beneficiaries and the physical environment of the northern sylvo-pastoral zone itself, no detailed analysis of the Senegalese implementing organization ever found its way into our project document.

In retrospect, this was a major mistake. "Even the best designed projects," Boyle says, "typically ignore how implementing structures can more effectively be established, and they do not anticipate what the likely and recurrent consequences of that ignorance may be."

A typical project will contain not one but several implementation structures, including the host government at several different levels (national, regional, and local), the donor agency (both its Western headquarters and its national field mission), and the contracting firm or agency (again, both its headquarters and its project organizations).

Typically, the different structures will misunderstand each other in ways similar to what occurs between agencies as a whole and the beneficiary populations they attempt to serve. In the process, culturally based biases and assumptions are revealed as arrangements shift or break down. Boyle analyzes the SODESP livestock project in Senegal from this perspective.

I was the anthropologist member of the design team responsible for writing the project paper—that is, the AID document that contained most of the framing decisions that would guide project development. The impact on the FulBe herders of the area was of concern to the design team, as well as the eventual impact on the environment of the sylvo-pastoral zone of the project. Our fieldwork and subsequent analysis focused mainly on these things.

In the process, however, we became aware of two other issues, which, as it turned out, were crucial in the project's demise. One was an issue of management style, the other of project goal or purpose. At a basic level, of course, these were interrelated.

The SODESP's Senegalese project director was a strong-minded individual who ran his organization in a top-down, highly centralized manner.

(continues)

MINI-CASE 7.1 (continued)

Trained as a veterinarian, he was inclined to take a technocratic approach to issues of planning and implementation.

The director and most of his staff, furthermore, did not really see the project in the same way as the American designers did. From our perspective, it was important to improve the lives of the local herders, at the same time preserving the fragile sylvo-pastoral environment. In our minds, beef production would only be successful to the extent that these basic goals were met.

The director had a different view. His job, as he saw it, was to produce beef for the urban market, and this he intended to do. Environmental changes were not really his concern. To the extent that they followed project guidelines, local herders were obedient clients. If they did not, they became obstacles. They were never partners in a real sense.

Our design team was aware of these differences in outlook. One of the few members of the American design team with fluent French, I was often called on to translate during meetings and negotiations between Senegalese and American technicians. The term "range management," it seemed to me, was fundamentally misunderstood in these discussions.

To the Americans, the term meant far more than raising cattle profitably; it meant doing so in a way that preserved the environment and the lives of those who inhabited it, on a long-term and sustainable basis. Although the Senegalese with whom we talked presumably understood—or could have understood—this concept, they tended to translate "range management" in different terms. "*Gestion de paturage*" was one; "*amenagement du territoire*" was another. Neither of these accurately conveys the sense of the English term "range management."

These issues arose not just because different actors wanted different things, but because, at a more basic level, they *saw* different things. They never communicated these things clearly to each other during the crucial framing phase of project development, with the result that these differences were never satisfactorily addressed in the final project design.

The design team, composed of specialists in anthropology, range management, livestock economics, and water became very aware of and sensitive to the issues of management style and focus that were, in the end, to doom the project. We not only discussed management issues with members of the USAID mission, but we also took care to write into the project paper an extensive section advocating closely monitoring environmental conditions in the project area, and described in detail the types of information that should be collected.

(continues)

MINI-CASE 7.1   (continued)

But—and this is the point—these important differences never found their way into the project's final design. There was simply no place in AID's framework for them. Although several members of the design team were aware of these differences and concerned to address them in the design, other stakeholders' views prevailed. It was important that the AID mission in Dakar get funding for this project—doubly so, since the French, the Canadians, and the World Bank were also interested in the project. The final project paper thus became essentially an advocacy document, intended to persuade AID/Washington to approve funding.

After my report was submitted, of course, my involvement with the project ended. AID approved the project, issued a contract for technical assistance to support it, and four American specialists arrived to work with SODESP on implementation. Eventually, all four either resigned or were fired by the project's directors. Subsequently, USAID canceled further project funding. The conflicts that led to this end were based on differences in organizational culture, as Boyle's analysis makes clear.

The Technicians

Boyle describes how the American contractors hired to help implement the project considered themselves independent professionals, whereas the project director considered them subordinates, required to carry out a variety of routine administrative tasks. The contractors were focused on what were to them crucial questions of environmental degradation and the welfare of local herders.

> The technical assistants had, in their [own] view, been hired to deal with the thorny questions of range management, provision of services to herders, and the monitoring of socioeconomic aspects of the herders' quality of life. Because of this, the technicians were particularly alarming to the [Senegalese] project leadership, which was much less concerned than USAID with socioeconomic effects on herders, and far more preoccupied with the purely technical objective of production of beef for the country's urban populations, specifically Dakar.

The SODESP Project's Leadership

The project's director, however, saw contractors' concerns as peripheral to the production of beef for urban markets. SODESP wanted to produce beef for the urban market. It also held to its own traditional view of top-down,

(continues)

MINI-CASE 7.1 *(continued)*

centralized management from a technocratic viewpoint. They considered the herders as obstacles or clients, not partners. "The director of the livestock project, who was clearly ill at ease with, even suspicious of, the new American personnel, did not intend to modify his organizational structure, objectives, or values, in order to accommodate foreign personnel who came with terms of reference he felt has been imposed upon him by USAID" (1984: 14).

The USAID mission, for cultural reasons of its own, adopted an arm's-length attitude in this struggle, and the contractors' home office, fearful of losing its contract, urged its field specialists to go along with local arrangements. Eventually, all the American specialists either resigned or were fired, and USAID decided not to renew the project's funding.

USAID in Dakar

From the outset, USAID had wanted not to be involved in the details of project implementation. It also wanted to continue its relationship with the Senegalese government. "When all four technical assistants were either fired or resigned, including the chief of party, the USAID mission was faced with a project organization that had obtained just what it wanted—financing on its own terms and with virtually no disruption of its original mission. Faced with the project's refusal to carry out the terms of the grant agreement, USAID determined not to renew funding for a second project phase" (1984: 16).

Conclusion

As the SODESP project shows, it is not enough to carry out social analysis on project beneficiaries alone. The entire implementation structure, including all of the major stakeholders, need to be looked at in terms of their capacity and willingness to do what is necessary to advance the project. Boyle comments: "Improper knowledge of the organizational sub-cultures called upon to cooperate in project implementation is responsible for many of the breakdowns of communication and cooperation in development schemes" (1984: 4).

In retrospect, it is possible—and perhaps likely—that the misunderstandings were both deliberate and mutual. USAID got a major project approved for funding, and as Boyle points out, the Senegalese got project financing on their own terms and conditions, with virtually no change in existing procedures and arrangements.

SOURCE: Boyle 1984.

Group Decisions

On any project, many of these key decisions are made by groups rather than individuals. Group decisions are particularly called for when a variety of ideas or viewpoints are needed to find solutions, when relevant expertise and knowledge is spread among different people, and—most important—when it is necessary to get consensus and to share risk.

Meetings are therefore an almost daily occurrence on many projects, and serve a variety of purposes. Meeting behavior is heavily influenced by the core values of a particular culture. Some cultures (for example, Japanese or Indonesian) prefer to discuss issues privately before a meeting, airing disagreements out of sight. During the meeting itself, there will be little public disagreement, and therefore no loss of face. In such situations, the chair's role may not be to lead discussion, but rather to express the will of the group. Such meetings are often characterized by efforts to maintain harmony and minimize surprise.

To Americans, however, meetings are occasions where issues are openly discussed and decisions are made on the spot. Americans are quite comfortable with overt disagreement during meetings, and with the give and take of public debate, which can sometimes become heated. Indeed, Americans often seek areas of disagreement as a way to test ideas, and many Americans are quite comfortable with argument as a mode of discourse, sometimes using it to cement relationships.[2] Once decisions are made, Americans often want to "see it in writing." Other cultures, of course, do things differently. They may emphasize relationships more than contracts, and see the relationship not as something fixed, but as evolving through time.

Helping People Take Sound Decisions

Despite these differences in meeting styles, project staffers must still find ways to discuss and decide important issues. Anthropologists can help facilitate these interactions in several different ways. One is by seeing to it that important items are put on the agenda. Another way is to help different groups determine their own preferred solution requirements, and by helping each group understand the other's requirements. A third role is that of helping to facilitate discussion.

Project groups typically must agree on what the issues are that they need to deal with, what kinds of information they will consider, and what types of solutions will be acceptable. The anthropologist can help facilitate discussion by making sure that key issues of context are consid-

FIGURE 7.1   A Framework for Group Discussion and Decision

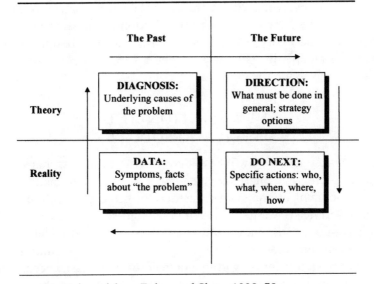

SOURCE: Adapted from Fisher and Sharp 1998: 79.

ered, and that appropriate voices are heard. The anthropologist can also make sure that appropriate information is available to participants and that the significance of this information is explained properly and understood by everyone. As various strategy options are generated and debated, the anthropologist can help people understand which goals and values underlie both their own preferences and those of others. Finally, of course, anthropological input can help guide choices in directions that are culturally feasible and appropriate.

When dealing with different cultural styles of discussion and decision, it helps to have a common framework. Fisher and Sharp offer a simple yet effective model for group work.[3] Group discussion, they point out, tends to shift and drift back and forth between theory and the real world, on the one hand, and between the past and the future on the other. All four of these domains are necessary for effective thinking, but they need to be managed during discussion. One role of the facilitator is therefore to put the contributions of the various participants into the appropriate domains, and to do this in such a way that the group can see how the domains are related.

In this process, diversity within a planning group can be a significant source of strength. Diversity—of skill, knowledge, experience, approach, values, or attitude—helps the group understand how situations can be seen in different ways by different people. Not everyone will see the same issues, and not everyone will see the same issue in the same way. Because solutions must satisfy everyone to some extent, discussion of different viewpoints is necessary before actions can be taken. When it is time for action, the group's diversity may provide a variety of good—but different—ways of solving the problem.

NEGOTIATION AND CONFLICT RESOLUTION

From time to time, there will be disagreements or conflicts that threaten to hold up progress. Such disagreements can arise from many sources: lack of communication; acute differences in perceptions or values; and variations in needs, wants, and desired outcomes. In these cases, discussion becomes *negotiation*, or, in extreme cases, *conflict resolution*. Here again, the anthropologist can play a key brokering and facilitating role.

Unmanaged, differences within a project team can easily become conflict. Conflict can consume vast amounts of energy, divert the organization's focus, and—in some cases—even bring things to a standstill. Conflict is essentially a relationship. Persons are in conflict, and they are in conflict because of their differences. Managed badly, conflict allows neither party to get what they need in the present, and jeopardizes further interactions in the future.

Like fire, however, conflict can be useful as well as destructive; not all outcomes are negative. As negotiators like to point out, conflict helps reveal what different people really need. Managed well, conflict gives everyone a chance to understand differences in viewpoints and to develop mutually satisfactory responses to them. This can strengthen a relationship and give both parties all or part of what they seek within a framework that encourages them to continue to work together. Conflict therefore provides organizations and individuals with opportunities to learn, grow, and develop.

Most conflicts can be negotiated. Conflicts arise from perceptions that something is wrong or unsatisfactory, and these discontents give the parties something to negotiate about. Often, what people disagree about is the allocation of resources. If each party in the conflict can, in effect, stop the other from getting what it wants, then both sides have an excellent reason to negotiate.

The groups involved, however, must want to solve the problem, and they must be able to solve the problem through some mutually accept-

FIGURE 7.2   Options in Negotiation

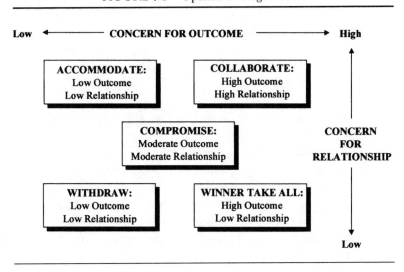

able procedure. Good negotiations do not take up too much time or energy, promote better relationships between partners, and result in outcomes that are satisfying to both parties, fair, and sustainable.[4] A group that simply wants to prevent the other group from getting what it wants is not really a negotiating partner.

Approaches to Negotiation

People who enter a negotiation generally have two things uppermost in mind: what they want from the *relationship* with their negotiating partner and what they want as an *outcome* for themselves. How negotiators feel about these two essential things will determine, in large measure, their approach to the negotiation process itself. Five basic approaches present themselves.

Winner Take All.   *Winner take all* is the strategy adopted by someone who is very concerned about achieving a particular outcome, but who cares little or nothing about the future of the relationship with his or her negotiating partner. "Be a winner at whatever cost" characterizes this approach to negotiation. This produces pressure tactics, take-it-or-leave-it positions, and intimidation. The negotiating relationship is seen as an adversarial one, with a win/lose outcome. Although such a strategy may be very effective in the short run, it does not produce positive long-term relationships, and may trigger a desire for revenge or getting even on the part of the loser.

Withdraw.   Parties to a negotiation will *withdraw* if they have little concern for either the outcome or the relationship. They may feel powerless to influence the negotiation, or they may dislike the other party. Perhaps they truly do not care one way or the other what happens. In these cases, the strategy becomes "Take whatever you can get, no matter how small, without making a fuss." Like the winner-take-all strategy outlined above, withdrawal may solve the problem in the short term, but create more problems later on. The outcomes of negotiations of this type tend to result in unfair and sometimes unworkable arrangements, and may engender feelings of resentment. Eventually, someone will try to get even. In the meantime, parties may opt out of their interactions with each other.

Accommodate.   Someone who adopts a strategy of *accommodation* is focused on maintaining the relationship, and will be much less concerned about the outcome of the negotiation itself. The theme is "Let's be friends." Using this strategy, people will work hard to promote harmony and will minimize and avoid dealing with differences. They will yield fairly easily to pressure on specific points, just to preserve the relationship. Here again, outcomes achieved using this strategy may eventually prove unsatisfactory and unsustainable.

Compromise.   Someone who adopts *compromise* as a strategy has an equal concern for both the outcome and the relationship. Efforts will be made to meet the other person halfway, make trade-offs, and compromise. The principle of "splitting the difference" characterizes this approach to negotiation. Each party is willing to give up some of what they want in exchange for other desired things. The strategy does not result in either an optimum outcome or an optimum relationship, but produces results that both parties can live with much of the time.

Collaborate.   Persons who adopt a strategy of *collaboration* have a high degree of commitment to both the outcome and the relationship, and they will seek to maximize both, often in very creative ways. "Let's both win" characterizes this approach. Partners will search for common interests, or, failing that, identify individual interests that can be satisfied at little or no cost to the other party. The idea is to work together to find ways to maximize each party's preferences.

Cross-Cultural Issues in Negotiation

Of these strategies, *compromise* or *collaboration* are the two most likely to preserve or strengthen an existing relationship, giving both parties some or all of what each wants. Collaboration, in particular, seeks to move beyond surface statements of position—or wants—to the underlying interests—or needs—that drive the partners. If partners turn out to need different things, then there is often no further reason to disagree. If partners need the same thing, they can often be persuaded to work together. Many negotiations in a project setting will of course be cross-cultural in nature. Although this makes them more difficult in some respects, it also enhances the likelihood that collaborative solutions can be found.

One collaborative approach that often works well is the *formula-detail approach*, consisting of three steps. The first is an initial diagnosis, in which the facts of the situation are outlined, and the issues and problems are described as clearly and fully as possible. The second step is the determination of a formula to guide agreement. The formula is an abstraction, but it sets out what will be negotiated, where the boundaries are, and what the values or principles are that will guide resolution. The third and final step is the hammering-out of the details, based on the diagnosis and the formula, both of which are used to guide offers, demands, and concessions.

I used this approach frequently in unfamiliar overseas environments as I hunted for necessities in local markets. On one particularly memorable occasion, winter had come early to western Russia, and one morning found me picking my way through the large black market area outside Moscow, searching for warm clothes.

The *diagnosis* stage of this process involved locating the part of the market where fur hats—chapkas—were sold, locating the sellers, and examining the range of items on offer. Chapkas come in a wide variety of styles. Did I want, they asked, an elegant hat or a plain hat? One made from rabbit fur or arctic fox? A Cossack hat, perhaps? Or a Soviet infantryman's hat, complete with hammer-and-sickle insignia?

Once we had focused on the relevant type of hat, we established the *formula*. This tended to consist of a few basics, including the language that we would be doing business in, and what I had to trade with. My Russian was poor, my German passable, my French good, my English fluent. No hat-sellers that day spoke English, French, or German, and so we used my limited Russian vocabulary plus a large number of what I hoped were universal nonverbal signals.

I possessed dollars, rubles, and finnmarks, plus the clothes I was wear-

TABLE 7.4   Differences in Negotiating Style

One Group Focuses On	The Other Group Focuses On
Principles	Details
Win/Lose Opportunities	Win/Win Opportunities
Secretiveness	Openness
Form	Substance
Relationships	Outcomes
Talk	Action
Symbolic Worth	Practical Worth
Consensus	Hierarchy
Prestige	Benefits
Argument or Debate	Smooth Relationships

ing. Although a great deal of attention was initially paid to both my Levis and my overcoat, we finally settled on dollars as an appropriate medium of exchange.

Once we had established the formula, negotiations began in earnest, as my partners and I worked collaboratively to establish the real price of the chapka under consideration. I left the market somewhat poorer but a great deal warmer.

Most negotiations in project development are much more complex than this, of course. When the parties to a negotiation come from different cultures, the process of separating surface positions or demands from underlying needs can sometimes prove difficult. In a cross-cultural encounter, not everyone uses—or even knows—the same set of facts; not everyone interprets and reacts to these facts in the same way. This can lead to marked differences in negotiating style. Some of these are set out in Table 7.4.

Naive realism is often a significant factor in cross-cultural negotiation. "We behave the way we do for perfectly valid reasons," one side may claim. "But *they* act the way they do because they are Arabs" (or Africans, engineers, or economists). In truth, all parties in a negotiation are acting out their interests from within the web of meanings their culture gives them.

In the early 1990s, I was in Tallinn, Estonia, helping to train foreign ministry officials in negotiation, to prepare them for discussions with the Russians about troop withdrawal. Our training team spent part of an afternoon describing what, from a theoretical point of view, a good negotiator should possess in terms of skills and personality characteristics. We then divided the Estonian officials into four groups and asked each to write down what they felt, from their point of view, the characteristics of a good negotiator were.

Three of the four groups independently put the ability to consume large quantities of vodka at the top of their list of essential characteristics. They then had to spend time explaining to the surprised American team exactly how important this was when dealing with the Russians. "We drink," they said, "because it's the only way to gain the Russians' respect."

We nodded uncertainly. "But why do *they* drink?" we asked.

"Why?" The Estonians shrugged. "Because they are Russians, of course."

The fact that cultures are different provides opportunities as well as obstacles. Indeed, it is precisely *because* different cultures categorize and value things differently that mutually acceptable solutions are often possible. If one culture is more concerned with form, for example, and the other culture emphasizes substance and cares less about appearance, we have a situation resembling that of Jack Sprat and his wife: Each party can get what it most values without damage to the other's interests.

This is not to say that such solutions are always immediately apparent. It is important, in a cross-cultural negotiation, to avoid jumping to conclusions about what the other side needs, wants, feels, or even sees. Patient discussion and questioning, combined with a nonjudgmental attitude, can help participants understand how issues—and possible solutions—are defined and structured.

Often, communication styles themselves must be understood in order to make progress. The *high-context-low-context* dichotomy, explicated by Edward Hall, distinguishes cultures in terms of how much attention people pay to the context surrounding communication, as opposed to the actual message itself.[5] Table 7.5 sets out some of these differences.

High-context cultures take a variety of things into account in interpreting a message, including who the speaker is and what their relationship is with the listener. In low-context cultures, on the other hand, although such cues are not irrelevant, people tend to focus on the message itself and the "facts" it conveys.

High- and low-context differences often characterized the project negotiations I participated in. Tunisians and Senegalese, although very different cultures in many respects, are both fairly high context compared to the very low-context culture that characterizes most American AID officials. In these discussions, Americans tended to interpret the some-

TABLE 7.5 High- and Low-Context Cultures

Low-Context Cultures	High-Context Cultures
• Information must be provided explicitly, usually in words. People prefer detailed background information and explicit and careful directions from someone who "knows."	• Much information is drawn from surroundings; very little must be explicitly transferred. Environment, situation, gestures, and mood are all taken into account.
• People are less aware of nonverbal cues, environment, and situation.	• Nonverbal cues and signals are very important for determining meaning.
• People may lack well-developed networks.	• People maintain extensive information networks.
• People tend to segment and compartmentalize information. Knowledge is a commodity.	• The physical context is heavily relied on for meaning. Meaning is "out there" and available to anyone who can read the situation.
• People control information on a "need-to-know" basis.	• Information flows freely.

SOURCE: Adapted from Hall and Hall 1989.

times emotion-laden statements of Tunisians or Senegalese as mere bluster, whereas these officials, for their part, tended to disregard the specifics the Americans were carefully explaining, and focus instead on the affective aspects of the relationship. Thus, attempts to build the relationship (that is, to enhance the context) by Senegalese or Tunisians tended to be brushed aside by the Americans in an attempt to "get down to business." On one memorable occasion, this so upset a Tunisian official that he broke off discussions and left the room. The fact that all parties were doing this in French—no one's native tongue—merely added to the complexity of the task.

High-context situations might be characterized as requiring a high degree of intuitive skill, whereas low-context situations call for more literal-mindedness. If both parties to a negotiation share a common approach to context, then things are somewhat easier. But often, parties do *not* have a common approach, and miscommunication occurs. Even when the parties recognize this difficulty, it takes time to develop the relationship—and hence, the appropriate facilitating context—between them.

TABLE 7.6   Some Basic Negotiating Principles

- Try to separate the problems under discussion from the people you are discussing them with.

- Focus on underlying needs, not just on stated wants or positions.

- Use whatever common ground you find as a platform from which to continue discussions. Talk as much about what you have in common as about your differences.

- Try to learn as much as you can about how the other side sees the issues, sees you, and sees itself. Try to avoid imposing your own judgments or standards. Show respect, and preserve everyone's dignity at all times.

- If the issues are complex, begin with simple things. Break larger problems into smaller ones if possible.

- Look for a variety of possible good solutions before settling on one. Make sure that the solution you settle on is sustainable and is seen as acceptable according to some set of standards or measures that both sides can acknowledge.

- Individuals do not negotiate in a vacuum; each person is a member of one or more interested communities, whose interests may also have to be taken into account in crafting a workable solution.

- Avoid contaminating discussions with broad declarations of principle. When issues of principle are raised, they tend to become obstacles to resolution.

TECHNICAL ASSISTANCE
AND COUNTERPART RELATIONSHIPS

Technical Assistance

Technical assistance—the provision of outside specialists at various points in project development—is a feature of most development efforts. Often, these outsiders are provided by the donor agency as a condition of the grant or loan that funds the project. Technical assistance for a given project may consist of a single individual or an entire team. It may be permanent, lasting throughout the life of the project, or it may be temporary. Outsiders may be narrow specialists and work only in one or two key areas or they may be generalist managers responsible for broad aspects of planning or implementation. In addition to supplying needed expertise, outsiders provided by the donor also ensure, to some extent at least, that donor interests are represented on-site during project development.

FIGURE 7.3   A Continuum of Technical Assistance Roles

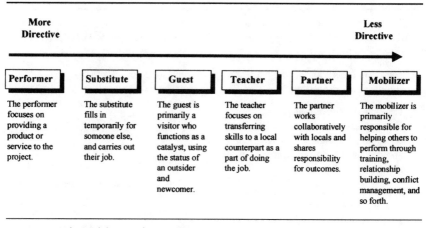

SOURCES: Adapted from Silverman 1984; Lethem and Cooper 1983; Honadle and Van Sant 1985.

Technical assistance roles can be seen as forming a continuum, depending on the degree of responsibility and authority outsiders have. At one extreme, an outsider performs a role or completes an assignment by working essentially alone. As we move more toward the middle of the continuum, however, the outside expert becomes a teacher and adviser, in what is essentially an apprenticeship situation. Moving further, outsiders and locals work together as equals. Finally, at the other end, outsiders function mainly as resource persons, coaches, or hands-off advisers. This continuum is presented in Figure 7.3.

Counterparts

Larger projects will contain several—perhaps many—outside specialists, and each will have a place somewhere on the continuum. Of particular interest are the roles that involve structured contact with a local expert, usually called a *counterpart*. The counterpart relationship is a common feature of projects that seek to build local management capacity in addition to providing project benefits.

Although the counterpart relationship is often crucial to project success and sustainability, it is frequently mismanaged. To begin with, neither the outside specialist nor the local counterpart usually has much say in the matter. Expatriates and locals are often frequently assigned to each other without much regard for compatibility, background, or other im-

FIGURE 7.4   A Continuum of Counterpart Relationships

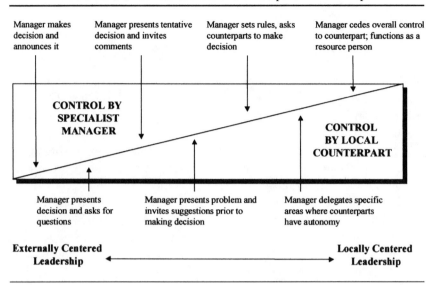

SOURCES: Adapted from Peace Corps 1983; Schein 1969.

portant considerations. Marginally competent people are sometimes as-signed as counterparts, or promising local staffers are paired with unwill-ing or indifferent outsiders.[6]

Most projects also assume that the flow of expertise will be primarily one-way—from the outsider to the local. However, local counterparts can often be an invaluable source of information and advice. In many projects, the relationship is often not planned in advance or even explic-itly discussed; it is assumed that collaboration and skill transfer will just somehow happen.

We can range counterpart relationships on a continuum based on the relative degree of control exercised by outside specialists and local coun-terparts. A successful counterpart relationship will normally progress, over time, toward more local control.

Although outside specialists on a project often have responsibility for getting things done, realizing this goal may depend largely on their coun-terparts and the quality of the counterpart relationship. Good counter-part relationships combine different sets of skills and knowledge. Each person in the relationship possesses a certain comparative advantage—a unique body of knowledge, set of attitudes, and tool kit of skills—highly useful for operating in parts of the work environment, but, by them-selves, not sufficient for success. One person's comparative advantage, in combination with that of his or her counterpart, can generate original and often superior results.

Creating Counterpart Relationships

Successful counterpart relationships require the commitment and involvement of the organizations from which the partners come. Creating this relationship and making it work are tasks and processes that should be built into the design of the project.

Typically, neither outside agencies nor local development organizations are particularly skilled at structuring and managing counterpart arrangements, so work must be done in advance to secure agreement on basic procedures, tasks, and timetables. This is another important area where anthropological expertise proves particularly valuable. Anthropologists often find themselves working as formal or informal cross-cultural trainers, showing project staff (both local and expatriate) how to communicate and work together more effectively.

Who Should Be a Counterpart? A good counterpart relationship starts with choosing the right people to be paired. Although planners may have little choice in the matter, they should exercise choice where they can. To the extent that partners have had previous cross-cultural work experience, they are likely to be better at forming and maintaining counterpart relationships. Both partners must be motivated to make the relationship work.

Since the ideal relationship is one of reciprocity, it's important that each partner have skills and experience that will be useful to the other, and that each person is willing to share what they know. Of equal important is their ability to do this. Often, project specialists have little experience with training or mentoring, but these abilities will be very useful.

It is also important that people who are paired have a reasonable chance of staying with the project long enough to develop an effective working relationship with each other. In many developing countries, the need for skilled personnel of any type is so great that counterparts rarely stay in one job long enough to absorb the necessary things.

How Should Transfer Be Effected?

Collaboration can best be achieved in relation to a specific set of goals or tasks. Setting clear expectations and objectives is a good way of framing the relationship to elicit discussion of each partner's skills and abilities with respect to the work to be done.

Three activities are important for promoting good counterpart relationships: creating good communication between partners; establishing a mutual learning environment; and reviewing progress regularly.

Effective cross-cultural communication begins with finding ways to show respect to each other. Counterparts do not have to actually like each other, but they must respect each other, and they must be able to show this in culturally appropriate ways. They must also learn to communicate effectively with each other. Since different cultures have different patterns of workplace communication, partners must find the appropriate ways of communicating basic speech acts such as asking for things, promising or refusing things, framing questions, and making assertions and declarations.

Once good communication has been established, the focus can shift to mutual learning. An outsider's technical knowledge must be blended with the context in which it is to operate in order to be effective. From this perspective, therefore, outside specialists and local counterparts must learn from each other to accomplish their work.

Having specific expectations for the transfer of skills and experience will also encourage partners to work together. All too often, outside specialists focus on getting the job done, rather than on training counterparts. A relationship centered on transfer as well as accomplishment will define realistic expectations, discover and discuss assumptions crucial to performance and transfer, and establish realistic measures of success. Discussion about these things will continue throughout the duration of the relationship.

One of the most important aspects of crafting a counterpart relationship is that of making explicit the procedures by which learning will take place. Partners—and their respective organizations—must understand what models of learning and collaboration are prevalent in each other's cultural environment, and what assumptions underlie these. Although one cultural pattern may indeed predominate within the project, learning, teaching, and working together will happen—or fail to happen—within the spaces created by the interactions between different cultural frames of reference.

Relationships take time to develop, and it is important to give counterparts the time to learn how to work with one another. As they do, both partners will change, in terms of what they know, how they feel, and what they do. As this occurs, the relationship itself will change, of course. It is important, therefore, to review arrangements regularly and make adjustments where necessary. The goal of a counterpart relationship is more than simply transferring knowledge or skills: it is to generate insight into how different cultural perspectives can be combined in productive and creative ways.

⁓ ⁓ ⁓

SUMMARY OF CHAPTER 7

Chapter 7 has continued the examination of project development by focusing on some of key aspects of project management. Because projects involve continued interaction between culturally diverse groups and individuals, management tasks center around managing these differences in productive and positive ways.

The chapter begins by looking at organizational culture, outlining the main elements of this, and discussing how these may vary cross-culturally. The chapter then takes up the topic of decisionmaking within organizations, noting some of the important differences across cultures in the way this is done, and presenting a simple model for the facilitation of group decisionmaking.

Negotiation and conflict resolution is then discussed, again from a cross-cultural perspective. A matrix of strategy options is presented, together with some recommendations for using these to best advantage.

A final important aspect of project management is the development of effective counterpart relationships between outside specialists and local project staff. Cultural differences pose both obstacles and opportunities in this situation of mutual cross-cultural learning, and the chapter outlines some effective strategies for getting the best out of the partners in a counterpart situation.

ENDNOTES

1. See Staudt (1991: 54). Few studies exist that focus specifically on how agency culture affects project development. One interesting example, from Malaysia, however, has been provided by Wolcott (1983), who describes the organizational culture of a religiously based development agency and how this influenced what it did in a rural village.

2. Argument and opposition are deeply ingrained in American—and indeed, Western—patterns. Our courts, boardrooms, classrooms, and legislatures all incorporate an essentially confrontational approach to getting at the truth, and

when we feel too easily persuaded by someone's argument, we often play "devil's advocate" expressly to provoke disagreement.

3. Fisher and Sharp (1998: 79).

4. Fisher and Ury (1981).

5. See, for example, Hall and Hall (1989: 6–10).

6. Few studies of counterpart relationships in technical assistance exist. Scott-Stevens (1987) is a notable exception. Lecompte (1986: 123–131) looks in a more general way at how technical assistance relationships should be structured for maximum mutual benefit.

chapter 8

ASSESSING PROJECTS

THE PURPOSES OF ASSESSMENT

Each project is a social experiment, generating important new knowledge about what works and what does not in a specified cultural context. Assessment is therefore a crucial part of project development.

During the project, assessment improves decisionmaking by helping planners cope with the inevitable surprises in project implementation. By testing project assumptions, hypotheses, procedures, and models against the project environment, planners gain insight into how sustainability can be achieved. By tracking project performance, staff will get needed feedback and management will be improved. If policies and procedures need to be changed, assessment data provide strong evidence for doing things differently.

As results appear, assessment helps planners and stakeholders understand the relationship between efforts and outcomes. This may permit them to improve or fix the present project, and should enable them to carry those lessons forward to the next project. Finally, end-of-project assessment provides the information necessary to document and justify the project to outside funders.

Assessment seeks to answer basic but important questions: What happened here? How and why did we get these results or outcomes? What does this teach us about future efforts?

Multiple groups have a stake in assessment. Locally, project staff, beneficiaries, and other participants have direct interests. National and interna-

FIGURE 8.1   A Framework for Project Assessment

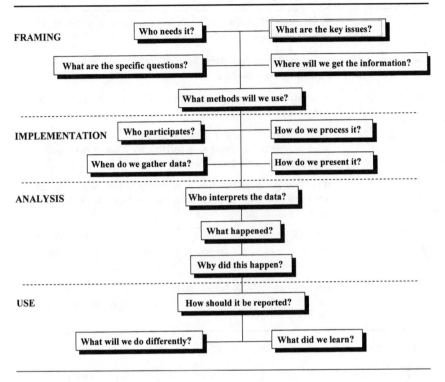

tional agencies are also important stakeholders. Further afield, policymakers and one's disciplinary colleagues can be considered stakeholders.

For assessment to work, clear procedures need to be set up, data must be collected accurately and impartially, and the results must be used to generate learning and improved performance.[1] Assessment must therefore be built into the design, and data must be collected systematically as the project unfolds.

Setting up a good assessment system means defining what data are most relevant for project purposes, deciding how to collect these data quickly and reliably, and delivering results at times when they will be useful.

Assessment planning is analogous to project design itself, and has four principal components: *framing* (deciding what to look at, how, and why); *implementation* (collecting the data); *analysis* (turning the data into information); and *use* (applying what has been learned).

TABLE 8.1   Management Decisions in Assessment Framing

Needs	**What types of questions do you need answered? What types of data will help provide these answers?**
Measures	Where will your data come from? What will you look at? Are these data available?
Methods	How will you collect, process, and analyze your data? What skills do you need to have in order to do this?
Timing	When should the various data-collection activities take place? What project needs shape data collection? What environmental considerations also shape data collection?
Resources	What will you need in terms of personnel, equipment, time, and money to assess the project? Will you need special skills? Where are these available?
Who's Involved?	Who within the project is responsible for data collection? Within stakeholder groups, who will provide the needed data? What other groups or individuals need to be involved?
Use	How will assessment results be fed into project design and management? What procedures or arrangements must be in place for this to happen?

Management decisions relating to this assessment framework are outlined in Table 8.1.

At the *framing* stage, several key decisions must be made. Who are the principal beneficiaries of assessment data, and what sorts of questions do they need answers to? Once user groups and main issues have been identified, methodological questions can be addressed. These include translating issues into more specific and detailed sets of questions, deciding where the answers to these questions might be located, and choosing the appropriate methods for uncovering these. This includes the collection of baseline (that is, preproject) measures if needed for later comparison with project results.

Once this frame has been set, *implementation* choices can be made. These include decisions about who will be involved in data collection and how and when data will be gathered. Other decisions must be made at this stage about how data will be processed and presented for analysis.

The *analysis* stage involves still other decisions, centering around who will carry out the interpretation of the data and how this will be done. During analysis, the results of assessment are compared with other measures. These can include baseline data sets, data from other projects, or predictions derived from theoretical models. At the same time, decisions need to be made as to the levels or standards of performance that will qualify as successful or acceptable in terms of what the project originally intended to do.

Finally, decisions about the *use* of assessment results must be made. These include making choices about how results should be reported, how often, to whom, and how the results will be transformed into learning and recommendations for future projects.

MONITORING AND EVALUATION

Assessment has two fundamental aspects: *monitoring* and *evaluation*. These are complementary ways to develop an understanding of project operation, but they ask different questions. Both are usually incorporated into an assessment design.

Monitoring

Monitoring—sometimes called *formative assessment*—tracks progress during project implementation. It looks at whether project inputs are being delivered and used as planned, and whether they do what they were expected to do. Monitoring information falls into three broad categories: information about *resources*; information about *activities*; and information about *results*.

Monitoring helps check key assumptions and hypotheses, identifies difficulties at an early stage, develops data on trends, accounts for resource use, and points to where things might be changed or improved.[2] Monitoring focuses on whether things are happening on time, within budget, and to standard. Monitoring, in essence, asks the question, "Did we follow our project design?"

Evaluation

Evaluation—sometimes referred to as *summative assessment*—makes judgments about project *outcomes* and *impacts*, especially as these concern stakeholders. Evaluation also looks at unplanned or unanticipated results of the project.

Evaluation, unlike monitoring, looks at the bigger picture to make judgments about the worth of the entire project, in its context. Has the

TABLE 8.2   A Summary of Differences Between Monitoring and Evaluation

Monitoring	Evaluation
• Tracks daily events	• Takes a long-range view
• Accepts policies and rules	• Questions policies and rules
• Accepts plans and targets	• Asks if plans and targets are accurate and appropriate
• Checks work against targets	
• Stresses input/output relationships	• Checks targets against reality
• Looks mainly at how project delivery occurs	• Stresses project purpose and goal
	• Looks also at unplanned things, causes, and assumptions
• Reports in terms of progress	• Reports in terms of lessons learned

project been successful in achieving its goals? Were these goals worthwhile? Are the results due to the project or to some other set of factors? What side effects or unanticipated consequences were there? What are the pros and cons of doing a project this way? How does this way compare with other possible alternatives? What, finally, did we learn from this experience?

Evaluation therefore does not ask, "Did we follow our plan?" but rather, "Was our plan a good one?" It is possible to have a project that proceeds like clockwork but is totally ineffective at producing the hoped-for changes. Projects may succeed on one level, only to fail on another. An example would be a project that succeeded in terms of its original goals and objectives, but generated a host of negative second-order effects later on. Or a project that succeeded initially, but could not be sustained.

CONTEXT-BASED ASSESSMENT

What Do You Need to Know and Why?

Context-based assessment starts with clarity of project outcomes. If these are vague, then it will be difficult or impossible to discover whether they have been achieved. Since assessment is really the only way that planners can establish project success or failure, methods and procedures must be closely matched to project aims.

Monitoring needs are fairly straightforward. Project managers need information on three main aspects of project implementation: what's been done (activities); what's been the result (outcomes or outputs); and what's been the cost (use of resources). They can then compare this information with their original plans, targets, or estimates to determine changes.

Evaluation needs are more complex, for as a concept, "change" is multidimensional. It includes considerations of amount, direction, rate, nature, and extent, in comparison with something else. Planners will need, for example, to compare project outcomes with conditions at the start of the project, so baseline data must be available. If these data do not exist, then they must be collected before the project itself begins.

Project outcomes can also be compared with control group data from elsewhere, with results from a similar project or with the predictions or extrapolations generated by a theoretical model. In each case, data must actually be available for these purposes, and their availability—and compatibility—needs to be determined before the project design is finalized.

The system should be kept as simple as possible. The natural tendency to overdesign data collection at the planning stage is often incompatible with the requirements of running a successful project in the field.[3] Complexity in data collection promotes breakdown and delay, to say nothing of taking up much valuable time and energy.

At different stages of the project development cycle, different assessment needs come to the fore, as Table 8.3 indicates.

Establishing Assessment Criteria

Assessment focuses on illuminating the relationship between arrangements and outcomes in a project. Whatever forms or methods of enquiry are adopted, planners need to understand how the different components of the project interacted to produce the results that were observed. The data they collect to determine this will become meaningful only in relation to some set of criteria.

These criteria must be established for each specific project, as part of project framing. Although each project is in some sense unique, certain broad criteria apply to most if not all projects. Table 8.4 sets out the most common project assessment criteria.

There are many ways in which these and similar criteria can be worked into an assessment design. One option is to match these criteria to the major project components that were outlined earlier, in Chapter 4. In

TABLE 8.3 Assessment Needs in the Project Development Cycle

Project Startup	• Is the design workable? • Are resources adequate? • Is the project team performing as expected? • Were our assumptions and estimates correct?
Mid-Project	• Are things happening on schedule? • Are there unforeseen problems? • Are peoples' reactions positive? • Do any modifications need to be made now?
Project End	• Are beneficiaries benefiting? • Are objectives being achieved? • Are modifications or design departures working? • Have other changes occurred? • Have any negative outcomes appeared?
Postproject	• Have changes stabilized? • Have benefits remained? • Have new possibilities been created?

this way, a more detailed understanding of how project arrangements relate to outcomes can be gained. Table 8.5 sets out a matrix by way of illustration.

How Will Planners Get Their Information?

In designing assessment, planners will deal with three different types of data: data on startup conditions (baseline data); data on how the project is progressing (monitoring); and data on outcomes (evaluation).

Planners must build their data collection procedures into all necessary phases of the project, keeping in mind the costs in time, energy, and money that data collection require. They will look primarily at tangible and measurable things, and try to get that information in more than one way, using local measures whenever possible.

Data collection should be comprehensive, but as simple as possible. Project staff and beneficiaries are busy, and data collection can be an all-consuming activity if it is not carefully planned and organized. Record-keeping, in particular, should be as streamlined as possible, to avoid overlap and unnecessary effort.

As with virtually every other aspect of project development, cultural factors enter into assessment planning. Deciding what to count, as men-

TABLE 8.4 Typical Project Assessment Criteria

Effectiveness	How well does it work? Do project technologies, procedures, and arrangements actually function to produce the intended results? If there are problems with producing results, why is this? What could be done to fix things?
Efficiency	How much does it cost? If results are forthcoming, how expensive are they in terms of the various resources (time, money, personnel, equipment, and so on) that must be used? Are these levels of cost sustainable?
Appropriateness	Do people like it? Are the results of the project acceptable to all stakeholders? Any stakeholders? If they are not, why not? Could the results be made acceptable? How?
Adequacy	If the project is producing benefits, how are they distributed? Do all stakeholder groups benefit? Do all benefit equally? Are any groups left out? If so, why is this occurring? Can it be corrected?
Side Effects	In addition to anticipated project benefits, are there other, unanticipated consequences of the project? Are these positive or negative? Who is affected by these, and why? Should corrective action be taken? If so, what?
Learning	What new knowledge has been gained through the project? Who has learned what, and why is this important or significant? How will this learning be used in the future?
Replicability	Given the experience of this project, can it be done again elsewhere? If so, what if anything should be changed or improved? If not, why not? Do better project models or options exist?

tioned in Chapter 4, is probably the most important of the cultural considerations in assessment design. It is important to choose relevant cultural domains from which to gather data, and within these, to identify indicators or proxy measures that are specific enough to be useful for project purposes, valid in terms of what they reflect, and actually obtainable using available means and methods.

The success of interviews, questionnaires, or other interactive methods will obviously depend in large part on how cultural considerations are incorporated into data collection methods and approaches. The cultural calendar, for example, will have a marked effect on data collection. Seasonal changes in the weather may affect patterns of work and leisure—and hence, who is available and willing to participate in assessment. Who is likely to know what (and be willing to tell an investigator)

TABLE 8.5   An Example of Criteria Applied to Project Components

Criteria	Objectives	Strategies	Activities	Resources
Effectiveness: How well does it work?	Do the objectives really address the problem?	Has the strategy attained the objective?	Are all the activities directly relevant to the project strategy?	Do the resources provided relate directly to the planned activities?
Efficiency: How much does it cost?	How much does it cost to do it this way, in terms of total outcomes?	How costly is this strategy compared with others available?	Have all activities been done quickly and within cost limits?	Have more resources been needed than were planned for? Is there wastage of resources?
Appropriateness: Do people like it?	Do people agree that the problem addressed is a real one for them?	Is the strategy accepted by the beneficiaries?	Do the activities seem worthwhile to people? Do people participate?	Are the resources provided appropriate to people's means and values?
Adequacy: Does everyone benefit?	Are aspects of the problem left untouched? Are some people's problems ignored?	Does the strategy allow everyone to participate? To benefit?	Is everyone included in these activities? Are groups excluded?	Have enough resources been provided? Does everyone have access to them?
Side Effects: What else has happened?	Has attainment of the objective created new problems?	Has a strategy of active participation, for example, provoked frustration?	Have the activities, for example, forced people to neglect other things?	Have new resources, for example, stimulated or depressed the local economy?
Learning: What have we found out?	Have people learned to analyze problems and set their own objectives?	Have people had a chance to compare strategies for themselves?	Can people take over running the activities themselves?	Have people learned to use resources better, to estimate resource needs more exactly?
Replicability: Can we do it again?	Do all potential project areas have similar problems?	Will the same strategy work elsewhere?	Can similar activities be used in other situations?	Can similar resources be made available for other projects?

will depend on a host of other factors too, none of which can be assumed, but rather discovered through sustained interaction with the populations concerned.

Most project assessment efforts use some type of *time-series design*, where data are collected at specified intervals. Control groups, for obvious reasons, are usually absent. Instead, correlations between project activities and outcomes are established through data collection at various points in the project cycle. This popular evaluation design depends for its effectiveness on adequate measurements before, during, and after the project's activities have taken place. Case studies are also often used to complement time-series data, and to focus on specific aspects of project operations and results.

Some Assessment Problems

Each project assessment presents special problems, but several types of difficulties occur frequently. One concerns baseline data that may be missing, incomplete, or otherwise unsuitable. Alternatively, initial baseline studies may have been done that did not incorporate key variables later found to be important in the project environment. In these cases, time-series comparisons become difficult, as does end-of-project evaluation.

Another problem concerns the types of indicators chosen for assessment. Given the often enormous demands on project staff, there is a tendency to focus on what is easiest to collect. Although this may be adequate for monitoring purposes, it is often much less satisfactory when one attempts to determine whether the project was ultimately successful from the beneficiaries' point of view. Aggregate measures, for example, may hide important differences within groups. Proxy measures may be culturally inappropriate, and therefore may not accurately portray local reality.

Finally, there is the essentially political problem of defining project objectives in clear and unambiguous terms. Here, the interests of project designers and implementers may conflict directly with the interests of other stakeholders, particularly donors or host country government organizations. From a planning standpoint, having clear and precise goals is a necessary condition for good project design. From an administrator's perspective, however, vague and general goals allow agencies to claim that nearly any result obtained—however inadequate it might appear to beneficiaries—is in fact a solid success.

LEARNING PROJECT LESSONS

Assessment results help planners make important decisions with respect to current and future project efforts. In the short run, information will permit planners to make modifications to the project to improve it. In the medium term, planners will be able to decide whether the project should be continued, extended, or replicated. In the longer run, they will be able to say important things about how subsequent projects of this type ought to be designed and managed.

To be useful, assessment must be documented. Although it is true that many project reports go unread, many do not, and a well-written report is often the only permanent record available of what happened and why. The preparation of reports must therefore be done carefully. As before, cultural considerations are important in determining how—and to whom—information is transmitted.

Project reports will have specific audiences and specific intentions vis-à-vis these audiences, which will usually include agency officials, donor organizations, and local stakeholder groups. Other groups—such as academic units—may also be included. Groups will have organizational cultures of their own through which the report's information will be filtered. To the extent, therefore, that such cultural considerations are known, acknowledged, and addressed, the information will have more impact.

In essence, assessment reports attempt to link project results to project arrangements. Depending on the audience, the report may begin with a background section that outlines the history of the project, its initial aims, and who the main stakeholders are. If appropriate, the assessment design will be described in terms of what questions were deemed important and what methods and approaches were selected to address them.

The assessment findings are, of course, the core of any report. These can be set out in detail or simply summarized, depending on the audience. Five common foci of project reports are *time, cost, performance, linkages,* and *surprises.*

Time, cost, and performance are aspects of project operation that fall more or less under control of the project management team, and have probably been previously outlined in the project's logical framework at the framing stage of design, in the connection between inputs and outputs. Linkages, on the other hand, refer to longer-term results (often appearing in the logical framework under purposes and goals) that are often not under the direct control of project staff but are nonetheless hoped for. Finally, surprises include outcomes—positive and negative—that planners did not anticipate as results of the project.

It is usually advisable to discuss assessment findings in some detail, to make explicit the connections between project arrangements and project outcomes. If areas of uncertainty still exist, these should be identified. The discussion of findings should conclude with specific recommendations for change in the current project or for the design and operation of future projects.

Learning During Project Implementation

All projects—no matter how well they are planned—encounter problems during implementation, and these will be revealed by assessment efforts. On one level are problems with performance, where some sections or parts of the project are simply not functioning as they should. Sometimes this is essentially a personnel problem. Sometimes it is a technical problem, involving the performance of machinery or other equipment.

At another level, however, there may be problems with the connections between inputs and outputs. In these cases, everything functions as it should, but the anticipated results do not materialize. Alternatively, negative effects may appear that overshadow the positive benefits of the project.

Finally, there may be changes in outside factors that affect the project. New legislation, economic changes, political events, adverse weather— these and other changes lying mainly outside the control or influence of the project staff may generate major changes in project operation.

To the extent possible, the project must be modified in response to these problems. If the project has been planned in a highly interactive manner, as outlined in Chapter 4, then it may be possible to make minor modifications to improve performance. Projects developed in a more rigid manner, of course, will be harder to alter once basic arrangements are in place.

In either case, successful modification depends on an accurate diagnosis of what is wrong and a realistic assessment of the suitable options that are available for redress. Just as cultural factors loom large in the initial framing decisions that underlie a project, so too, the same factors inform efforts at project modification.

Learning for Next Time

Whether or not the current project can be fixed, assessment provides valuable insight into how future projects might be planned and implemented. If properly documented, each project becomes a kind of extended case study that can provide planners and stakeholders with answers to important questions. What, for example, are the main similarities and differences between this project and others, in terms of goals, structures, processes, and results? What were the main strategies and techniques used here, and how successful were they? What assumptions played a key role in how events unfolded?

Understanding Project Failure

Not all projects are successful, of course. Indeed, most projects fall short of expectations in one way or another. Another way of learning from projects is therefore to focus on failure, to embrace error and examine it.[4]

Although project success is more desirable than failure, failure attracts our attention, and it is important to be able to understand why projects fail, in whole or in part. A successful project that works well but has been inadequately documented may add little to understanding how to promote development goals. A failed project for which good assessment data exist provides clear and valuable lessons for future planning.

Connecting failure to context is an essential step in learning. Some failures stem from circumstances largely outside the control of planners and participants. External policies, for example, are often responsible for project failure, even though their effects may have been indirect and muted. Agency procedures and regulations, as well, often contribute to project failure. In both cases, assessments that do not look outside the project itself may not even identify such causes of failure, much less discuss them.

Other failures, of course, are linked to the relationship between the project and its stakeholders, particularly in the beneficiary community— the aspect of context that I have referred to as the proximate environment. If the project has been designed and managed with close attention to stakeholders' characteristics and preferences, such failures will be minimized, but this conjuncture cannot be assumed; rather, it must be demonstrated in tangible outcomes.

But it is with respect to the internal environment of the project—aspects of design and operation that lie largely under the control of staffers—that there may be the most to learn. To a great extent, project personnel cannot anticipate, much less control, what the proximate and the external environment will do. They can really only control what they do, reactively and proactively, to shape and direct the project.

The choices made by the project as events unfold therefore become a crucial part of understanding why and how failure occurs. Although each

TABLE 8.6 Categories of Project Failure

At the Framing Stage	• Failures of *intelligence*: not knowing enough at the early stages of project formulation, with the result that crucial aspects of the project context are ignored.
	• Failures of *decisionmaking*: drawing false conclusions or making wrong choices from the data that are available. Underestimating the importance of key pieces of information.
At the Management Stage	• Failures of *implementation*: bad or inadequate management of one or more important aspects of the project.
	• Failures of *reaction*: inability or unwillingness to modify the project in response to new information or changes in conditions that come to light as the project proceeds.
At the Assessment Stage	• Failures of *evaluation*: not paying attention to the results.
	• Failures of *learning*: not transferring the lessons back into future plans and procedures.

failed project, as Tolstoy might have said, fails in its own particular way, there are several broad categories of error that seem to recur with some regularity. These are outlined in Table 8.6.

DEVELOPMENT ETHNOGRAPHY

Learning from projects is much more difficult than it might appear. Development professionals are often ill-equipped to understand the local environment and to learn from it. The development agencies they work for may, in direct or indirect ways, filter information and therefore learning from the field, as they move reports up through their structures. Large development donors, heavily involved in the politics as well as the practice of development, may have even more compelling reasons to ignore or downplay certain types of information. Some of these issues are discussed in more detail in Chapter 9.

Beyond all this, however, is the fundamental problem of the project environment itself, which because it contains so many factors that interact in so many ways is immensely complex. The true results of many projects do not really appear for years in some cases, and we have few reliable means for tracking and analyzing this. Although we know that beneficiary worldviews are crucial to project success and that agency cultures are equally important, we have not yet developed effective ways of incorporating these key factors into our planning and assessment.

Despite all that has been written on project planning and implementation, we really know very little—in an ethnographic sense—about how projects actually develop; about the way in which stakeholders at multiple levels negotiate meanings and outcomes with each other.[5]

Anthropologists are particularly well equipped to examine the context in which development projects develop, to uncover and examine the concepts and premises underlying project design, and to relate these back to issues of organizational culture and how agencies learn or fail to learn. But at the practical level, little has been done.

What is needed is *project ethnography:* detailed, long-term analyses of how projects develop and operate on a day-to-day level to produce the outcomes that are summarized in reports. Such ethnographies could provide the thick description of project events that is now largely lacking in development documentation, and would help to situate this description within an overall framework that includes not only the stakeholder community but also the agency and its parent organizations.

Project ethnography would use anthropology to examine the core processes of development itself, not just the details of project implementation or policy formulation. All of the actors in a project situation are behaving rationally, but they think and act differently, and this multicultural behavioral stew needs to be understood, not just as a slice-of-time snapshot for assessment or appraisal purposes, but over the length of the undertaking, and indeed, probably some way beyond it.[6]

Why has there been so little project ethnography? Until quite recently, most anthropologists have not considered development and development projects as suitable research topics. Most anthropologists working directly with projects are paid to design or to manage them, not to write ethnographies. Some useful examples of development ethnography—defined rather loosely—do exist, however.[7]

Many more are needed. Although the models in use by many agencies still insist that projects can be planned and implemented in a fairly linear and segmented manner, according to external rules and standards, long experience dictates that projects are interactions, a complex game between stakeholders with diverse values, perspectives, and interests.[8] As the game unfolds, meanings associated with the project become clear through a process of negotiation between participants.

Formal models of administrative decisionmaking are unlikely to be of much help in understanding how this happens. Goals are multiple and shifting, the environment is uncertain and at times ambiguous, and information is incomplete. It is through project ethnography that we will gain understanding about how "experts" and beneficiaries construct meaning, how they frame their problems, and how they structure options or solutions. Only then can we truly begin to understand why we get the development outcomes that we do.

Project ethnographies would serve two very specific purposes. They would establish the effect of certain variables on the process of project development and outcome formation and they would in the process generate other hypotheses that could be tested more widely.

To produce such ethnographies, anthropologists must restrain their tendency to emphasize uniqueness in the situations they study, and instead concentrate also on finding and describing regularities or pattern variables. They must also broaden their research horizons to encompass multiple project stakeholders, rather than focusing on a single ethnic group or community.[9]

By broadening the range of issues and questions to be examined, it will be possible to understand more fully why a particular project failed or succeeded; by comparing and contrasting such project ethnographies, one can finally begin to understand the patterns of regularity that underlie the development of all projects.

Having the right kind of social knowledge will not make development planning easier. On the contrary, it will probably make the task of project development in a given context more complex. Nor will it necessarily lead to greater clarity in a wider sense; projects or approaches that work well in one situation will not necessarily work well elsewhere. Nonetheless, it is necessary to develop and elaborate our understanding of how context influences project development, if we are to become more effective at what we do.

MINI-CASE 8.1   THE MASAI RANGE PROJECT

This is an example of how an in-depth look at the way a project develops day by day can illuminate the relationships between stakeholders, agencies, and project arrangements, and in the process, can shed light on why the project had the outcomes it did.

(continues)

MINI-CASE 8.1 (continued)

In this example, the project was impacted by a number of factors from different parts of the environment, including the inner project environment itself, the proximate environment of the project's principal stakeholders, and the outer environment of the national policy context in which the project took shape.

The Masai Range Management and Livestock Improvement Project operated in Tanzania from 1970 to 1980. After ten years, the project was judged a failure, and USAID assistance was terminated.

The reasons for failure are complex, and might not normally be apparent from official documents. Jon Moris served first as the project sociologist and later as team leader, and his 1981 account of the project provides an insider's ethnographic account, over a considerable amount of time, which adds enormously to our understanding of how the project developed and why it ultimately failed.

Western notions of "range management" were central to the project (see also the SODESP case outlined earlier), and depended, as Moris shows, on several unstated assumptions. Key among these were:

- An identity of interest between producers and range advisers
- Mechanisms to cope with adverse seasons
- An orientation toward beef production
- An adequate information base
- Producer control of land use

Moris comments: "In the African contexts where USAID and the UNDP intended to transfer range management technology, the settings fail to meet these conditions at almost every point" (1981: 102).

Producer strategies in the project area, although rational in themselves, diverged from those of a system oriented toward the production of beef, and project technicians found it difficult or impossible to control land use. Furthermore, technicians and pastoralists tended to distrust each other.

Moris describes in detail the beginnings of the project, and points out that in many ways, it was an "anomaly" within the socialist-based *ujamaa* movement of the time. The project's relationship to regional plans and to regional officials always remained problematic. As these struggles were enacted, the project was changed several times. Along the way, staff turnover and morale surfaced as problems. Moris notes, "The project was continuously under reconsideration, either by Tanzanian leaders or USAID" (1981: 106).

(continues)

MINI-CASE 1.2 (continued)

In 1973 a number of key decisions were made involving the resettlement of Masai herders into villages, setting up a database on livestock production, and accelerating the development of water sources. USAID-mandated range management techniques emerged as a major bottleneck in the project delivery system, as did USAID's complex procurement system for project materials. Finally, the limitations of the Western concept of range management, combined with the constraints of the project environment, were becoming clear. Moris observes: "The project was working against the grain of local economic trends and sociological views. Several visitors assured us it had taken forty years to change similar perceptions in the American West. We were attempting to do it in ten" (1981: 110).

By 1976, the project was given additional responsibilities for other projects outside the original scope of work.

These were desirable and worthy projects, but the demands they placed on team technicians destroyed the continuity of effort we had begun to achieve. The root problem was that the most information about a project's environment is required during project formulation. US planning procedures tend to assume that adequate information already exists. In the Masai situation, formulation of a new project entailed a huge investment in information acquisition. (1981: 111)

Eventually, "battle fatigue" set in, as the result of struggles to keep all of these activities afloat. By mid-1977 most of the original expatriate team had left the project, as well as several key Tanzanian counterparts. In 1979, USAID announced that it would no longer continue project funding. Little by little, the infrastructure created by the project began to crumble and disappear.

What lessons can be drawn from this project? Moris lists several. To begin with, he says, there is an enormous gap between "ought" and "can" in planning—that is, between statements about what should be done and what actually can be done, given local means and expertise. "The Masai Project," he says, "suggests the importance of modifying prescriptions to fit capabilities in the short run and not vice versa" (1981: 112).

The second lesson is that it is very difficult to swim upstream—that is, to expect a project to work that goes counter to local trends and practices. In high-risk projects, he says, it is very important to design "fall-back objectives" that will benefit people even if the project's main goals are not attained.

(continues)

MINI-CASE 8.1   (continued)

Moris points out that modernizing pastoralism is essentially a systems problem, where many forces connect and intersect. He lists seven of the most important from the Masai experience: control over land use; development of alternative food supplies; identification of individual animals; ways of keeping animals alive during extremes of drought; adequate disease control; making people feel responsible for ranching operations; and efficient transport and marketing. "Unless we can learn how to improve the inter-agency matrix of services in a coordinated fashion (integrated rural development), individual project investments will remain relatively ineffective. It does seem that many other types of rural development programs share this dilemma" (1981: 112).

Finally, Moris points out that benefits are harder to sustain when they occur only within the context of a temporary project. "In the Masai Project there was no operational base where resources could be lodged that might survive the project itself. Once the project funding ended the better staff were transferred to other regions (often at their own initiative); the many reports, maps, etc. we had accumulated were dispersed; and the entire fabric of what had been a large program fell into pieces" (1981: 113).

There is a need, he emphasizes, to institutionalize program resources independently from their individual project base.

All of these points might be applied to many other failed projects. Moris's account is exceptional, however, in that he remained with the project throughout its life, and was able to describe, in detailed terms, how and why decisions were made that had a major effect on subsequent events. In this way, we are able to learn more about the process of negotiation through which projects find their identity and purpose, and how these might differ in significant ways from what planners assumed—and hoped—at the outset.

SOURCE: Moris 1981.

SUMMARY OF CHAPTER 8

This final chapter on project development has focused on assessment—that is, on how project results are judged. Assessment has two aspects: monitoring and evaluation.

Monitoring looks primarily at internal project operations as implementation proceeds and compares results with planned targets. Evaluation, on the other hand, looks more broadly at how the project affects its proximate environment: Was this project a successful way of producing results? Were the results obtained in fact useful ones?

The main task for planners, as with other aspects of project development, is to ensure a high degree of fit between project arrangements and the context in which they must operate.

Assessment is only effective, however, if something is actually done with the information generated. Chapter 8 discusses the reporting of assessment results and their use in understanding the relationship between design and outcomes.

The chapter concludes with a discussion about the contribution that an ethnography of development projects could make to the process by which such projects are developed and implemented. By looking at how projects are shaped through time by interactions with their surrounding context, we can gain insight into the relationships between arrangements and outcomes in a given situation, thereby increasing our understanding of how cultural factors influence development plans, procedures, and outcomes.

ENDNOTES

1. See OECD (1992: 133) for more discussion.

2. Eade (1997: 131).

3. R. Chambers (1993: 31).

4. The phrase "embracing error" is David Korten's. See Korten (1980) for more discussion.

5. Years ago, Spicer (1976: 132) proposed a "comparative ethnography" of public and private policymaking bodies.

6. Rew (1985: 194–195) makes the case for project ethnography this way: ". . . while some disciplines will treat development planning work as a set of wholly technical exchanges and examinations, the social anthropologist will want to place such research within a sociological context and examine the social relations of the team, its enterprise, its clients, and how groups within society will be affected by the studies and the decisions taken in their light. This is an area in which there have been very few empirical studies. Their absence means there are correspondingly few anchors, other than general theory or prejudice, with which to stabilize the search for explanations of, say, the performance of development projects or the reasons for policy formulation in particular or general cases."

7. Pressman and Wildavsky's (1973) excellent study of the Model Cities project in Oakland remains an outstanding model of how a day-to-day examination of projects as negotiating arenas can illuminate the gap between policy and outcome. Tendler (1975) and Bruneau et al. (1978) have provided inside looks at development agencies (AID and CIDA, respectively) in an attempt to understand how behavior that appears irrational from an outsider's perspective actually makes internal sense. Clements (1993) provides an example of organizational analysis of the large agencies. Grindle (1980) has looked at the process of project implementation. Moris and Hatfield (1982) described a range management project in East Africa. Ferguson (1990) provides a detailed account of a development project in Lesotho. Klitgaard (1990) describes what it was like to work in Equatorial Guinea, and is one of the few accounts of how the World Bank actually operates in the field. Dr. Goeffrey Griffith, working in the Maldives on a VSO project, wrote a series of "dispatches" from his project over a four-year period, from 1987 to 1991. Entitled "Shaviyani Nights," these were published in *Anthropology Today*, the bimonthly publication of the Royal Anthropological Institute. Maren (1997) provides a fascinating picture of development efforts in Somalia.

8. See, for example, Pottier (1993b: 27–28), Peattie (1970), Garber and Jenden (1993: 53), and Hanchette (1999). Other investigators have stressed the same point. Kottak (1991) pointed out that only ethnographic study is likely to reveal how and why development problems arise and continue. Honadle and Van Sant (1985: 99) say: "Explanations for the minutiae of implementation often fall on deaf ears because they stress details that do not interest planners, economists, and policy makers, who are more attracted to the power and prestige attached to the overall situation. But without an appreciation for what happens after policies are declared and plans set in motion, grand designs are likely to be unrealized and the means for attaining them unsustained. Until this situation is rectified, development efforts will continue to encounter the same traps and pitfalls as in the past."

9. See Pottier (1993b: 19); Rew (1985: 187–188).

PART THREE

---

the way ahead

PREVIOUS CHAPTERS DISCUSSED how anthropology can make important contributions to project development, and has been highly successful in many situations.

Despite this, anthropology has had a relatively low level of impact on the development industry as a whole. In Part Three, "The Way Ahead," I look at both the development industry and anthropology to identify ways in which these two could be made more compatible with each other.

Chapter 9, "Reforming the Development Industry," looks at why development has not worked as well as it might, and what needs to be done to change the ways in which development agencies think and act. Chapter 10, "Redirecting Anthropology," turns our attention to how anthropologists are trained in the academy, and suggests possible improvements in this training to make practitioners more effective in development work.

Chapter 11, "A New Development Paradigm?" concludes the book by taking up the question of reformulating the way we conceive of development, and how anthropological insight will be central to this change in thinking.

chapter 9

REFORMING THE
DEVELOPMENT INDUSTRY

DEVELOPMENT AT CENTURY'S END

Uneven Results

Over the past fifty years, substantial progress has been made on several development fronts. World GNP, estimated at $1.3 trillion in 1960, rose to nearly $30 trillion by the end of the 1990s. During the same period, child mortality has been more than halved worldwide, the rate of school enrollment has risen by almost 50 percent, and life expectancy in poor countries has gone up by seventeen years.[1]

Despite these gains, however, disparities between the rich and the poor have continued to grow, both within countries and across entire regions. As one development decade turned into another, it became clear that many countries were simply not making the progress they had hoped for. Exploding populations, internal strife, and external debt often swallowed whatever gains had been made. From 1950 to 1990, the world's population doubled, and so did the number of people living in poverty.

In 1950, differences between per-capita GNP in the First and Third Worlds was approximately $2,200. By the mid-1970s, this difference had grown to over $4,800.[2] A number of countries—many of them in Africa—are poorer today than they were in 1960; other regions—notably in Asia—have boomed.[3] In the 1950s, for example, Congo and South Korea had the same income levels. By 1997, South Korea had a per-capita income of about $10,000 per year, but Congo's stood at $150.

Real per capita income in fifty-one low-and middle-income countries was lower in 1993 than it had been in 1980.[4]

Widening Criticism

Development agencies and their policies have come under increased scrutiny and criticism in recent years.[5] Previous attempts to recast development efforts (such as AID's New Directions mandate in the 1970s) produced little substantive change in either aid procedures or in poverty alleviation.

At the same time, the spectacular growth of some East Asian countries appeared to have been achieved in ways other than those prescribed by the World Bank, AID, and the IMF. The economic success of Singapore's so-called guided democracy, in particular, seemed to upset the long-held Western axiom that prosperity was dependent on an open and democratic society.

The most telling aid encounter, however, occurred in Eastern Europe and the newly independent states of the former Soviet Union. Here, established Western aid structures and procedures failed—often spectacularly—to address economic and social problems, despite initial promises, rhetoric, and optimism.

By the mid-1990s, critics had begun to focus particularly on the IMF and the World Bank.[6] Increasingly powerful and influential, these institutions appeared to be in effective charge of economic—and hence, social—policy in some of the poorer countries. Some critics saw this as the new face of colonialism.[7] Others asked why, if it was indeed so powerful, the World Bank hadn't "fixed" poverty by now. Many concluded that the development industry simply didn't know what it was doing, and—worse—was unable or unwilling to admit ignorance.[8] The secrecy surrounding the internal operations of the large multilateral agencies hardly improved public perceptions.

A Retreat from the Field

But as the power of the development industry grew, its direct connection with the world's poor appeared, on many levels, to lessen. The 1980s and 1990s had seen larger development agencies turn away from direct involvement with the grass roots toward issues of national policy, expressed through, for example, programs of governance or structural adjustment. Attention shifted away from the realities of poverty and toward more abstract workings of "the market."

Although this shift had a definite ideological aspect, it also resulted from the simple fact that locally centered development had grown too cumbersome and frustrating for many of the larger agencies. Internal policies and procedures now constituted a major constraint on their ability to respond to development needs quickly and selectively.

Seeking to improve efficiency, large agencies continued their previous pattern of opting out of many of the tasks of design and implementation, and contracting these instead to outside firms. Governance and structural adjustment programs, it was found, could be managed at a distance, involving agencies in little or no sustained engagement with the realities of the local scene. The aggressive promotion of the private sector, with the market the final arbiter of development outcomes, seemed to absolve the agencies from any need to be concerned about equity.

As a result, agency officials—whatever their areas of specialization—now needed to know less and less about the conditions under which ordinary people lived their lives in the poor countries of the world. Dialogue between poor countries and the larger agencies became more a discussion about finance and relationships to an impersonal world market, focusing on such things as rates of exchange, subsidy, and current account balances. Development goals, to an increasing extent, had become externally defined and managed.

This shift was particularly marked in AID, where, by the 1970s, few agency staffers were actually directing projects, but instead spent their time managing the labyrinthine paperwork associated with them. Over the years, the agency has increasingly relied on contract specialists, consulting firms, and NGO groups to be their eyes and ears on the ground, and to design, manage, and evaluate projects and programs. By the late 1980s, over 60 percent of AID's employees were contractors or foreign nationals, compared with only about 25 percent in the early 1960s. At the same time, AID budget and staffing levels overall have declined steadily. In the 1990s, over twenty-five overseas AID missions were closed, and staff were cut by one-third.[9]

Donor Fatigue and Public Opinion

By the end of the 1990s, there was a clear sense of *donor fatigue* in many agencies. In 1999, aggregate official aid was about $55 billion, down from over $60 billion (in constant dollars) from the beginning of the 1990s.[10] Nowhere was aid fatigue seen more clearly than in the United States. In the mid-1950s, the United States alone accounted for over 60 percent of all of the world's foreign assistance, but by 1998, this had fallen to 17 per-

MINI-CASE 9.1   PUBLIC OPINION AND FOREIGN AID

One problem with reforming the development industry is that foreign aid has no natural constituency, and its procedures and effects are invisible to voters, for the most part. Partly in consequence, foreign aid has been captured by what might be called "special interests"—including diplomats, the military, economic theorists, free traders, and others.

Domestically, foreign aid has never been a particularly popular idea, although as polls show, Americans—hostile to foreign aid programs—are generally in favor of aid itself. But Americans have by and large been relatively uninformed—except at moments of crisis—about what development is, how aid is used in it, and how results are achieved.

More to the point, perhaps, the public seems puzzled by the continuing stream of disaster stories, of pictures of starving children and strife-torn villages. A certain amount of what might be called "donor fatigue" seems to have set in. Levels of aid have decreased in many cases, and even where aid continues to flow, there is increased skepticism about its utility, coupled with more insistence on accountability and control.

There is disagreement about how strong public opinion actually is for foreign aid and about what the available figures actually mean. A 1982 Gallup poll found that two-thirds of the public thought that U.S. economic assistance benefited the rich more than the poor. In 1987, another survey found that almost 90 percent of the general public thinks that aid is largely wasted by the U.S. government, and misused by foreign governments (in Hellinger et al. 1988: 5).

In 1994, a polling company summarized the findings of twenty-six surveys and polls. The results showed no clear mandate for foreign aid, with support declining from 54 percent to 47 percent. But people consistently overestimate the amount given in aid, and they also say, when asked, that they would give five times as much as the current amount (less than 1 percent of the budget). Assistance for humanitarian purposes and for the environment were high on the list, not the "security concerns" of past years. Nonetheless, people surveyed had a low level of confidence in the overall effectiveness of our programs (Tilman 1995: 42–43; ODC and InterAction 1987).

Smillie (1995: 125) argues that data showing declining support for aid are "debatable, transitory, or actually false." He cites a 1995 poll in the United States that found that 80 percent of those polled were in favor of aid to countries in genuine need. The U.S. public believes that they give about fifteen times as much foreign aid as they actually do. When informed about actual levels of aid, a strong majority favored maintaining or increasing it.

When asked how they felt about 1 percent (the real figure), only 18 percent of those polled thought that this was too much (CISSM 1995). Forty-

(continues)

---

six percent of respondents felt this was "about right," and 34 percent felt that it was not enough. Fifty-eight percent of respondents agreed with the statement "If I knew that most foreign aid was going to the poor people who really need it, rather than to wasteful bureaucracies and corrupt governments, I would be willing to pay more in taxes for foreign aid." On the other hand, 64 percent agreed strongly with the statement that "taking care of problems at home is more important than giving aid to foreign countries."

In recent decades, disasters in the developing world have pushed longer-term development issues out of the public spotlight. Today, when people think of the developing world, they tend to think of famine, starvation, disease, displacement, and warfare. These require very different types of responses from the West than the more mundane and less dramatic issues of local participation, capacity building, and institutional strengthening, which form the focus of much development work.

Although public support of aid seems about the same, a number of *institutions* are now much more negative on the subject of foreign aid, both from the left and the right. Partly, one supposes, as a result, recent studies (quoted in Smillie and Helmich 1998) found that 68 percent of U.S. policy makers believed that the public has a negative attitude to foreign aid.

Is there actually donor fatigue, or is it compassion fatigue? The public now gets more information than ever before on foreign events, which probably influences how they perceive foreign aid. The media has a lot to do with this. Smillie and Helmich (1998: 26) comment:

> The public in [Western industrial] countries—conditioned by images of disaster, bad weather and conflict—has developed an overwhelmingly negative set of beliefs about the plight of the Third World. If it is not famine or flood, it is slums and poverty; if not ethnic cleansing and genocide, then wanton destruction of the environment and the slaughter of elephants for ivory. Much of the public is increasingly unwilling to accept that the picture could be otherwise.

The media may not be the only culprit. Smillie and Helmich point to the fund-raising tactics employed by NGOs, saying that the essentially paternalistic messages sent in this way may be "dumbing-down" development education and hence public awareness of Third World issues (1998: 35).

They conclude: "While there may not be aid fatigue, there is little understanding, and there is certainly aid *agency* fatigue, the result of a series of

(continues)

MINI-CASE 9.1 (continued)

deep and often damaging cutbacks to development budgets through the DAC" (1998: 35).

SOURCES: Overseas Development Council and InterAction 1987; Tilman 1995; Hellinger et al. 1988; Center for International and Security Studies at Maryland 1995; Smillie 1995; Smillie and Helmich, eds., 1998.

---

cent.[11] U.S. appropriations for foreign aid, which had been as high as 3 percent of GDP in the 1960s, were now down to one-tenth of 1 percent of GDP, the lowest level in history, and the lowest level of aid of any major industrialized nation.[12] In fact, Japan is the only bilateral donor that has dramatically increased its development aid in the past twenty years.[13]

The Rule of the Market

In the 1990s, after the fall of the Berlin Wall, the word *globalization* began to be used to characterize the emerging post-Soviet world. Globalization refers, in essence, to a coming together of the major components of world economic activity—including finance, production, information, and technology—within an overarching market-driven framework. This framework now extends in one way or another into virtually every corner of the globe. The World Bank estimates that today, fewer than 10 percent of the world's workers remain disconnected from world markets.[14]

Globalization has been accompanied by a substantial increase in the power of transnational corporations and banks. There are an estimated 40,000 transnational corporations today, which, together with nearly 300,000 foreign affiliates, have holdings worth over $40 trillion.[15] Some transnational corporations are now more powerful than many national governments.[16]

Of the world's hundred largest economies, for example, fifty-one are corporations. Although the 200 largest corporations only employ less than 1 percent of the world's population, they generate 28 percent of the world's economic activity. The top five companies in each major market—for example, aircraft, autos, microprocessors, grains—typically control 35–70 percent of world sales. Taken together, the 500 largest corporations account for 70 percent of world trade. Table 9.1 sets out a few of

---

MINI-CASE 9.2   THE FAILURE OF DEVELOPMENT
ASSISTANCE IN EASTERN EUROPE

When the Soviet Union fell apart, the development landscape changed fundamentally. For one thing, the tension that had informed so much of development assistance to the Third World largely disappeared. For another, millions of additional people now entered the ranks of the world's poor. At the same time, the countries where they lived were opened to Western institutions.

The West, particularly the United States, lost no time in assembling packages of development assistance. The early 1990s were a period of intense activity, as AID missions and offices were set up in Moscow and the capitals of other former Soviet republics and client states. One year after the fall of the Communist bloc, the United States authorized nearly $1 billion in aid to promote democracy and the private sector. Led by USAID, ambitious programs were quickly designed to promote the "transition." In the United States alone, some thirty-five federal agencies were involved in the aid effort.

Several years later, disillusionment had set in on both sides. People in the former Soviet Union had all but concluded that Western aid was insufficient, insincere, inefficient, and largely irrelevant to their needs. Their cynicism was confirmed as they saw aid dollars being spent mainly on foreign consultants and contractors, siphoned off by local politicians, or wasted on projects that seemed to have little to do with improving their daily lives. In the West, frustration mounted as few visible results appeared and as the realization dawned that large quantities of Western aid had simply disappeared without a trace.

What was largely unappreciated at the time was the gap in perspectives, experience, and needs between Americans and Eastern Europeans. Wedel (1998: 2) comments: "In the years ahead, that gap would grow wider before it narrowed and would create a situation in which many were far from enchanted with aid efforts."

Wedel charts three main phases in Western aid to the East. The first phase, which she calls "triumphalism," was a period of euphoria quickly replaced by the second phase, "disillusionment." In some countries—notably Poland, Hungary, and the Czech Republic—this was eventually followed by "adjustment," as donors and recipients learned to live with each other and to be generally more realistic about what could be accomplished (7).

Wedel found that U.S. development officials and agencies, despite many years of previous experience, paid little attention to the relationships between themselves and Eastern Europeans. She states:

(continues)

MINI-CASE 9.2   (continued)

In the study of aid and development, little attention has been paid to how aid actually happens. Yet how aid happens—through whom and to whom, under what circumstances, and with which goals—determines not only the nature of what recipients actually get and how they respond to it, but its ultimate success or failure. (1998: 6)

Although recipients often are viewed as passive and voiceless, their responses, agendas, and interests influence aid administration, implementation, and outcomes. Recipients can, actively or passively, frustrate, encourage, subvert, facilitate, or otherwise alter aid programs as they are conceived by the donors. (1998: 9)

There were other problems as well, arising from differences in thinking between Western aid officials and their clients and counterparts in the newly independent states.

Western aid agencies, for a start, did not know whether to classify countries in the region as "underdeveloped" or "developed." If the Third World was—or had been—underdeveloped, the Second World had been, in the view of some U.S. officials, "misdeveloped," and as a result, all traces of Communist legacy now needed to be wiped away. Time was of the essence, as it was feared that without massive Western aid and accompanying change, the region might slip into chaos, or even back into communism.

In contrast, Wedel says (1998: 39): ". . . many Central and Eastern Europeans considered themselves exemplars of European culture and civilization and saw communism as a forcibly imposed alien system. They were insulted to see their nations likened to Third World ones and not to be consulted about the course of development."

As before, however, the development paradigm that had driven so much of U.S. aid in the past was now applied, virtually unchanged, to the countries of the former Soviet Union. Wedel comments: ". . . although donors perceived the Second World as unique, they had little real understanding of it, and little organizational capacity to deliver new programs. . . the aid programs most available were those that had been implemented in the Third World. Almost by default, donors set many of them into motion. Many were ill-matched to recipient needs and stifled innovation" (1998: 33–34).

Diplomatic and security issues, as before, drove much of the planning of aid. Econometric models, based largely on Western experience, formed the theoretical backdrop to advice and programming. Administration on the ground was carried out, for the most part, by AID staffers with previous experience in Asia, Africa, and Latin America—few of whom had spent any time in Eastern Europe or Russia, did not speak the local languages, and

(continues)

MINI-CASE 9.2 (continued)

were largely unfamiliar with the differences between these countries and the places where they had previously served.

Aid was contracted out to consulting firms and other providers of technical assistance. Most of the contract winners proved to be the same "Beltway Bandits" that had been so active earlier in the Third World. As before, pressures to spend money quickly were intense.

Wedel concludes that aid to Eastern Europe might have worked, but that our own structures and approaches proved inadequate. The players in this drama consisted of "distant, if mutually fascinated nations and people. Cultural ignorance—coupled with the idea that cultural knowledge is either irrelevant or easy to achieve—configured the first phases of the aid story" (1998: 190).

Wedel insists on the value of anthropology in the development process—clearly missing here—to help understand how relationships shape, and are shaped by, the development encounter: "It is only through a grounded, real-world focus on political, economic and social relationships that we can understand the 'chemical reactions' of the development encounter and make progress toward disentangling—and changing—the world system we know as development" (1998: 196–197).

All of this demonstrated, in the end, how difficult it is for large aid bureaucracies to learn either the lessons of previous experience or to learn about new situations that they may encounter. AID's response to opportunities in Eastern Europe and the former Soviet Union was to apply standard procedures and standard thinking, despite clear evidence that this had not worked particularly well in the past.

SOURCE: Wedel 1998.

---

the largest companies and compares their market capitalization in 1999 with selected countries.

One result of this is that as official aid flowing to the developing world has either stagnated or declined, private direct investment has grown. Private investment flows to developing countries in 1988 were three-quarters the volume of official aid. By 1997, private capital flows to developing countries exceeded $250 billion per year, compared with $66 billion in official aid.[17]

In one sense, this was good news. In another, however, it was not; private finance went mainly to the fast-growing economies of Asia. Poorer countries—particularly many in Africa—were receiving little if any private investment.[18]

TABLE 9.1   Corporate Power and National Economies

Company	Market Capitalization	Comparable Country GDP
IBM	$201 billion	Colombia
Wal-Mart	$296 billion	Argentina
Microsoft	$593 billion	Spain
Intel	$246 billion	Poland
General Electric	$456 billion	Thailand
Cisco Systems	$344 billion	Iran
Dell Computer	$109 billion	Vietnam
Lucent Technologies	$227 billion	South Africa
America Online	$194 billion	Philippines

SOURCE: Adapted from *New York Times,* December 26, 1999: Section 3: 1.

Indeed, for many of the world's poorer countries, the cumulative effect of development policy and globalization forces has made development options virtually synonymous with world trade. To an increasing extent, a poor country's ability and willingness to open itself to outside investment and the rule of a global—and impersonal—market, has come to be, for better or worse, its best hope of success. Outside investment, coupled with pressure from development agencies to privatize national industries in poorer countries, has increased foreign ownership of local assets, at the same time as funding has lessened for broad social support programs in many countries.

Information, in the view of many observers, had now become the new global currency, with some claiming that the information revolution would transform the coming century, just as the industrial revolution transformed Europe in the 1800s.[19]

There are serious disparities between countries and regions with respect to information technology, however, and these gaps will probably widen in the years ahead. Eighty percent of the world's population does not have access to reliable telecommunications, and three-quarters of the world's telephones are found in just eight industrialized countries. In Manhattan alone, there are more telephone lines than in all of sub-Saharan Africa (excepting South Africa). Something like 90 percent of the data about Africa itself is held on computer systems outside the continent. Of the 50,000 African Internet hosts, 48,000 are in South Africa.[20]

A FAILURE TO LEARN

Why haven't development agencies done better? Criticisms of development work have an almost timeless quality: The same things that are wrong today were wrong twenty and thirty years ago.[21] On the whole, development agencies have consistently shown themselves to be poorly equipped to design and support effective policies, programs, and projects that directly address problems of poverty.[22]

In large part, this is because the agencies have difficulty learning from their experience. Although individuals within these agencies may learn a great deal, this learning tends not to find its way into the organization. So we are drawn to the question of what development organizations know and how they learn what they know.

At the most basic level, the reason why large agencies do not learn is because they do not have to.[23] Few agencies directly experience the effects of their plans, projects, and programs. Their internal operations, largely opaque to outsiders, are not particularly disposed to self-criticism or the discussion of failure.

There are three broad reasons for this organizational inability to learn: the *paradigms* that dominate development work, the scripts or *development narratives* that this paradigm generates, and the collusive *structures* in which the development partners seem to be locked. I'll look at each of these in turn.

Paradigms: The Technicist Mindset

The mindset of the development industry—often referred to as "technicist"—constitutes a major obstacle to organizational learning.[24] Derived from the disciplines that have historically dominated the industry—economics, engineering, accounting, and finance—this mindset limits what is looked at, what questions are asked, and how answers are interpreted.

Although the technicist perspective is useful for many purposes, it is also constraining. Its insistence on quantifiable certainty places too much confidence in numbers and formulae. Its concern with simplicity tends to reduce complex situations to the policy equivalent of soundbites. Deductive and prescriptive, the approach tends to define reality in advance of investigation, thereby rendering new information irrelevant. It is preoccupied with efficiency, which pushes planners into applying past models to current—although different—situations. It is based on expertise, which means that often its operations and conclusions are couched in arcane terms, mysterious and inaccessible to ordinary people. Finally, it considers growth axiomatic. More—bigger, stronger, further, and so on—is, by definition, better.

Like all worldviews, the technicist outlook has important consequences for the way in which development agencies operate. What is considered real—and therefore important—is almost wholly confined to what which can be measured. Further, the reductionism in this approach encourages a divorce of measurements from context. The *implicit* forms of knowledge contained in a specific cultural context are all too often ignored or overlooked. Specialists can develop theory and make plans without ever having to learn much about what ordinary people are actually like.

The much-vaunted rationality of the technicist approach is a particularly Western construct, centered on control, speed, and efficiency. People, in this view, are almost always male individuals acting out of short-term self-interest. But although these assumptions are Western-derived, they are applied in other situations with little regard for local context.

The technicist approach generates large areas of ignorance and provides the illusion of precision, control, and understanding. Problems are narrowly defined, precise methods are applied, and data are gathered and compared. The numbers then tell the story. Things that cannot be counted or whose significance is unclear tend to be ignored or downplayed. Larger questions are often not discussed at all. What the specialists do not know, in many cases, is considered not worth knowing.[25]

Despite its drawbacks, such an outlook is clearly attractive. As several observers have pointed out, it can become almost a religion, with its followers unable to comprehend why others might think differently.[26]

Development thinking is still dominated by the technicist mindset, despite the lack of evidence that such a perspective is effective at resolving problems in cross-cultural situations. The models imposed by this way of thinking, in fact, are remarkably resistant to change. The mindset encourages agencies to take essentially conservative postures with respect to the situations they encounter, with a bias toward criteria such as simplicity, quantifiability, predictability, and similarity to past experience. Local data, in this framework, tend to contaminate and destroy the simplicity of the models thus constructed, and so are avoided whenever possible. This is partly why so much agency analysis has a curiously flat, one-dimensional character, where data are laid out in neat sets of quite simple categories, and where the conclusions derived from this information are sometimes startlingly black and white, leading some critics to speak of "cookie-cutter analysis."

This is not to say that agencies cannot discriminate among shades of gray. But there is a tendency toward premature closure in analysis, toward the overextension of wide-ranging conclusions from narrow sets of data, and toward data that are already judged safe by the agency.[27]

Development Narratives:
Stories About Us, Stories About Them

One of the products of a technicist mindset is the creation of *development narratives*—stories or scripts about why the developing world is the way it is.[28] The narratives or scripts are cultural constructs that help define relevant data, interpretations, and exclusions, thereby pointing the way toward possible solutions, or at least options for choice.[29]

The "tragedy of the commons" is one such development narrative. Others include the notion of the "noble savage" and the "tradition-bound peasant." These are allegories or fables that implicitly or explicitly underlie much development planning. Such narratives provide a model for thinking about a situation and a way of identifying heroes, culprits, and connections between events.

People everywhere use simplifying narratives to help them think about complex things.[30] Development narratives help us to simplify uncertainty and smooth out complex data sets into neater patterns. Narratives arise and prosper partly because they are a way for experts to claim ownership of the development conversation. Landes illustrates how this works with the question of why some are rich and others poor.

> One [narrative] says that we are so rich and they so poor because we are so good and they so bad; that is, we are hard-working, knowledgeable, educated, well-governed, efficacious, and productive, and they are the reverse. The other [narrative] says that we are so rich and they so poor because we are so bad and they so good: we are greedy, ruthless, exploitative, aggressive, while they are weak, innocent, virtuous, abused, and vulnerable. It is not clear to me that one line of argument necessarily precludes the other, although most observers and commentators have a strong preference in the matter. What is clear is that, insofar as we may want to do something about the gap between rich and poor, each of these explanations implies a very different strategy.[31]

Frances Moore Lappé, in her critique of American development aid, also draws the contrast between two opposing narratives:

> As AID sees it, the poor are poor because they lack certain things: irrigation, credit, better seeds, good roads, or what have you. But we ask: *why* are they lacking these things? The reason is that the poor lack power, power to secure what they need. . . . The official diagnosis assumes that the poor are living in static backwardness and that foreign aid's function

is to get things moving by offering material incentives and other benevo-
lent prods.[32]

Narratives, at best, draw attention to things in the environment that
might otherwise be ignored. At worst, they enable us to avoid directly
encountering the other cultural worlds in a development situation. If a
narrative becomes elevated to the status of an axiom or theoretical orthodoxy, planners then have little need to go into the field where they
might encounter discrepant and varied patterns of data.

Structures: Collaboration and Collusion

The structure of agency work also contributes to the learning problem.
Agencies tend to favor larger rather than smaller projects, if for no other
reason than to achieve economies of scale with their funds. The complexity of design and approval procedures also makes it attractive to opt
for larger undertakings, since the level of effort is about the same as for a
smaller project.[33]

As a consequence, approaches to a particular development problem
tend to be reduced to those that are most easily manageable by the
agency at the widest possible level of scale. This reduces both the number of design options available, and later, the opportunities to learn from
a wider variety of both success and failure. Because agency staffers move
frequently between departments and overseas missions, they rarely have
to live with the outcomes or consequences of the projects they initiate.
There is little accountability and little opportunity to learn at firsthand
about how projects actually work.

Since larger agencies often prefer to manage programs and projects
through contractors, the experience of project development tends to be
fragmented. People who participate in project development—agency
staffers or contractors—often do not see projects through to completion,
and hence never develop a firm stake in the outcome.

Contractors and outside firms, moreover, have little power to influence
agency decisions. They seek instead to maintain good long-term relationships with these agencies that are, after all, their principal customers.
Unsurprisingly, there is a general disinclination within firms to criticize
the industry.

Individual contractors and firms, however, often accumulate a great
deal of practical knowledge about what works in development and why.
But only certain types of information are actually absorbed by the agen-

cies that employ them. Agencies tend to be preoccupied with moving money down the aid pipeline, and bad news tends to impede the flow. Success, for most agencies, means disbursing the maximum amount of money with a minimum of problems.

Host country bureaucracies are at the other end of the money pipeline, of course. Their relationship to large agencies is often symbiotic: the agencies need to spend their budgets and the local ministries could not function without the external funds that agencies provide. Host countries will therefore have a "wish list" of projects, all of which require funding, if not in this fiscal year, then surely in the next.

Agencies, particularly bilateral agencies, will have their own set of funding priorities, usually emanating from their own oversight or regulatory bodies. The job is to match these as smoothly as possible to the requests of the host country—or at least, to give the appearance of doing so—to keep the pipeline open. One result is that national development priorities can sometimes wind up being determined by what specific donors are prepared to fund.

There is thus a collusive web of relationships linking agencies (and their oversight bodies), host country governments, and contract specialists. Agencies depend on their regulatory agencies for funds, and once they obtain these, spend most of their time pushing money through the pipeline. Host country ministries need development aid for their survival, and hence provide justifications for projects requiring these funds. Consulting firms supply the manpower to plan and manage these projects. Each member of the network has an interest in communicating some types of information, but not others, to their partners.

In the process, critical analysis tends to be muted. There is little opportunity for careful analysis of projects and programs, and little institutional learning. Bad news from the field about results and outcomes may pose problems to the smooth operation of the pipeline, which is why experience and knowledge are so often presented in the form of carefully shaped and sanitized reports. These reports serve as compliance and advocacy documents, essential for securing the next round of appropriations, rather than as rigorous analyses of what happened and why. Failure is rarely discussed in such documents, so the opportunity to embrace error and learn from it is usually bypassed. Often, completed projects are by definition successful ones, since they pave the way for more projects—and more funding.

Within this pattern of relationships, agencies have little incentive either to learn or change, and few mechanisms for converting what is learned into better planning. Project planning will be driven primarily by the rules for project approval and funding. Project designs tend to be conventional, emphasizing quantitative aspects—such as money and equipment—that can be easily documented and controlled and that can be displayed to constituents as proof of accomplishments.

POSSIBILITIES FOR REFORM

Players in the development game are locked into a self-reinforcing system that clearly needs to be reformed. This will not be easy; changing an organization's culture is usually best done by the organization's leaders, but this would mean relying on the very people who got to the top under the existing arrangements.[34] But I can at least suggest some directions which reform might take. They fall into three broad categories: *accountability*, *incentives*, and *mechanisms for learning*.

Accountability

Development agencies may have little incentive to learn or change, but they *can* be made more accountable, more sensitive to context as they do development, and more capable of learning from experience. What sorts of reforms might be suggested?

One approach is to look at organizations that are already more accountable and context sensitive, and to try and see what they might have to teach the development industry. The military, for example, has elaborate systems of accountability, and intelligence agencies emphasize the in-context analysis of information. Although neither of these are probably good models in their entirety, aspects of their operations might be successfully adopted by development agencies.

Another approach is to look at mechanisms for oversight. Even the so-called "free market" is far from free, and must operate within a complex web of regulation. Right now, bilateral agencies are accountable only to portions of their respective governments, and the larger multilaterals are effectively accountable to no one. What sorts of oversight arrangements, already in place for other industries, might work well for development? Might it be desirable to create independent boards to review and regulate the operation of development agencies?

Host governments must also be made more accountable. This will mean altering aspects of conditionality—that is, the basis on which development assistance is given. All too often, conditionality becomes an adversarial tug-of-war between donors and recipients, each side attempting to impose its will through pressure or manipulation.

Ideally, conditionality should be a mutually agreed upon set of principles underlying project development, arising from a clear and realistic assessment of the conditions necessary for project success, and at the same time, of the ability of local stakeholders to create, deliver, or sustain such conditions. There is simply no point in requiring stakeholders to do things they cannot (or will not) do.

Such an assessment should be an integral part of the earliest phases of project development, and donors should be prepared to delay or even cancel projects where preconditions have not been satisfied. In cases where these conditions *have* been met, projects should include provisions for the building of local capacity, so that project benefits, once they appear, can continue after donor funding has disappeared.

Incentives

At the moment, there is simply no direct connection between development agencies and the results they obtain from their projects in the field. There are no institutional consequences for failure, no rewards for success. Nor are there any consequences, most of the time, for individuals who work within those agencies. As pointed out earlier, the main criterion for success appears to be, in virtually all the agencies, the ability to move money through the system with a minimum of friction.

Agencies do not differentially reward their staffers according to project results, and agencies do not normally compete with one another. But outside the development industry, competition is often held up as one of the major ways to ensure innovation, quality, responsiveness, and performance. Might it make sense to encourage competition between agencies? To break larger agencies into smaller ones?

At the moment, agencies work mainly to satisfy their own internal requirements and those of the boards or legislatures that vote their budgets. Would there be advantages to creating a system of shareholders? Would it be feasible for countries to solicit bids for development projects from a variety of agencies, and then select the most advantageous?

Within agencies themselves, what would be the effect of linking staff salaries to project performance? Taking a cue from the private sector, salaries, bonuses, and overall budgets could be directly linked to the success of projects, using any of a number of simple measures. Staffers whose projects were successful would benefit directly; those who designed or promoted unsuccessful projects would find their income and promotion prospects diminished accordingly.

Mechanisms for Learning

But the most critical change of all regards information and the ability to learn from experience. Unless agencies are able to alter the way they see the project environment and learn from it, to connect this learning with planning and implementation, and to remember the lessons afterward, very little in the way of improved outcomes can be expected.

Because they deal with the lives of human beings, projects are one of the most difficult aspects of development work to plan and manage. Every project is in some sense unique, a special case. It would make sense, therefore, to acknowledge that the environment in which projects unfold must be approached as something to be understood and worked with, rather than as an obstacle to be overcome. As this book has tried to show, planning and management styles that seek to understand the local environment and use it to guide project elements will stand the greatest chance of success.

This would mean adopting a much more interactive approach to project development, being willing to invest time and manpower in fitting plans to people, and being prepared for error, delay, change, and ambiguity at all phases of the project cycle. In situations where local capabilities are unknown or where the commitment of local stakeholders is uncertain at the outset, projects would need to be designed as "learning process" experiments, segmented in such a way that delay or cancellation has as few negative effects as possible. In this way, the experiences of early stages of planning and implementation can reliably inform later stages. And if, after all, the project must be halted, a minimum of damage has been done.

Finally, it is clear from the wreckage of littered projects of the past that one of the biggest weaknesses of the present approach is its disregard of local capacities. Here, as in every other sphere of life, groups have different comparative advantages. A thorough project analysis will pinpoint the human resource capabilities of the local population, make an intelligent assessment of how these can be incorporated in present form into the process of planning and implementation, and from this, indicate which skills or capabilities should be strengthened so that the project truly becomes a locally run and locally controlled affair.

The overall effect of these changes will not necessarily require donors to increase their present levels of involvement, but to do two other things: shift that involvement more toward people and away from things; and bring policy, planning, and project development down much closer to the grassroots level.

MINI-CASE 9.3 ORGANIZATIONAL LEARNING

Peter Senge's influential book *The Fifth Discipline* (Senge 1990) discussed in detail the need for organizations to develop and improve their ability to learn. Learning, in essence, is the ability of an organization to "maintain or improve performance based on experience"(DiBella and Nevis 1998: 28). All organizations learn, of course. What is important is what they learn, and how. This is determined, as DiBella and Nevis (1998: 21) point out, largely by the organization's culture.

Organizational learning has three fundamental processes: creating or acquiring knowledge; spreading knowledge within the organization; and using knowledge. An organization's *learning orientations* will determine what is learned and how. What is learned reflects organizational values to a large extent. Organizations will typically concentrate their learning efforts on areas of high importance to them. How this learning is stored, communicated, and used also reflects organizational values and priorities.

Some organizations, for example, pay attention to only part of their surrounding environment, ignoring the rest. Some organizations distrust "outside" information and learn primarily from data that they collect themselves. Some organizations pay particular attention to outcomes, whereas others also look closely at the process by which outcomes were achieved. Some organizations attempt to formally codify and explicate their learning through manuals, standard procedures, and checklists; others prefer to let organizational learning remain within individuals, to be shared informally. Some organizations seek to challenge existing knowledge, and other organizations seek mainly to deepen their understanding of what already exists.

Organizations learn more and learn better, DiBella and Nevis claim, if certain facilitating factors are in place. These include:

- People willing and able to seek out new information externally.
- An organization's recognition of gaps between current performance and desired results.
- A commitment to definition and measurement in the process of learning and improvement.

(continues)

- Curiosity about new approaches, coupled with a climate that encourages openness, risk taking, and continual learning.
- Internal operational variety, where multiple methods and approaches are used in pursuit of organizational goals.
- Multiple advocates, with new ideas coming from different people at different levels.
- Leaders who are visibly and actively involved in developing organizational learning and who encourage new ideas from people at all levels of the organization.
- A systems perspective within the organization, where everyone is aware of how their efforts connect and interact.

Clearly, the development industry is not well set up for organizational learning. Because of the current dominance of the technicist mindset, only some signals from the environment are recognized as significant. Bureaucratic procedures and internal patterns of incentives and sanctions make it difficult to try new approaches, to express skepticism or disagreement with organizational orthodoxy, and to learn from outside groups. At the same time, defensiveness in the face of pressure or criticism from other outside groups—many of them unfriendly—discourages open discussion of shortfalls or problems.

Because development work at the project level is an emergent problem, development agencies must be able to learn. Projects, operating at the interface where an implementing agency's way of doing things meets that of the locals, provide an excellent cross-cultural environment for learning.

In individuals, cross-cultural learning proceeds in five stages:

- The first stage involves becoming aware of differences.
- The second stage is about gaining some understanding about how these differences are structured and linked, and what they "mean."
- The third stage involves finding ways to cope with the differences on a day-to-day level.
- The fourth stage is reached when someone not only can cope with differences, but can manipulate them in the process of reaching goals and objectives.
- The fifth and final stage is where some aspects of difference are incorporated into one's permanent operating framework.

(*continues*)

MINI-CASE 9.3 (*continued*)

Although most development agencies can do the first and second of these things, not many of them have developed effective ways of coping with difference that are mutually acceptable. Few large agencies have been either willing or able to incorporate cultural difference into their own internal policies, procedures, and mindsets.

SOURCES: Senge 1990; DiBella and Nevis 1998.

SUMMARY OF CHAPTER 9

The results of development, although positive in many respects, have been disappointing overall. Poverty continues to define life for billions of people, and the gap between rich and poor continues to grow. Chapter 9 looks at the development industry in terms of the reasons for this uneven performance, and what might be done to improve matters.

The development industry is under considerable pressure from a variety of quarters to do better, at a time when many of the larger agencies have actually distanced themselves from the field. Despite public criticism of the industry and its practices, there also seems to be a lessening of public support for development aid in general. Private investment money is now many times the volume of development aid, but very little of this money finds its way to the poorest countries.

Chapter 9 focuses particularly on the difficulties development agencies have with learning the lessons of experience. There are several reasons for this difficulty. One concerns the dominant pattern of thinking within many development agencies; another is linked to the structural relationships between agencies, specialist contractors, and host country governments. Making agencies better learners will involve changing some fundamental things about how the industry works, and these are discussed in the final sections of the chapter.

The chapter concludes with some recommendations for reform, including changes in accountability, incentives, and mechanisms for organizational learning.

ENDNOTES

1. See World Bank (1999: 319).

2. See McMichael (1996: 80). Raymond Baker, writing in the *International Herald Tribune* (February 5, 1999) claims that the gap between rich and poor is widening rapidly. The difference between the top and the bottom 20 percent in terms of income, according to many estimates, was estimated to be about 60 to 1 in 1993, and this had risen to 74 to 1 by 1998. But Baker maintains that depending on whose data you use, the difference might be as high as 135 to 1.

3. Sub-Saharan Africa is the most heavily aided region in the world, receiving some $15 billion yearly in official assistance. At the same time, it is in danger of being forgotten, as new crises emerge elsewhere and as other countries and regions forge ahead in the race to globalize. A *New York Times* article (January 3, 1995), "Global Economic Prospects Are Brighter for Most," did not even mention Africa at all. The United Nations Development Programme (UNDP) calculates that eleven Africa countries were richer per capita in 1960 than they are today (*New York Times*, May 20, 1997). Africa's share of world markets has fallen by 50 percent since 1970, and per capita income has dropped by 25 percent since 1987 (in McMichael 1996: 196).

4. World Bank figures quoted in Hook (1996: 2).

5. Here again, the literature is voluminous, and emanates from the political left, right, and center. Among the influential books are Payer (1982) on the World Bank, Hancock (1989), Rich (1994), Brecher and Costello (1994), Danaher (1994), Bandow and Vásquez (1994), and Samoff (1996).

6. In addition to the 50 Years Is Enough Campaign in 1994, other groups also began to call into question the entire technicist paradigm. See, for example, the full-page ads that ran in the *New York Times* (for example, August 28, 2000: A11; November 15, 1999: A7) from the Turning Point Project, "a coalition of more than 50 non-profit organizations that favor democratic, localized, ecologically sound alternatives to current practices and policies."

7. In this view, the international system was set up to exploit the Third World to advance the interests of Western capitalism. The poor countries would provide raw materials at rock-bottom prices, which the Western industrialized countries would turn into expensive consumer goods for the world market. Efforts by the Third World to opt out of this system or to rework it to their own advantage were to be strongly resisted.

8. One of the early, powerful statements of this appeared in 1973, in *We Don't Know How*, a book by William and Elizabeth Paddock.

9. Black (1999: 66); *New York Times* (February 19, 1995); *New York Times* (July 6, 1999: A4).

10. *The Economist* (June 17, 2000: 21).

11. See Hook (1996: 6); USAID (1998).

12. For a recent analysis of U.S. trends in foreign aid, see O'Hanlon and Graham (1997).

13. Tisch and Wallace (1994: 120).

14. World Bank (1995: 1).

15. Feeney (1998: 143).

16. See Kaplan (1997); also McMichael (1996: 94).

17. Feeney (1998: 141).

18. World Bank (1999: 320). See also McMichael (1996: 196). *The Economist* estimates that only 1 percent of the world's private investment goes to sub-Saharan Africa (*Economist*, April 8, 2000: 46).

19. McMichael (1996: 89).

20. All figures from *Developments* (4th quarter, 1998).

21. These problems have been recognized for some time. A 1973 study (Posz et al. 1973: 106) of the organization of development assistance within AID noted this: "The data [of the present study] clearly show that many aspects of the present bureaucratic structure of AID are dysfunctional in terms of effective professional performance. Many of the dysfunctional elements in the mission structure originate at the macro-level—the federal bureaucracy, the U.S. legislative press, the political-administrative aspects of the client system, and, ultimately, in the international environment."

22. Hellinger et al. (1988: 125). Opportunities to change and reform aid have been largely missed. Zimmerman and Hook remark: "Though the emphasis on sustainable development suggested a possible new paradigm for U.S. foreign policy in the 1990s, in practice many established aid programs remained unchanged, with only their rhetorical goals changing" (1996: 65). Later (p. 70), they add: "U.S. leaders seem to understand the importance of concepts such as self-determination, ownership, and empowerment, but their aid strategies and project proposals continue to reflect established bureaucratic and political routines."

23. Louis Lapham, writing about what he perceived as a similar characteristic of President George Bush *père*, observed: "This lack of development is fairly common among people born to the assumptions of wealth and rank. They can afford to believe what they choose to believe, and they seldom find it necessary to revise the texts of the preferred reality" (*Harpers*, March 1992: 7). The end of the Cold War may have made it even more difficult for our aid agencies to learn. Speaking of the attitude of "triumphalism" in the West following the breakup of the Soviet Union, where, in the view of many, capitalism and the market "triumphed" over socialism and centralized planning, Samoff (1996: 616) notes: "This triumphalism has (at least) two powerful consequences for the relationship between aid and policy making. Those who have triumphed need no longer listen. Since they know what is right, and since it is their power, rather than negotiation, that secures their interests, they can instruct rather than learn. Moreover, since the triumph, they believe, proves the correctness of their perspective, they need to feel reticent or guilty about telling others what to do."

24. Bowers (1988: 8–9).

25. Browne (1996: 225) and others have pointed out that noneconomic studies are often not even reviewed within the large development agencies. When I worked for the World Bank in the late 1980s, I once spent the better part of an afternoon explaining to an Indian economist how the system of religious *marabouts* in Senegal affected the way in which peasant farmers made decisions, hoping thereby to illuminate his discouraging regression results linking reductions in fertilizer subsidy with groundnut output. He listened politely, and then said in a kindly voice, "This is very interesting, but it cannot really be part of my analysis. All of these things that you have told me are what the Bank calls non-price factors."

26. Others are less charitable. Robert Chambers (1997b: 54) characterizes this viewpoint as a "professional prison."

27. Some agencies—such as the World Bank—are also very concerned to "speak with one voice" to their clients, and the notion that alternative perspectives might emanate publicly from the same agency is usually rejected out of hand.

28. The term "development narratives" was first used by Emery Roe (1991, 1995). See also Hoben (1995).

29. Hoben (1980: 362) has pointed out that some "folk" beliefs are held at the level of the local national AID mission.

30. See Hoben (1980: 352), also Douglas (1986).

31. Landes (1995: 74).

32. Lappé et al. (1987: 78).

33. Again, this problem has been recognized for years. McNeil (1981: 9) writes: "Much that is wrong with foreign aid is caused not by incompetence or corruption but by the complex machinery which has been developed to enable aid to be transmitted from donor to recipient. This machinery had been designed and constructed mainly by the donors, with the stated intention of making the aid process more efficient, but it actually causes or exacerbates many of the very problems that aid is meant to alleviate."

34. Baré (1998: 321).

chapter 10

REDIRECTING
ANTHROPOLOGY

Development anthropologists can play several key roles in project development, in addition to their more traditional functions as data providers and cultural brokers. In recent years, anthropologists have begun to work as team leaders, project managers, and policy makers.

Despite this success, anthropologists continue to have difficulty with development work on several levels. New anthropology graduates are rarely able to fully contribute to development efforts "straight out of the box," primarily because the universities from which they come do not, on the whole, provide them with training adequate to the increasingly sophisticated demands of development work.

In this chapter, I look first at the kinds of problems anthropologists have typically had with development work, before moving to a discussion of how academic training might be changed to address some of these issues.

ANTHROPOLOGY AND DEVELOPMENT:
THE DIFFICULT ENCOUNTER

Engagement

Anthropology's problems with development begin with a general lack of engagement. Despite a long history of application, anthropology as a discipline has always had a decidedly ambivalent attitude toward programs of planned change and toward development work in particular. Anthropology remains deeply troubled about the use of power to effect change, and indeed, about the usefulness of directed change as a way to achieve "betterment" in human affairs.

Anthropologists have had surprising little to say until relatively recently about development issues. In the past, anthropologists have tended to assume that their work was value-free and without political implications, preferring to believe that their role as provider of knowledge was sufficient—or that the knowledge itself was sufficient—to assure a positive outcome. When anthropologists *did* engage with real-world problems, they were often accused (by outsiders as well as colleagues) of upholding the status quo and resisting changes that might improve the lives of local people.[1] Despite dramatic growth in the numbers of anthropologists working outside the academy, controversy continues within the discipline concerning the proper role of practice and the appropriate status to be accorded practitioners.

Representations

Once engaged, however, development anthropologists face a fundamental dilemma in terms of how to represent themselves and what they do. Whereas university-based anthropologists can, if necessary, retreat to their primary academic identity, practitioners must choose their roles carefully. Defining one's abilities as somehow "unique" may promise more than it can deliver. On the other hand, claiming to be a jack-of-all-trades can relegate anthropologists to secondary assignments with little direct impact on the way things happen.[2] For if anthropology has no special insight and is simply a collection of methodologies that anyone, with a little practice, can pick up and use, then there is no real need for an anthropologist per se.

Teamwork

Anthropologists have not been particularly good at interacting with other specialists in the field. We often don't know much about what they do, and even if we are somewhat familiar with economics or range management, we have usually been trained in the lone-wolf mode of independent field research. Our relative unfamiliarity with other disciplines (which is often matched, to be fair, by equal ignorance of us on their part), coupled with the demands and skills of teamwork in general, make us less effective players in the development game.

But as we have seen, projects are group efforts, planned and implemented by coordinated teams. Because virtually all development work is, in one sense or another, a team effort, the ability to work with other specialists and stakeholders is an important professional attribute.[3]

Project staff work under continual time pressure, and specialists must work quickly and smoothly together to resolve differences in research approaches, personality, and management. Our academic training has, by and large, given us little experience with the requirements of teamwork, which emphasize compromise, adjustment, the integration of other disciplinary worldviews, and a willingness to settle for outcomes that may be merely adequate rather than optimal or ideal. Anthropologists are often seen as individualists and loners, people who are likely to turn out to be critics of the project they've been hired for, rather than as team players. All too often, anthropologists seem to view their main role as that of contributing disassurance to the enterprise, by calling its assumptions into question.[4]

In many development agencies, furthermore, there is no established network of senior anthropologists who might play a mentoring or socializing role for newcomers. One important exception to this, however, was discussed in the mini-case in Chapter 3 on the role of anthropology at the World Bank.

Results

Fieldwork-based ethnography, which is anthropology's stock in trade, tends not to impress project planners. It takes too long and may not actually generate what planners consider to be useful information.[5] As one writer put it, anthropology uses nonreplicable methods to gather overdetailed information that is nongeneralizable.

Although we know that traditional ethnography is not what is needed, we sometimes find it hard to change our presentation style, using jargon that tends to obscure rather than illuminate the hard questions faced by project planners. Although phrases such as "cultural integration, cultural dynamics, [and] socio-cultural systems in contact" may roll off the tongue in a graduate seminar, this may come across as meaningless jargon to most project administrators unless such statements are explicitly connected with some recommended course of action.[6]

Just because we can demonstrate the elegance and appropriateness of local practices does not make us particularly good at formulating recommendations. We are most comfortable providing data, explanations, and sometimes alternatives, instead of specific suggestions for what to do next.

ANTHROPOLOGISTS AND ADMINISTRATIVE CULTURE

Many of the problems that anthropologists encounter in the development industry are clearly cultural, arising from differences between themselves and the planners and policy makers who direct their work. These differences appear most sharply in terms of the collection and use of knowledge. Figures 10.1 and 10.2 set out, in simplified form, some of the differences between anthropologists and others with respect to these two areas.

Although over time anthropologists have become more comfortable with administrative culture, differences persist.[7] One of these could be expressed as a question: "How much knowledge is enough?"

Policy makers, by and large, are perfectly aware that they deal with complex situations. But in their work, they often seek to simplify and prioritize elements of their environment—to limit, so to speak, the size of the playing field. Knowledge is useful to them to the extent that it helps make decisions, justify decisions, or manipulate the context in which decisions are made.

Whereas these decision makers seek to pare down reality, as it were, to make decisions of the moment, anthropologists are essentially interested in developing more detail, in learning more. Given a planning problem, for example, anthropologists are inclined, both by training and temperament, to question basic aspects of the situation, many of which policy makers consider axiomatic.[8] In sum, although anthropologists essentially want to *learn about* the situation, policy makers want—indeed, need—to *make decisions about* that situation.

Another major difference between anthropologists and policy makers might also be expressed as a question: "Whose side are you on?"

Policy makers, for their part, know that no plan is ideal. Once a decision is made, however, they will expect their staff to climb on board and support it. They know that they must advocate for and defend their ideas and decisions, not just present them. Policy makers also know that polit-

FIGURE 10.1   Problems with the Collection of Knowledge

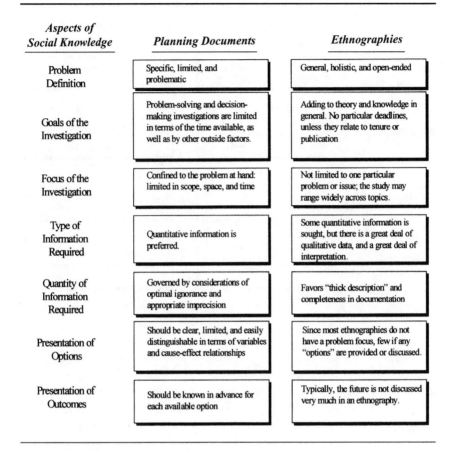

Aspects of Social Knowledge	Planning Documents	Ethnographies
Problem Definition	Specific, limited, and problematic	General, holistic, and open-ended
Goals of the Investigation	Problem-solving and decision-making investigations are limited in terms of the time available, as well as by other outside factors.	Adding to theory and knowledge in general. No particular deadlines, unless they relate to tenure or publication
Focus of the Investigation	Confined to the problem at hand: limited in scope, space, and time	Not limited to one particular problem or issue; the study may range widely across topics.
Type of Information Required	Quantitative information is preferred.	Some quantitative information is sought, but there is a great deal of qualitative data, and a great deal of interpretation.
Quantity of Information Required	Governed by considerations of optimal ignorance and appropriate imprecision	Favors "thick description" and completeness in documentation
Presentation of Options	Should be clear, limited, and easily distinguishable in terms of variables and cause-effect relationships	Since most ethnographies do not have a problem focus, few if any "options" are provided or discussed.
Presentation of Outcomes	Should be known in advance for each available option	Typically, the future is not discussed very much in an ethnography.

SOURCE: Adapted from Curtis 1985: 105.

ical as well as scientific factors enter into decisionmaking, and they will therefore compromise if necessary.

Anthropologists, on the other hand, are often prone to argue for ideal solutions under ideal circumstances. They tend to see policy questions as problems for research, sometimes forgetting that for policy makers, research is only one of many ways of arriving at decisions. Because the type of research that anthropologists do best has the effect, not so much of confirming present arrangements, but of generating new and often discrepant information, policy makers can come to regard anthropologists as dissident voices.

FIGURE 10.2   Problems with the Use of Knowledge

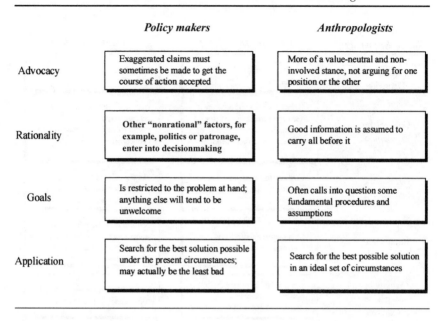

	Policy makers	Anthropologists
Advocacy	Exaggerated claims must sometimes be made to get the course of action accepted	More of a value-neutral and non-involved stance, not arguing for one position or the other
Rationality	Other "nonrational" factors, for example, politics or patronage, enter into decisionmaking	Good information is assumed to carry all before it
Goals	Is restricted to the problem at hand; anything else will tend to be unwelcome	Often calls into question some fundamental procedures and assumptions
Application	Search for the best solution possible under the present circumstances; may actually be the least bad	Search for the best possible solution in an ideal set of circumstances

At best, the anthropologist-as-dissident is merely an annoyance and irritation to others. At worst, they are loose cannons on the deck. Neither role endears them to others in the development industry. This is what one World Bank official had to say about anthropologists in development work:

Anthropologists are inclined to argue . . . that their skills in social understanding transcend those of economists and that they could therefore get under the crude questions of cash flow and marginal rates of return to the deeper social realities. Maybe, but one recalls the not altogether unfair stereotype of an anthropologist living in a village for years and emerging at the end with the view that the villagers are all splendid chaps who ought to be allowed to get on with agriculture in their own way regardless of the fact that the world around them will not allow them to do so . . . any generalized adoption of social anthropology would be, I believe, merely an expensive way of avoiding a few, not very costly, mistakes . . . [9]

Finally, and in part because of these cultural differences, agencies and administrators within agencies often do not know how to actually use anthropologists to best advantage. Anthropologists frequently complain that their involvement with project development is sporadic and piece-meal, too late in the process to influence crucial framing decisions.[10]

BECOMING A PROFESSION

Our discipline lacks an overall model or framework for the application of anthropological knowledge. Partly for this reason, anthropology has come to be considered by many as a soft social science, preoccupied with the exotic and unusual, generating curious bits of data whose utility was uncertain. Anthropologists, when not viewed as misfit adventurers à la Indiana Jones, are often seen as eccentric academicians, conversant with strange languages and customs, but with little interest in the world out-side the library or museum.

Despite the centrality of real-world fieldwork, traditional anthropol-ogy is actually one of the more theoretical disciplines, marked by a gen-eralized reluctance to engage in public debate and a marked aversion to public controversy. As Ralph Bishop once remarked, Margaret Mead dead is better journalistic copy than most living anthropologists.[11]

To the extent that most anthropology students are still trained to be researchers and academics, they are unfamiliar with and unprepared for the demands of development work. Many of them lack an understanding of how policy-relevant knowledge—and its creation—differs from tradi-tional field research. They find the notion of working for clients uncom-fortable, and they are particularly ill at ease with the requirements for partisanship, advocacy, confidentiality, accountability, and loss of auton-omy that agency work often necessitates.

Profession and Discipline

To a great extent, development anthropology does not constitute a sepa-rate, identifiable profession, but has remained at the level of a pure disci-pline.

A discipline is a worldview, a way of generating understanding about the world, based on a set of rules and precepts. To a discipline, knowl-edge is inherently fascinating, but its utility is not necessarily either as-sumed or sought. A discipline's conversation, so to speak, is largely with itself.

A profession, in contrast, strives to *make* knowledge useful. Although a profession is theoretically based, it is essentially outward-looking, and its conversations, consequently, are largely with clients. A profession exists in relation to a universe or body of groups and individuals who value what the profession claims to offer, and are willing to pay for it.[12] A profession is flexible and responsive to the needs of its market, alert to similarities as well as differences that exist between it and other professional communities.

Professions usually engage in problem solving for relatively unambiguous ends—health, profit, justice, and so forth. A profession generally encompasses a clearly defined realm of problems or issues, and claims ownership of a body of knowledge, technique, or understanding that is particularly—perhaps even uniquely—suited to the diagnosis and resolution of problems within this realm.

In these terms, anthropology is not yet a profession, and the knowledge that anthropologists tend to produce is seen by the public as interesting rather than useful.[13] Within the academy, there is still intense debate over how far anthropology should go in pursuit of public goals, what means and methods should be used, and what roles anthropologists should adopt. Some within the discipline argue that the most that one can expect from anthropologists is to be providers of esoteric information, ex post facto critics, or—at most—advocates for the downtrodden.

Others disagree. One development anthropologist commented: "The notion of a value-free, non-directed applied science that is uninterested in achievement is absurd. Most anthropologists . . . are crippled as applied scientists because they are unwilling—or simply unable—to accept service in the search for improvement as a measure of professional performance."[14]

CHANGING THE ACADEMY

Like the development industry, anthropology itself is in need of reform, if it is to be truly effective in development work. The growth of practice has vastly altered the career choices available to anthropology graduates, but academic training still focuses almost exclusively on preparing them for academic careers, even as the rapidly growing practitioner community continues to define and develop itself in ways that continue to distinguish them from their university-based colleagues.

Despite the growth of practice, many traditional anthropology departments seem barely aware of job possibilities for their students outside of the academy. If members of the academy do sometimes acknowledge the presence of this market, they do not necessarily see it as their job to prepare students for it in any meaningful way. This attitude perpetuates a situation in which each succeeding cohort of anthropology graduates finds itself essentially unprepared for the world outside the university, and where each cohort must learn to work in this world, not from their professors, but from each other.

Fortunately, this is beginning to change, thanks to various practitioner-organized activities.[15] For development anthropologists in particular, the most important source of extrauniversity support has been the Institute for Development Anthropology. This organization is discussed in more detail in Mini-Case 10.1.

Professional Schools of Anthropology?

Becoming a profession will mean altering many things about what we do, starting with how we train our students. An anthropology department committed to training practitioners would more closely resemble the professional schools that exist for law, medicine, engineering, or public administration, where training is oriented less to the needs of the discipline than to the needs of the market.[16]

A professional school of anthropology would differ from its current academic counterpart in several important ways. It would teach new skill sets together with more traditional offerings, and would provide opportunities for interdisciplinary coursework and project work during training. It would explore different ways to provide field experience, using models from service learning and cooperative education. Finally, it would bring experienced practitioners themselves into the training process as equal partners with their academic colleagues.

Bringing Practice In. Because they are largely excluded from the academy, practitioners have little influence on the structure and content of academic training for anthropologists. One result, therefore, is that anthropology students have few professional role models within the university. Intending practitioners are taught by academicians, individuals who, whatever their research, writing, theorizing, and teaching skills, may never have worked in an applied setting. They cannot really serve as a model for practice the way, say, a consulting engineer, doctor, lawyer, or business school specialist can. They have neither the professional networks nor the hands-on experience with application problems that are so important in preparing students for the marketplace.

Many if not most of anthropologists who have been involved with development work as practitioners—in some cases for decades—have had

MINI-CASE 10.1   THE INSTITUTE FOR
DEVELOPMENT ANTHROPOLOGY

In 1976, three anthropologists—Michael Horowitz, Thayer Scudder, and David Brokensha—set up the Institute for Development Anthropology (IDA), with the aim of applying the approaches and insights of anthropology to efforts to improve the condition of the world's poor. "Although anthropologists are well aware of the fact that development as planned and implemented has not worked out as it was supposed to and have documented adverse effects in case studies and general articles, there is little agreement in the profession as to what should be done about the situation" (Scudder 1988: 366).

Based in Binghamton, New York, the institute grew slowly into one of the most outstanding examples of applied social science, engaging in a wide range of research, training, and project development activities. IDA has an advisory council, a college of fellows, and a database of hundreds of associates, who are all development specialists of one sort or another. In addition to anthropologists, these include economists, engineers, agronomists, and others.

IDA's intention was to provide social science input to the development industry of such high quality that it could not be ignored. Although the institute has been highly critical at times of the development industry, it is committed to working with existing structures to improve development planning and implementation, and in particular by focusing the skills of anthropologists on problems of world poverty, thereby increasing anthropology's voice and influence within the industry.

Scudder (1988: 371–373) has explained this orientation in clear and succinct terms: "Our problems are not so much with the goals of such agencies as AID and the World Bank . . . *but with the difficulties these agencies face in implementing these goals*" (emphasis in original).

As to why IDA became involved in large engineering projects, Scudder provides a pragmatic answer:

The point is this: regardless of its ideological stance and the nature of a nation's political economy, large-scale river basin development projects are going to continue. The options, therefore, are to stand on the sidelines complaining about the negative impacts of such projects but having relatively little effect on their number, location, design and purpose, or to try to influence—both from within and, where necessary, from without—their planning, implementation, and management in ways that incorporate local populations in project benefits

(continues)

MINI-CASE 10.1 (continued)

in an environmentally sound way. That is what the Institute for Development Anthropology is trying to do.

IDA's first grant was from USAID for a workshop on rural development. Soon, IDA was involved in development efforts in the Sahel. Eventually, they extended themselves into Asia and Latin America, North Africa and the Middle East, and into China.

IDA's activities have spanned virtually all development sectors and concerns: resettlement, rural-urban linkages, household production systems, pastoralism, agricultural extension and marketing, rural cooperatives, river basin development, community forestry, and employment generation.

One of their most successful undertakings has been the multiyear program of research carried out in the Senegal River Valley. Not only was this work begun well in advance of planning for river basin development, but it also developed some innovative methodologies for data collection and analysis.

IDA's main funding sources are USAID, the World Bank, FAO, and the UNDP. Other donors that fund IDA activities include the Inter-American Development Bank, the OECD, the International Fund for Agricultural Development, the National Science Foundation, the Ford Foundation, and the World Conservation Union.

The institute has attracted funding from all of the major donors, has participated in the planning and management of development projects and policies around the world, and has produced an impressive list of publications on important aspects of development, including over twenty monographs and nearly 100 working papers. IDA's newsletter, the *Development Anthropology Network*, has been in existence since 1981.

In a 1994 article, Horowitz outlined some of the salient contributions that anthropology has made to our understanding of development. Most of them stem, directly or indirectly, from the work of IDA professionals.

- Anthropologists have provided critical understanding of development processes.
- Anthropologists have demonstrated the need for in-depth social research as an integral part of development planning, and have convinced donors to support this.
- The results of this research have led directly to recommendations for changes and improvements in the ways in which development is carried out.

(continues)

MINI-CASE 10.1   *(continued)*

- Anthropologists have moved into leadership roles in projects, and are now involved in many more aspects of development planning and implementation—including policymaking—than before.
- Anthropologists have begun to connect cultural issues with environmental issues, and have forged links across disciplines to broaden our understanding of how these are related.

IDA has played a particularly useful and crucial role in bringing local people into development in a number of different ways. IDA has played a key role in training younger professionals and in collecting and disseminating information about development. They have organized numerous training workshops and other programs.

IDA has also been instrumental in several rather far-reaching policy discussions. Their work with pastoral systems, river basin development, and resettlement have produced serious academic work combined with related policy changes.

Finally, IDA has been at the forefront in using Third World social scientists in their work. These specialists have been involved in the development of projects, programs, and policies, and have helped collect needed data and analyze it. Host country social scientists now figure prominently among IDA research and development programs.

SOURCES: Brokensha 1986; M. Horowitz 1994; Scudder 1988.

---

neither the time nor the opportunity to share their findings, experiences, and insights with the discipline. One imperative, therefore, is to bring practitioners into the academy, if only on a temporary basis, and integrate them into training. This may require rethinking tenure, research, and publication arrangements, and creating special positions for practitioners, of both a temporary and a full-time nature.

Teaching Skills for Practice.   Skill sets are also important. Anthropologists working in development do one or more of three things: they collect and analyze *information;* they make *policy;* and they design and carry out *action.* And they do these things in context—that is, not theoretically or abstractly, but with specific reference to place, people, and project.

To do this, they need a specific combination of functional and technical skills.

TABLE 10.1 Skills for Anthropological Practitioners

Functional Skill Categories	What These Skills Do	Examples of What You Need to Know to Be Skilled
Finding Out	Uncovering salient facts within a specific context; asking the right questions and being able to understand the answers	Survey design; rapid assessment; literature and database search; interviewing; needs analysis
Analyzing and Learning	Figuring out what the facts mean within the context; figuring out what results and outcomes teach us	Data analysis; statistics; summarizing; checking; redesign; iterative methods
Communicating	Telling others what we've learned	Presentations; reports; briefings; teaching and training skills
Planning and Designing	Knowing how to get things done within the context; keeping things moving smoothly	Project and program design; proposal writing; budgeting; design of procedures
Managing	Being able to organize and sustain action toward established goals	Working with others; facilitation; decisionmaking; negotiation and conflict management; delegation and supervision
Judging	Measuring accomplishment and assessing what the results mean	Evaluating outcomes; troubleshooting and modification
Documenting	Writing our stories persuasively for different readerships	Reports, articles, briefings, monographs

These skills are best learned within programs that provide opportunities for application. Of particular importance would be practice-oriented field experience.

There are many models of field experience, from internships through field schools, cooperative work assignments, and service learning. Whatever the model chosen, it should involve significant time spent on project work in an other-cultural environment. The field experience should emphasize teamwork within organizations, exposure to project development activities, and the application of anthropological techniques (including rapid assessment procedures) to these.

Although fieldwork is a necessary condition for practitioner training, it is by no means sufficient. Other specific training in professional skills and abilities should be incorporated into the regular curriculum. Of particular importance is a reading program that extends beyond traditional anthropological texts to include the fundamentals of economics, public administration and other relevant disciplines, and practice in clear and effective writing for a professional—as opposed to academic—audience. Finally, skills should be developed in various areas of change management, including consulting, conflict resolution, and organizational analysis.

Changing Our Academic Culture

Teaching anthropology differently will mean changing the academic culture in important ways. One of these would involve departments taking more responsibility for connecting students with the world of practice. This would mean developing mentoring and networking programs, actively helping students with their job searches, tracking where graduates go and what they do, and developing strong alumni associations of practitioners.

Second, practice-oriented programs would need to be well connected with outside organizations if they are to help students succeed. Links to development organizations of all types need to be developed and maintained by programs.

Finally, to achieve professional credibility, programs will need to be willing and able to measure themselves against clear standards. These standards will be set, by and large, by clients, not by academic peers.

THE WAY AHEAD

Our discipline cannot contribute effectively to the public dialogue on development unless it is also willing to learn from that dialogue. Developing anthropologists who are reflective practitioners is an essential step in this process.

Finding Our Voice and
Leading the Development Agenda

In the past, few other specialists cared to visit areas of the world that anthropology took as its field, and the professional community was content to let anthropology be its main point of contact with exotic and remote areas. Today, thanks to improved travel and communication, much of what anthropology knows and does is accessible to others. Other disciplines now move confidently through areas once considered our private preserves. Like old-style Sovietologists, the raw material that we used to trade in is now much more freely available on the open market. Ethnographic methods and qualitative analysis, once the almost exclusive domain of anthropology and a few sociologists, is now being taught—and used—in a variety of other contexts, for example, nursing schools, education classes, and so on. Others now can and do check our facts and interpretations.

Does this mean that anthropology is on the way out in fields such as development? That there is no further place for someone with an anthropologist's skills and training? Not at all. But today, anthropology needs to make decisions about what it knows, what it can do, and how this can be presented to others.

It is clear that the way ahead for international development efforts must involve both the acknowledgment of difference and the incorporation of these differences into satisfactory and sustainable working relationships between partners. Anthropology's most valuable contribution to development probably lies in this area, more than any other. If anthropology can make the necessary changes within itself, it has a chance to lead the development agenda. The creation of a new development paradigm (the subject of the next chapter) is unlikely to occur from within the industry as presently constituted. But the broad characteristics of the paradigm, to a large extent, are things with which anthropology is already familiar, and where it can lead, rather than follow.

The new development paradigm will, of necessity, place people at the center of planning, and allow local preferences and practices to assume the determinant role in both process and outcome. Although the key elements in this paradigm are obvious, it will remain for a professionally trained group of anthropological practitioners, working together with others, to establish and elaborate it.

The biggest single thing we'll need to do is to get more anthropologists into policymaking roles within the development industry. Years ago, Laura Nader urged us to "study up"—today, we also need to "move up"; to take a more central role in development policy and planning. Such a role is natural for anthropology.

During the past thirty years, anthropological practice—and particularly development anthropology—has come into its own. The experience of practice has been the primary catalyst for a profound paradigm shift within anthropology, a shift whose final dimensions are as yet only dimly outlined. The professional application of anthropology to development work will demand new skills and abilities from anthropologists. These, in turn, will generate new insight.

The first generation of anthropologist practitioners are already at work in that world. It is the next generation of practitioners that will secure anthropology's place in the great public forum. We owe it to them—and to the rest of the world—to begin training them for the important tasks which lie ahead.

SUMMARY OF CHAPTER 10

Chapter 10 has looked at anthropology as a discipline, in terms of how well it has been able to respond to the needs and demands of development.

Despite considerable recent success with getting anthropologists into planning and policymaking, there are still problems with the application of anthropology to development needs. These do not arise because anthropology is irrelevant to development, but primarily because anthropology graduates do not receive the type of training that would equip them to operate outside the academic sphere.

To become more effective at development work, anthropology must become a profession, not simply a discipline. This in turn will mean changing the way in which graduates are trained. Specifically, graduates need to be equipped with skill sets that are relevant to development work and effective at getting anthropology's insights into planning and practice. If the necessary changes can be made within our discipline, anthropology has a chance to lead the development agenda in the future.

ENDNOTES

1. See Batalla (1966).

2. Most observers note the conflicted and sometimes ambiguous roles that anthropologists have in development agencies (see Gardner and Lewis 1996: 131–132 for Britain, for example).

3. Not all anthropologists, of course, are unfamiliar with interdisciplinary teamwork. Few detailed accounts exist of exactly how an interdisciplinary conversation occurs in the field, but for an interesting example, see Bentley and Andrews (1991), which focuses on the differing (and often complementary)

perspectives that an anthropologist and an entomologist brought to a pest management project in Honduras.

4. Gatter (1993: 177) puts it this way: "Though anthropologists working in multi-disciplinary research teams will assert, at a practical level, the need to learn the languages of other specialists, there is a tendency for anthropologists to take apart [those] languages and look at what kinds of premise they are based on, thereby appearing to subvert the work of others. This does not make for easy professional relationships."

5. Morey and Morey (1994: 20).

6. Hamilton (1973: 128–129) provides a discussion of this example that is particularly illuminating.

7. Hoben (1984: 16–17).

8. This is not an altogether bad thing, of course. Indeed, I would argue that one of the reasons anthropological practitioners have had such a difficult time both in the development industry and in the academy is because they report from the frontlines, as it were, and the news they bring is often disturbing and unsettling. Practicing anthropologists, in truth, live and work in worlds that bureaucrats and academicians often only write about.

9. Simmonds (1985: 51).

10. Rhoades (in Pottier 1993b: 14) thinks that such piecemeal involvement leads directly to project failure. Even if they are brought in at the right time, their position—both to them and to others—may be uncertain and ambiguous (compare with Hamilton 1973: 120–127).

11. *American Anthropological Association Newsletter* (April 1985).

12. See Greenwood (1957) for more discussion.

13. Hoben (1984).

14. Fleuret (1987: 217).

15. I have already mentioned the important role of local practitioner organizations. Other groups, such as Practical Gatherings, now organize training and discussion sessions on a wide variety of practice-related topics in major cities and at professional meetings. These alternative forms of practitioner education will probably grow in number and importance.

16. Although there are now several dozen training programs in the United States (see Trotter 1988), we still do not have anything resembling a true professional school.

chapter 11

___

A NEW DEVELOPMENT
PARADIGM?

WHERE WE ARE

Development is humanity's first global project, carrying enormous risk as
well as high promise. Although ending world poverty is now within our
means in a technical sense, it is increasingly unclear as to whether we
have either the political will or the sensitivity and intelligence to accomplish this. Our early optimism that everyone could live a decent life,
and that this would not take very long to achieve, now looks naive
and—to some—hopeless.

Poverty has become regionalized and virtually institutionalized in
some areas. Growing populations and shrinking resources add to already
existing tensions between groups. In some areas, warfare and crime—often indistinguishable from each other—have pushed development priorities off the table altogether, as people battle for dominance or simple
survival.

Today, international development is a veritable industry, dominated by
a small but powerful group of multilateral organizations, among them the
World Bank, regional development banks, and various agencies of the
UN. These organizations control most development finance and have the
lion's share of many of the other resources necessary for development, including information, personnel, and influence. Such agencies function
largely independently of democratic control, and although each has a distinct institutional personality, all are tied together in a variety of ways.

Although these larger development agencies have steadily increased their influence and power, particularly among the world's poorer countries, they now operate in an increasingly distant fashion, removed from the daily realities of poverty and need. The recent trend toward market-driven globalization has only reinforced this movement away from the grass roots.

To an increasing extent, concern is being expressed in the West and elsewhere over the goals and procedures of this industry and over the extent to which it actually can accomplish its original purposes. The initial energy that accompanied U.S. involvement in the Third World, based on an optimistic vision of economic and political liberalism, has been replaced by fatigue and pessimism, the goals of development largely subordinated to diplomatic, security, and market interests.

Today, development is increasingly capital-centered rather than people-centered, and is guided by an economic model that is itself framed by the intersection of technology and market behavior.[1] Private capital, as we have seen, now dwarfs official development aid. But private aid flows are markedly uneven; investment choices are governed by the possibility of profits, not by development priorities or considerations of need, equity, or sustainability.

There is no doubt that in important ways globalization has eroded state power in some countries, and made most countries more dependent on the market. In this sense, it could be argued that development efforts have been absorbed by globalization trends, and that today, development has come to be seen, more and more, as linked to issues of world trade and economic competition.[2]

In this vision, there is virtually no room for consideration of local cultural factors. Bodley comments: "Global poverty has been consistently treated as a technological problem partly because professional elites who are far removed from the daily realities of poverty formulate and finance development policies. Development . . . has become a thoroughly institutionalized and highly complex industry with important political and economic functions for the wealthy donors, which may be unrelated to the needs of the poor."[3]

Although it is widely recognized that these models and approaches are flawed, agencies have been slow to develop alternative methodologies. They learn with difficulty if at all, and have few compelling incentives to change the way they operate. For these agencies, development is increasing defined by them—and for others—as "that which we do."

It is time, clearly, to rethink development.

OPPORTUNITY AND DANGER

The gradual spread of global commerce, communication, and transport has given us the illusion that we now have more control over events in the world, and therefore more collective security, whereas in many respects, we probably have less. Indeed, increasing economic integration seems to be accompanied by rising levels of ethnic and regional conflict.[4]

Problems once viewed as confined to the Third World are now recognized as having global spread and significance. The AIDS epidemic is one case in point, but there are many others. Issues of the environment, migration and immigration, women's rights, child labor, crime, inflation, and unemployment are now thoroughly global in their scope and impact, affecting rich and poor alike. Within the wealthy industrialized countries, questions of growth, distribution, sustainability, participation, and the environment—heretofore considered primarily as "development" issues—are now part of every national policy dialogue.

The emerging global system carries with it an implicit version of reality—a culture—that limits to a large extent our thinking about events and situations. Driven by the needs of producers and marketers, this new culture places its faith in the market, and counts money as the measure of most things. It tends to view the world in abstract quantitative terms and to ignore local details unless they are directly and obviously relevant to profit and loss. It assumes scarcity, competition, and individual action, and is comfortable with—or indifferent to—the notion of losers as well as winners. It is rooted in no one particular popular or elite tradition, and is located nowhere in particular except perhaps cyberspace.[5]

What impact this system will have on problems of poverty and inequality remains to be seen.[6] Some observers feel that globalization, left unchecked, will impose a kind of natural selection on the world's cultures, creating a competitive arena in which some will win at global games, and others will lose.

Such a scenario raises troubling questions. Are we headed into a world characterized by a few hugely wealthy countries surrounded by a sea of poorer, overpopulated ones? Or are we all destined to become poorer and more desperate as available resources shrink?[7] Can we solve problems of poverty, at the same time preserving the richness and integrity of the world's diverse cultures? Or will we, so to speak, wind up destroying the village in our attempt to save it?

Our dilemma is very simple: To continue industrial growth along present lines will ultimately endanger everyone on the planet. To deny poor countries the opportunity to industrialize, however, may condemn them to permanent poverty.[8]

The greatest danger is not that we will do nothing, but that we will simply continue as before. In the view of many, industrialization, population growth, and the continuing exploitation of the earth's natural resources are essentially taken for granted. The resulting problems will be solved, it is assumed, by further advances in technology. Others of course disagree:

> The answer cannot be more of the same. And the answer is surely more than simply hoping for the best, more than vague ideas about "strengthening over time the institutional forms and activities associated with global society." Simplistic exhortations to "accelerate the transfer of technology" after decades of disastrous technology transfer, are not only counter-productive, they are (and here, the percussion) *stupid.*[9] [emphasis in the original]

Relaunching Development

For all of these reasons, it is imperative to relaunch the faltering development effort. In order to do this, we need to imagine—and then create— an image of the future that is different from simply an extension of what we have now, and where current trends, left unchecked, seem bound to take us.

Anthropology has an unparalleled opportunity to lead this change. Despite the setbacks and the frustrations of the past development decades, anthropology has accumulated a valuable store of experience about what works and what does not. For anthropologists, the present challenge is to find ways to use their experience wisely and effectively. But the world does not necessarily need more anthropologists; it needs more anthropology professionals, capable of translating our discipline's considerable insights into useful ideas and strategies for building a better collective future than the one we seem to be, largely by default, constructing for ourselves.

Two contradictory tendencies are at work as we face the task of relaunching development. On the one hand, some observers detect a certain world-weariness among Americans. Exhausted from the Cold War, no longer convinced that their daily lives are connected with events beyond the shoreline, many people in the United States and elsewhere in the developed world seem increasingly reluctant to invest the time, energy, and resources in helping the less fortunate.[10]

On the other hand, Americans are still, in the view of some, intent on transforming the world in their own image. One observer comments: "Americans are the worst example of the coming world, wherein technology, automation, and the marketplace will dominate. They are loud, bold, full of themselves, socially inept in international affairs, yet good-hearted and charitable to a fault. They are preoccupied with success measured in dollars, material possessions, fun and leisure activities, and most important, they want everybody else to be just like them."[11]

Neither of these will work for very long. What is needed is a reengagement with the developing world, but on equal and respectful terms. This can only be done if we first transform our basic notion of what development is.

A NEW DEVELOPMENT PARADIGM

What Do We Know So Far?

A *paradigm* is a way of seeing, a framework to guide action; a "mutually supporting pattern of concepts, values, methods."[12] The present development paradigm is ethnocentric, largely unsuited to the realities of the developing world. Development, in this view, is growth, technology is its engine, and quantification is its measure. It assumes that people are rational actors making individual decisions primarily in terms of short-term individual benefit, that this benefit is economically defined, and that this occurs in more or less the same way across the globe. The paradigm further assumes that technical advances are essentially the same thing as progress, that growth can continue indefinitely, and that any problems that we may encounter along the way can ultimately be solved by new technology.

At the moment, the development industry sees its mission as one of providing "opportunities" to the developing world, via transfers of money and technology. These opportunities turn out, most of the time, to be pale copies of what the West has. The policies and arrangements that guide this transfer do not need to be tailored to fit, and can be basically plugged in. This mode of operation permits the poor of the world to choose from the options presented, but does not allow them any real choices of their own. They become owners and operators of existing models, rarely creators of their own. The technicist model tends to inhibit local expression and create structures of dependency, thereby weakening the mechanisms by which people might develop and express their own visions of betterment.

But our experience with development over the past fifty years reveals fundamental shortcomings in this paradigm. For one thing, quantification alone cannot provide us with adequate or accurate indicators of the quality of life, and aggregate measures give us no useful information about how gains and losses may be distributed. For another, a focus on short-term economic gain pays much less attention than it should to issues of long-term sustainability in broader and less economic senses.

Most important, the current paradigm fails to link development activities to their surrounding context. Actions are isolated and discrete, experiments performed *on* the environment rather than *within* the environment.

Because the local context is so often disregarded, our development institutions have built up very little understanding about this context and how to operate within it. At the same time, however, development projects often succeed—by design or by default—in altering these contexts in negative ways.

It is becoming increasingly clear that in development work, one size does not fit all; that policies and prescriptions emanating from the world's financial capitals cannot serve as the basis for a sustainable response to problems of poverty and inequality. We are beginning to comprehend the fundamental importance of according primacy to local reality in our plans and policies, of involving local actors, and of connecting those at the top of the hierarchy with those at the bottom. And we are beginning to accept that doing this successfully will take much longer—and be much harder—than we originally imagined.[13]

Ironically, the end of the Cold War has not opened up new possibilities for development, but rather has restricted them. Whereas before there were at least two competing ideologies and visions of the world to come, now there is really only one.[14] At the same time, there is the realization that few countries that received aid and development assistance in the past under either arrangement have succeeded in "developing" along the desired lines.[15]

It is clear that we have reached—or are about to reach—the limits of the current model of development. A new approach is needed.

The Goals of a New Paradigm

Our attempts to solve problems of poverty have been hampered by an approach that is too culturally specific and that does not encourage us to learn about—and use—cultural diversity. A new development paradigm must be one in which all of the world's cultures can participate as equal partners, and one through which, furthermore, we can all learn what we do not yet know, even as we make progress toward our common goals.

The fundamental premise underlying the creation of a new paradigm is that what we must understand in order to make development successful is not contained in any *one* cultural system, but in the dialogue and interaction *between* cultural systems.

Creating a new development paradigm would therefore begin by reversing current practices, by letting the world's poor define goals and priorities, and by building up our knowledge and wisdom from below.[16] ". . . The best definition [of development] would appear to create a process in which people's own voices define development rather than accept imposed definitions. Those voices must be male and female, rich and poor, in—and outside—the state. To enhance voice, people must be able to make choices about their lives—lives that are not dangling at the margin of survival—in a political structure accountable to them."[17]

Ideally, this would produce a kind of "cosmopolitan localism" where local problems could be addressed in ways compatible with the solution of more global issues.[18] For it is clear that at a certain level, the problems facing rich and poor are identical: how to increase prosperity and decrease negative side effects.[19]

Elements of the New Paradigm

A new development paradigm would contain several key elements.

Place and People.   To begin with, we will need to change our technicist view of development into one centered on people and place. Development planning must become highly context-specific, integrating local cultures into its models and processes, and using local resources to carry out its plans. In this way, people—and the physical environment they inhabit—become beneficiaries and partners, not obstacles to be overcome.[20]

Plans and practices introduced in the name of development must then seek to expand human capabilities and enhance the value of the surrounding environment. Particular attention would need to be paid to at-risk situations within this context. These might be social—as in the case of marginalized or disadvantaged groups—or physical—involving, for example, fragile ecosystems. The new paradigm would recognize that human and environmental problems cannot be addressed in isolation from other another.

It is possible, of course, and others have pointed out, that a development paradigm centered on people might not always find economic growth (at least as presently defined and conceived) at the top of one's list of needs and wants. Indeed, it is likely that much of what the poor actually want will be either incompatible with, or irrelevant to, the dominant development paradigm.[21] This incompatibility, of course, is an additional reason why large agencies have, in the past, found it difficult to "hear" the people they purported to serve.

Process. A World Bank official once observed, apropos development, that "what you get is how you do it."[22] A focus on context will require planners to involve people fully in the decisions and actions that affect their lives, determine their futures, and connect them with others across the planet. As we have seen in Chapter 6, participation in project development can take many forms, and these should be adapted to the requirements of the local context. In the process of participation, stakeholder capacities must be enhanced and extended to permit local populations to better control future events. Some NGOs have gone beyond this, adopting a rights-based approach to development that incorporates standards such as diligence, nondiscrimination, accountability, and redress, drawn from human rights legislation.[23]

Sustainability. The new development paradigm must also emphasize sustainability. One aspect of sustainability is of course environmental, requiring minimum disruption of local ecological processes and maximum conservation of materials and energy. A second aspect concerns the institutionalization or sustainability of program arrangements and outcomes. It is relatively easy to design projects for short-term results, but much harder to do this in ways that will stand the test of time. Institutionalization, not mere innovation, is the true indicator of social change.[24]

Learning. Finally, doing development should make us wise. Our actions should be based on a learning model that helps everyone involved understand how and why we get the results we do and how to use this learning to improve future outcomes. For local populations, a learning orientation will help build local capacities for the planning and management of change. For outside specialists, a learning orientation will break down the barriers to interdisciplinary collaboration, enabling individuals to enhance their skills and experience though a process of comparison and contrast with others. For agencies, a learning orientation will enable them to steadily improve processes and practices and to learn and remember the lessons of experience. A concern with context will necessarily require the development industry at all levels to become more open to change and learning, and to be both responsive and accountable to those they purport to serve.

Implications for Development Work

The adoption of such a paradigm would have profound effects on the way development is done. Methodologies for the discovery and incorporation of local cultural and environmental factors would improve considerably, and would play a central rather than a marginal role in planning.

Agencies and individual specialists would become much more tolerant of discrepant information, and skilled in working with it to produce results acceptable to a wider range of stakeholders. Planning would need to become more decentralized and flexible to facilitate decisions that match local realities.

Development would focus not just on plans and outcomes but on process, particularly on ways to involve local populations as controlling partners, at the same time building their capacities in directions that allow them to extend themselves in new areas of endeavor.

Development outcomes would be measured and evaluated not just in terms of quantifiable material goals, but also in terms of spread, equity, and follow-on effects.

Such an approach would require us to listen and learn before we act, and to work with local stakeholders to design interventions that are truly needed, that can be fully supported locally, and that will involve all partners in a mutually reinforcing process of learning and capacity development.

There are signs that a paradigm shift or change is now beginning to happen.[25] The needed changes will not, however, be easy:

> The shift toward equitable, sustainable and participatory development requires a whole new culture in which organizations think of sustainable development in terms of whole communities in relation to their respective habitats, rather than in terms of sector-specialized enterprises and capital projects. It demands a whole new discipline to combine in feasibility appraisals, such that social and ecological criteria are integrated with economic criteria. A new breed of managers must emerge that manages communities toward integral goals where economic efficiency is defined to

include social equity and ecological wholeness as integral outputs from the use of resources.[26]

Mini-Case 11.1, "We Have Met the Enemy and He Is Us," looks at how the work of one development specialist reflects the slow but steady emergence of this new paradigm.

The differences in viewpoint and approach that characterize the various "real worlds" of the development encounter can lead us to sustainable solutions, but only if we can learn to tap the storehouse of creativity and innovation contained within the diversity of the world's cultures. Development work represents a chance for us to use human cultural diversity as a way to both shape and achieve a coherent vision of the future. The ability to work across different cultural worlds, as we have seen, requires a particularly anthropological approach to learning, understanding, and doing, and is, finally, more than just a set of skills—it is a way of thinking.[27]

CHANGING THE WAY OUR INSTITUTIONS THINK

Changing our development paradigm will mean changing the institutions that do development. A society's institutions, as Mary Douglas reminds us, shape the way we think about problems, and—more important—determine to a large extent the solutions seen as available and acceptable.[28]

Institutions seek to stabilize and classify the surrounding environment, assigning "rightness" to certain ideas and initiatives and "wrongness" to others. In this way, they organize our public memory and block, to some extent at least, our public imagination. To an important extent, therefore, these institutional cultures create and shape reality.

Large development agencies define, in ways large and small, what development is, for the world at large. The agencies frame our perception of problems, direct our analysis of alternative solutions to these problems, and influence our judgments about the results obtained. Since development agencies, like all such institutions, tend to believe that they see the world as it is, development becomes that which they do. In important ways, the institutional forms and cultures we have allowed to evolve for development purposes function today not only as important obstacles to effective development, but to our very understanding of what effective development might be.[29]

MINI-CASE 11.1
WE HAVE MET THE ENEMY AND HE IS US:
THE WIT AND WISDOM OF ROBERT CHAMBERS

Robert Chambers, one of the most influential thinkers in development practice today, is also a poet. He is a much better development thinker than a poet. He has pioneered much of the rapid appraisal movement, and his writings on "rural development tourism" have been widely read.

Chambers is a rare bird: a fully committed, very experienced development professional who is highly critical of the development industry, and who has managed to make his voice and his ideas heard at the highest levels.

The visions of the 1950s and 1960s for a better world with full employment, decent incomes, universal primary education, health for all, safe water supplies, a demographic transition to stable populations, and fair terms of trade between rich and poor countries, have in no case been realized. The beliefs of those times—in linear and convergent development through stages of growth, in central planning, in unlimited growth, in industrialization as the key to development, in the feasibility of a continuous improvement in levels of living for all—these have now been exposed as misconceived and, with the easy wisdom of hindsight, naïve. (1997b: 1)

Chambers has moved, seemingly without effort, between the worlds of academia, the development industry, and the grass roots. His books, written simply but persuasively, have been aimed at practitioners at all levels. His articles, published in a wide variety of journals, have reached an even wider audience. Despite his sometimes scathing criticisms of the development industry and the professionals who work within it, he has been an influential and respected voice within the development community.

Although Chambers acknowledges the frustration and discouragement that has accompanied development efforts, he is optimistic. "This is a good time to be alive as a development professional. For we seem to be in the middle of a quiet but hugely exciting revolution in learning and action" (1997b: xvii).

Chambers believes a new development paradigm is coming: less centralized, more heterogeneous, and less dominated by "experts." This emerging paradigm will have people at its center, and well-being will be defined by the poor themselves. Progress will not be tied to a Western unilinear model. Instead, it will be open-ended and flexible. The emerging consensus on this new vision of development is contained in five key terms, as outlined below.

(continues)

MINI-CASE 11.1 (continued)

Five Aspects of Development

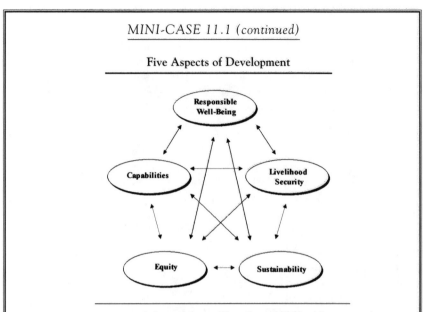

SOURCE: Adapted from Chambers 1997b: 10.

In Chambers's view, development professionals themselves are the main obstacle to the emergence of this new paradigm, and it is therefore through changes in the ways professionals think that we will find development solutions. He says:

> I am referring to us as a group. . . . The radical activist in a remote village in Bihar may not identify with the president of the World Bank, nor he with her. But we are all actors in the same "upper" system of organization and communication which is even better linked; and our decisions and actions impinge on those in the "lower" system of local rural and urban people and places. We are all trying to change things for others, we say for the better. We are all development professionals. (1997b: 3)

Development professionals, in a word, need to learn to *see differently:* "The early project process is dominated by engineers and economists, and preoccupations with infrastructure, budgets, schedules and quantification. The way professional and organizations think and operate biases the process against poor people"(1993: 76).

Chambers believes that wrong thinking is embedded in the concepts, values, and methods that many development professionals use, which come from their disciplines and their training. It is not the poor and powerless who have been wrong in development, Chambers says; it is us: "Per-

(continues)

---

haps the most neglected aspect of development is the personal psychology of what powerful professionals believe and do" (1997b: 232).

Chambers is highly critical of the development industry, as his poems (which are sprinkled throughout his books) show.

> Beneficiaries here I come
> Donor with a tidy sum
> Father Christmas is my name
> Spending targets are the game
> All will gain, that is the notion
> You get cash, I get promotion
> Help me be a good provider
> Open up your mouths much wider
> What I bring is sure to please
> Sacks with stacks of free goodies
> All you have to do is take 'em
> Evaluations? We can fake 'em. (1997b: 225)

Those who serve the industry also come under fire:

> Consultants with contracts to win
> wear colors they know to be "in"
> Chameleons, they
> fake a fashion display
> Camouflaging for cash is no sin. (1997b: 212)

As do academics:

> And northern academics too
> are seasonal in their global view
> For they are found in third world nations
> mainly during long vacations. (1983: 21)

He reserves most scorn, however, for economics, which he has termed a "cult."

Economists differ from dogs in several ways. But some behavior can be similar, as in the principle of the lamp-post. Dogs leave boundary marking signatures on lamp-posts, and mad dogs chase their tails. Some economists look for answers not in the dark areas where they are to be found, but under the lamp-post where they can see numbers in light. they, too, mark their boundaries of professional specializa-

(continues)

MINI-CASE 11.1 (continued)

tion, illuminated by the circularity of reductionism and measurement." (1997b: 53–54)

The result of such "professionalism," he says, is standardized thinking and standardized development prescriptions at odds with local needs and realities. Development fads and fashions (for example, basic needs, equity, governance, and so on) originate in the cores, and are imposed on the peripheries.

> Old Henry Ford the First, now dead
> reputedly, while living, said
> Americans should never lack
> their Model-Ts, so long as black.
> This way of thinking still persists
> Professionals are reductionists
> And bureaucrats embrace the norm
> that programs should be uniform.
> The poor are look-alikes and weak
> We know their needs. They need not speak.
> Our mass production's sure to please
> Let's make our programs Model-Ts. (1997b: 67)

Training produces experts versed in orthodoxy. A cognitive map of the way development professionals think, according to Chambers, would reveal a set of binary categories which shape perceptions, reactions, prescriptions, and plans. He describes these categories in simple terms: upper and lower, first and last, core and periphery. "Core" or "first" thinking characterizes the perspective of most development professionals, because they have been trained to think that way.

> The most brilliant and ambitious students are drawn to the master (more rarely, mistress) and are clever enough to learn the language. Having invested time, effort and their not inconsiderable ability in learning, they are co-opted by the concepts, modes of thought and jargon, and are bright enough to be able to use them. In this way a school may coalesce which talks to itself and impresses others in proportion to its self-sustaining separation from the world of real people. (1997b: 51)

He compares this with the people in Plato's cave: "Unwitting prisoners, professionals sit chained to their central places and mistake the flat shadows of figures, tables, reports, professional papers and printouts for the

(continues)

MINI-CASE 11.1   (continued)

rounded, dynamic, multi-dimensional substance of the world of those others at the peripheries" (1997b: 55).

Development professionals, by and large, do not see their worldview as culturally constructed. For most of them, it is a neutral and reasonably accurate—and useful—representation of the world as it is. Chambers presents numerous examples of how this worldview contrasts with others. Here, for example, are the contrasts between "core" and "peripheral" thinking regarding technology use in projects. Given these tendencies, he says, it is no wonder that engineering and economics carries more weight than anthropology.

Core Versus Peripheral Approaches to Project Development

Core or First	Peripheral or Last
Large-scale	Small-scale
Capital-intensive	Labor-intensive
Inorganic	Organic
Market-linked	Subsistence-linked
Mechanical	Human or animal-powered
Developed in the core	Developed in the periphery
"High" technology	'Low' technology

If we want to change what outside experts do, Chambers says, change the way they learn about rural conditions. This can be done, in his view, through a process of "reversals."

Reversals in thinking—for example, "putting the last first"—can change the way experts learn about rural conditions. This in turn will help offset bias and bring balance to their interactions with locals. Applying the notion of reversals to development practice, for example, would change a great deal of what professionals do. "For some professionals, development is still, consciously or unconsciously, seen as convergent; in the paradigm of reversals, development is decentralized and divergent. While normal bureaucracy and normal markets centralize, standardize and simplify, it is in contrast by becoming more complex and diverse that ecosystems and livelihood strategies become more stable and more sustainable" (1993: 120).

Chambers has outlined a set of simple principles for professionals to use in the work they do.

(continues)

MINI-CASE 11.1 (continued)

Reversals in Thinking

	Normal Tendencies	*Needed Reversals*
Behavior	Dominating	Facilitating
	Lecturing	Listening
	Extracting	Empowering
Professionalism	Things first	People first
	Men before women	Women before men
	Professionals set priorities	Poor people set priorities
	Technology packages	Technology choices
	Simplify	Complicate
Bureaucracy	Centralize	Decentralize
	Standardize	Diversify
	Control	Enable

SOURCE: Adapted from Chambers 1997b: 204.

- Sit down, listen, watch, and learn.
- Use your own best judgment at all times.
- Unlearn.
- Be optimally unprepared.
- Embrace error.
- Hand over the stick.
- They can do it.
- Ask them.
- Be nice to people. (1997b: 216)

Taking personal responsibility for one's work is central to Chambers's vision of the new development paradigm. "Basic to a new professionalism is the primacy of the personal. This recognizes the power of personal choice, the prevalence of error, and the potential for doing better in this thing called development. The personal, professional and institutional challenge is learning how to learn, learning how to change, and learning how to organize and act" (1997b: 14).

Chambers ends his last book this way: "We can have a vision of a future where . . . responsible well-being for uppers means privileging and respecting the realities of lowers; where development means change that is good for the poor in their terms, where it is their reality that counts.

"Why not? What stops us?" (1997b: 240).

SOURCE: R. Chambers, 1983, 1993, 1997b. Permission to use poetry granted.

Teaching our development institutions what they need to know must be done in many different ways, over time, with patience and persistence. Development is our grand human project. We can neither abandon it nor allow it to fail. But it is time to rethink its ends and its means, to reshape its structures and processes. In this process anthropology will play a central and critical role, but only if anthropologists themselves are equal to the challenge.

Anthropology has demonstrated its ability to contribute positively and innovatively to international development, but much more remains to be done. At the project level, we need to ensure that anthropologists are fully involved in all phases of project development, and that the perspectives that anthropology brings to development become an integral part of the way in which all projects are undertaken.

We also need to ensure that anthropology graduates are fully prepared to function effectively in the project environment. This will mean altering both the goals and the methods of professional training, ensuring that fundamentals are safeguarded at the same time.

Anthropologists will need to produce more and better documentation of the development experience from an explicitly anthropological viewpoint. As I have suggested earlier, one of our most useful contributions would be the creation of a body of development ethnographies, enabling us to better connect practice with theory.

Institutional and paradigmatic change will not come from piecemeal improvements to individual projects, nor will it come from critical articles written for a largely academic audience. It will only come when anthropology has become a fully-fledged profession, fully engaged in development work, no longer mainly on the sidelines. To the extent that we—through circumstance or by choice—remain fundamentally outside development structures, working primarily as hired hands, we will have only a marginal impact on the core activities, values, and priorities of the development industry.

There can be no more fitting arena for the application of what anthropology knows, no better dynamic for revitalizing and transforming a discipline into a profession, and no higher mission than the creation of a just, equitable, and prosperous future for all of humanity. Sue Estroff reminds us:

> The next decades will present us with choices we have avoided making explicitly and with intention for a very long time. The fabric and values of our culture will be stretched and revealed in many ways. Who is deserving?

What will we value most? Will we choose to be comfortable or comforting? . . . None of these agonizing choices can be made humanely without the kind of understanding of these "different others" and their worlds that anthropologists can provide.[30]

We have no other way, ultimately, to effect change on a global scale than through our institutions. These are human creations, built by us, products of our minds. As we created them, so can we reshape them.

And that, I suggest, should be the main goal of development anthropology in the years to come. If we neglect this task, then we—and the rest of the world—will continue to have development defined and done for us by organizations that know much less than they should.

SUMMARY OF CHAPTER 11

Chapter 11 has looked at the components of a new paradigm to guide development. The chapter began with an examination of globalization and its effects on efforts to eradicate poverty, and moved from that to a discussion of the need for a reconceptualization of development.

A new development paradigm, borrowing insights from anthropology, would be based on context as the key to successful development. Place and people would be central to the new paradigm, which would also emphasize local participation in planning and implementation, a concern for long-term sustainability, and finally an explicit learning orientation.

The adoption of such a paradigm will have profound and far-reaching consequences for the way in which development work is conceived and carried out. The understanding of cultural difference and its integration into plans and procedures would become a central part of development, rather than an afterthought. In order to change development thinking, we will need to change our development institutions.

Anthropology will play a central role in the development and application of this new paradigm and in the institutional transformations that accompany it. Anthropologists must continue their engagement with development at all levels, but particularly in the policy sphere, and find ways to make their contributions and insights both relevant to the needs of the developing world, and used by the agencies and institutions that operate there.

ENDNOTES

1. McMichael (1996: 11).

2. See McMichael (1996).

3. Bodley (1994: 339).

4. Emergency relief spending has increased by more than 500 percent since the early 1980s and now dominates foreign aid. Half of the funding of the UN agencies now goes for emergency relief. See J. Jones (1997: 111).

5. Black (1999: 2–4).

6. Horowitz (in Hanchette 1999: 47–48), for example, characterizes globalization as an "assault" on the family, producing several social costs whose true impact has yet to be measured. He asks: are people better off today as a result of development? If not, are we capable of putting the situation right?

7. Paul Kennedy (1993) notes: "It is inconceivable that the earth can sustain a population of 10 billion people devouring resources at the rate enjoyed by richer societies—or at even half that rate. Well before total world population reaches that level, irreparable damage to forests, water supplies and animal and plant species will have occurred, and many environmental thresholds may have been breached."

8. See Greider (1997).

9. Smillie (1995: 245).

10. See Zakaria (1998).

11. Naylor (1996: 96).

12. R. Chambers (1993: xvi).

13. See Dichter (1988: 177).

14. See Lewellen (1995: 249).

15. See also Grant and Nijman (1998: 6)

16. Hellinger et al. (1988: 179).

17. Staudt (1991: 272).

18. McMichael (1996: 256).

19. R. Chambers (1997b: 189).

20. One clear implication of putting people in the center of a new development paradigm—but one infrequently discussed—is that development will have to acquire a moral and ethical dimension. The current development model, as Tisch and Wallace (1994: 122) point out, has always lacked a moral sense, and ignores, for the most part, the social wreckage that its favored prescriptions—industrialization, mechanization, infrastructure development, and structural adjustment—are often apt to produce. Moran (1996: 229) states: "The moral goals of communities need to become part of the goals of development, and such goals are best seen as long-run in nature."

21. See Cobb (1999: 130).

22. Serageldin (1995).

23. Feeney (1998: 147–148).

24. Barth (1966).

25. See, for example, Finger and Verlaan (1995); Griesgraber and Gunter (1996); Korten (1997).

26. Roxas (1996: 22).

27. Fisher (1988: 131).

28. Douglas (1986: 92).

29. Finnemore (1997) discusses how this has operated to define poverty within the World Bank. As Finnemore points out, the organization of the Bank and the kinds of people the Bank employs constitute an elaborate filtering and transforming mechanism, taking in ideas at one end and turning these into policies, programs, and projects at the other end. Only certain ideas are taken in, of course, and only certain solutions are produced. Originally, development was conceived of as simply an attempt to raise GNP, and this was to be done through industrialization. This, in turn, was promoted through capital-intensive infrastructure projects. Between 1968 and the mid-70s, however, the alleviation of poverty was "discovered" by the Bank, and subsequently institutionalized. The Bank functions, therefore, as a major arbiter of development norms and meanings. One result of this is that until a problem, issue, opportunity, or concept has been "noticed" by the Bank, it does not really exist. And once it has been noticed, it tends to become, as it were, the Bank's intellectual property.

30. Estroff (1984).

appendix: becoming a
development anthropologist

*. . . there are no such things as anthropological problems,
there are only client problems or community problems.*[1]

To get a job in development, you'll need two essential things: *qualifications* that go well beyond just having a degree in anthropology; and an effective job search *strategy*. This appendix takes up these and other aspects of becoming a development anthropologist. We begin with the question of qualifications.

THRESHOLD QUALIFICATIONS

To a great extent, your training will determine your employability within the development industry. If you are already in school—or about to enter graduate school—you will need to make sure that your academic training is appropriate and useful. If you have already graduated, you may need to think about retraining yourself in some specific ways.

Although each development organization—and each job within it—will have specific needs and requirements, successful job seekers in development possess a set of specific *threshold qualifications* that get them in the door, so to speak, in a highly competitive job market.

There are four major threshold qualifications necessary for jobs in international development:

- Academic background
- Cross-cultural experience
- Language proficiency
- Workplace skills

You should have all of these in hand before beginning a serious job search. Threshold qualifications by no means guarantee you a job—they simply make you competitive in the marketplace. I'll take up these threshold qualifications one by one.

Academic Background

Although for some development jobs—particularly of a highly technical nature—a Ph.D. is necessary, the M.A. is quite acceptable for most entry-level jobs in international development.

Although no one course of study is required for international work, you need to be *generally* well grounded in the basics of international knowledge—through courses in area studies, history, geography, politics and economics, international affairs, and/or other clearly relevant subjects.

At the same time, you'll need the *specific* knowledge you get from anthropology. This lends you professional credibility and gives you certain essential tools, concepts, and networks helpful to you overseas.

The particular anthropology program you went through would probably be highly significant—and in some cases, determinant—if you were headed for an academic career, and your GPA would certainly be a factor. Sadly, perhaps, neither of these matter very much on the outside.

What *does* matter is how you have used your academic time to prepare yourself for a development career. Thus, the types of courses you've taken are important, as well as extracurricular activities you've chosen.

Coursework should include electives, where possible, from areas that complement your anthropology. For development work, courses in economics, management, and area studies are obviously going to be helpful. Courses in which you did independent research or carried out a project on your own will demonstrate to people that you have analytic skills and don't need extensive supervision. Courses where you collaborated with others to produce a group result will show that you have experience working with teams.

I'll say more later in this chapter about how you can use your time at the university to best advantage.

Cross-Cultural Experience

Employers are taking an enormous risk every time they send a new hire overseas. Since there's no sure-fire way to judge someone's suitability for overseas work, development organizations will be very interested in whether you've had previous experience in adjusting to new situations and people.

By insisting on this previous experience, employers hope to minimize the time it takes you to get up to speed. They also hope to minimize the risk of failure and maximize performance, by having you fit in quickly and smoothly with the overseas environment.

At the same time, you yourself will benefit enormously from the opportunity to experience another culture firsthand, and to practice applying your anthropological skills in that environment, *before* you go looking for a job.

Almost any international experience you've had will be to your advantage: summer abroad, semester abroad, work/study, travel, or volunteer experience. Service in the Peace Corps or similar organizations tends to be highly valued by

TABLE 12.1 Characteristics of Cross-Cultural Experience

Characteristics	Examples
Having to operate in a new or different frame of reference	Using another language; learning new technical procedures
Working in an unfamiliar environment	Working away from home
Working with people of a different background	Working with senior citizens, children, hospital patients, or people from a different ethnic or cultural group
Working with people who have a different value system	Working across lines of ethnicity, gender, socioeconomic class, or occupation
Working in a situation where two different value systems intersect	Working in a relief agency, community outreach organization, social service agency, police force, and so forth
Working in a situation of scarce resources	Working for a nonprofit group, charity organization, student group, and so on
Working in situations of ambiguity and/or uncertainty	Working for a political cause or campaign
Needing to be flexible in what you do	Working with community groups or on highly charged issues
Needing to learn in an uncertain environment, or under pressure	Research projects in unfamiliar areas; emergency response teams

most development agencies, since Peace Corps volunteers have spent several years overseas, often in difficult situations, usually emerging with a fluent grasp of at least one foreign language.

Even purely domestic experience will qualify, however, if it required you to develop cross-cultural sensitivities and skills. Domestic work in places or situations that are significantly out of your own cultural mainstream can be used to convince an employer that you'd be a good bet for overseas work. Table 12.1 sets out some of the characteristics of a good cross-cultural experience, domestic or foreign.

LANGUAGE

One of the quickest ways to get the attention of an international employer is to cite your fluency in a major world language. Note that I've said "major" world language: although it will be interesting for people to know that you can speak fluent Cebuano, Badyaranké, or Melpa, it's far more advantageous to come in with a good command of one of the vehicular development languages.

A "vehicular development language" is one that is spoken by large numbers of people in areas of the world where significant development activity is taking place; used administratively by significant numbers of development agencies themselves to communicate and exchange information; or both.

What are the most important of these vehicular development languages?

- Spanish, spoken throughout most of Central and South America, is probably the single most important development language, next to English.
- French is spoken across approximately half of Africa, and in a scattering of other places in the Pacific and the Caribbean.
- Arabic is widely spoken across North Africa and the Middle East, but variations make it difficult to understand some of the local dialects.
- Portuguese is spoken in Brazil, the largest country in Latin America. It is also spoken in Mozambique, Angola, Guinea Bissau, and several other places.
- Russian is widely understood outside Russia itself, in many Eastern and Central European countries, and indeed, in most parts of the former Soviet Union. Russian is also close to a variety of other Slavic national languages, such as Bulgarian, Ukrainian, Polish, and Czech.
- Indonesian (or Bahasa Indonesia) is the vehicular language for the world's fourth-largest country. An only slightly different form of the language is spoken in Malaysia, where it is known as Bahasa Malay. The Philippine national language, Tagalog, is also a Malay-based language, and although not intelligible to Malay speakers, there is wide overlap in vocabulary and structure.
- Turkish is a language that is widely useful across parts of the Middle East and Central Asia, because of its links to other neighboring languages.

Finally, there are *regional languages* that, although perhaps less widespread, are useful in certain areas. Hindi, Swahili, Maghrebi Arabic, Urdu, Bambara, Fulani, and Hausa would fit into this category, as languages spoken across national boundaries.

How fluent in another language do you have to be? The most widely used rating system is that of the Foreign Service Institute (FSI), which grades on a 5-point scale, with "0" denoting no ability whatsoever, and "5" representing native fluency. Most agencies that require you to speak a foreign language to a professional level will consider an FSI score of 3 or 3+ to be the minimum. The Foreign Service itself considers 4 to be acceptable for representational duties.

TABLE 12.2   Foreign Service Language Rating Scales (speaking)

Level	Abilities
0	No functional ability in the language.
0+	Able to satisfy immediate needs using learned utterances.
1	Able to satisfy basic survival needs and minimum courtesy requirements.
1+	Able to satisfy most survival needs and limited social demands.
2	Able to satisfy routine social demands and limited work requirements.
2+	Able to satisfy most work requirements and show some ability to communicate on concrete topics relating to particular interests and special fields of competence.
3	Able to speak the language with sufficient structural accuracy and vocabulary to participate effectively in most formal and informal conversations on practical, social, and professional topics.
3+	Able to speak the language with sufficient structural accuracy and vocabulary to use it on some levels normally pertinent to professional needs.
4	(Representational Proficiency) Able to use the language fluently and accurately on all levels normally pertinent to professional needs.
4+	Speaking proficiency sometimes equivalent to that of a well-educated native speaker but cannot sustain performance.
5	(Native or Bilingual Proficiency) Speaking proficiency equivalent to that of a well-educated native speaker.

Workplace Skills

Workplace skills are probably the most important part of your package. They are often divided into three types: *technical* skills; *functional* skills; and *self-management* skills. Table 12.3 sets out some examples of each of these.

Technical Skills.   These are highly specific to a particular field, profession, or situation. They are usually rooted in a particular context, and learned through special training or on-the-job experience.

Your employers know you're not omniscient. Your anthropological training will give you some, but not all of these skills. You'll be expected to pick up specific technical skills on the job. Some agencies have training programs designed for that purpose.

TABLE 12.3   Three Types of Skills

Technical Skills	Functional Skills	Self-Management Skills
writing a computer program	writing a job description	managing time
speaking Swahili	negotiating a business deal	managing priorities
designing a training program	supervising another person	communicating effectively
analyzing a farming system	planning a project	accepting disappointment
designing a survey	running a meeting	managing conflict
diagramming a kinship structure	preparing a presentation	making decisions
operating a radiotelephone	writing a report	flexibility
making a soufflé	drafting a budget	tolerance
performing a regression analysis	proposal writing	cooperativeness

Functional Skills.   These can be transferred from one job to the next. These skills arise partly from "natural" aptitudes—for example, the ability to communicate—but they are also learned through education and experience. It's your functional skills that can be most dramatically improved through training or practical experience. These are also the skills that you may lack if you're fresh out of school or if your background is in another field entirely.

Self-Management Skills.   Although these skills can be acquired, they are really based on your personal qualities: rather than knowing how to do these skills, you *are* these skills. Self-management skills are, in a sense, basic: employers will expect you to arrive with these and to use them intelligently. Few employers, obviously, are interested in training you to be on time for work or to be considerate of others. In the professional world, these things are simply a given.

USING SCHOOL EFFECTIVELY

Much of your preparation for international development work will take place in graduate school. While you're there, you need to use your time effectively. Regardless of the type of anthropology program you are in, you should aim to graduate with a grounding in the basic skill sets used by all anthropological practitioners.

   Skill sets are collections of skills focused on particular aspects of practice. All of your academic preparation, as well as your extracurricular activities, should ideally be designed to help you develop and practice putting these basic skill sets together. These are outlined in Table 12.4.

   You may not be in an applied or practice-oriented anthropology program. You may not even have a wide range of international courses and programs at your school. But even with limited options, there's still a lot you can do to prepare yourself for development work.

TABLE 12.4 Practitioner Skill Sets

Skill Sets	Applications
Finding Out	Survey design; literature research; interviewing; needs analysis
Communicating	Presentations; report-writing; training; briefing constituents
Planning and Designing	Designing programs and projects; designing office procedures; handling bureaucratic requirements
Analyzing	Data analysis; statistics; summarizing documents, findings, and reports
Managing	Working with other people; delegating and assigning; negotiating; monitoring and assessing
Judging	Evaluating projects and programs; troubleshooting and fixing things; identifying strong and weak points

Every university will have activities and resources outside the classroom, and you should take advantage of as many of these as possible, as a way to build knowledge and skills. They include:

- Career counseling: Most schools have career guidance centers. Some of the people in your school (professors, students, staff) may also have worked internationally. Start talking to them and asking advice.
- Career fairs and workshops: Many schools train their students in job-hunting and career-planning through workshops on subjects such as interviewing, networking, résumé writing, and so forth. They may also arrange career days or job fairs or some other form of structured introduction to the world of work.
- Internships: Schools (or faculty members inside schools) can often arrange internships for you, either credit or noncredit, which will help you get additional qualifications for international work.
- Field trips and conferences: Schools can often help you to attend conferences and meetings in your field, where you can meet other people and exchange ideas. Such gatherings are often held in cities like Washington, New York, or Boston, giving you the chance to visit the offices of development organizations.
- Consulting and research opportunities: These give you a chance to be involved in a short-term consulting assignment or a research project, usually in partnership with a senior faculty member. Consulting is, by

and large, more valuable to you than straight research, if you intend to be a practitioner.

- Fieldwork: Sometimes, too, schools make it possible for you to spend short periods of time overseas in the field, as part of an internship or research/consulting project.
- Grant-writing: Since much of the development industry is involved in writing reports and proposals, graduate school is a good place to acquire those skills. Many faculty members will be delighted to accept your offer to help them put together proposals or reports.

Internships and Volunteer Work

Two types of extracurricular experience will be particularly useful to you: *internships* and *volunteer* work. You may be able to arrange these through your school, or as a summer job.

Most volunteer work is unpaid, as are many internships. Sometimes, both can be done for credit or as completion of part of the degree requirements. What you're seeking, after all, isn't the money—it's the experience. To contribute to your employability, the experience should be cross-cultural if at all possible, and should use skills that are transferable to development work later on.

If part of a school's program, internships are usually supervised by a faculty member. Often, they have specific learning goals or objectives. Whether these are formal requirements or not, you should have some of your own.

Internships and volunteer assignments can serve many purposes:

- They can help fill gaps in your academic training.
- They can help you apply or practice what you have learned in the classroom.
- They can show you what kinds of organizations, people, and activities await you in the world of work.
- They can provide you with a testing-ground for your own ability to function inside a development organization.
- They can help you form a network of professional contacts that may lead to information, future jobs, or more contacts.
- They can provide you (and your employer) with a no-risk period to get acquainted.

Even in a very traditional anthropology program, you can, if you plan carefully, equip yourself with the threshold qualifications necessary for work in international development. In addition to a Master's or Ph.D. in anthropology, you will graduate with a set of functional skills that can be applied to whatever job you take; a working knowledge of at least one vehicular foreign language; and

TABLE 12.5 Internships and Volunteer Assignments

Characteristics of the Job	What You Should Look for in an Internship or Volunteer Assignment
Internships and volunteer work are usually not paid, or are paid very little	If you're not doing it for the money, make sure you know what you're going to get out of it: prestige, experience, knowledge, skills, contacts, exposure.
You are usually exposed to more than one job	Try to get as diverse an experience as possible. Learn about more than one aspect of the job environment.
You are often less experienced than the people you work with	Try to team up with someone who knows more than you do about something you'd like to learn about, and who has the time and willingness to teach you some of it.
You often have a counterpart	Use that relationship as a way to learn about counterpart relationships in general, and how you can manage them most effectively.
It's usually a learning experience for both you and the organization	Try to have a relationship that's mutually beneficial, where your work makes a positive contribution. It will give you a focus, make you conscientious, and produce a lasting good impression on others if you do a good job.

experience working in other-cultural settings, whether in the United States or overseas.

Now, you're ready to find work.

GETTING A JOB

Employers

There are seven major employers in the development industry:

- Large multilateral agencies such as the World Bank, the IMF, and the United Nations
- National bilateral agencies such as AID in the United States or CIDA in Canada
- NGOs in the United States and in other countries such as CARE, Save the Children, World Vision, or Oxfam
- Foundations in the United States and elsewhere with an interest in international development
- Universities in the United States and elsewhere that are active in international development.

- Independent institutes and think-tanks active in international development
- Consulting firms in the United States and abroad that supply the development industry with specialists and managers.

Although your ultimate goal may be to work for a large multilateral like the World Bank, you should consider your career as a work in progress. Job opportunities can be used strategically, to build skills and experience, to explore different varieties of application and practice, and to compare and contrast different types of projects, different regions, and different organizations.

So although work with, say, the UN or the World Bank is often viewed as highly desirable, these organizations are hard for most people to get into until they have built a network of contacts and a portfolio of relevant experience. Each of the major agencies—that is, the World Bank, USAID, and the UN—will have only a limited number of full-time positions open each year, and very few of these will be for anthropologists per se.

People entering the market therefore stand a better chance of finding assignments with NGOs or private consulting firms, since turnover tends to be high and there is a continuing need for qualified entry-level people. Such assignments are often temporary, lasting only a few weeks, but they constitute excellent preparation for later, more permanent assignments.

Initially, assignments may be limited to the headquarters office, but after an initial trial period, field assignments are likely, and these will provide extremely valuable experience. Anthropologists tend to begin field assignments as collectors of data, eventually moving to planning and implementation tasks, and finally, to policy work.

Specialist or Manager?

Within these broad categories of activity can be found a fundamental distinction between development workers who are considered primarily *specialists*, and those considered as *managers*. Although these roles overlap in some cases, job seekers should be aware of the differences, and what they imply for recruitment and career patterns.

The development industry needs highly skilled *specialists* in a wide variety of areas. Epidemiologists, for example, are specialists; so are statisticians, computer programmers, or trainers. Anthropologists might be specialized in pastoral land use systems, cross-cultural survey design and analysis, or technology transfer, to cite only three of many possibilities.

In many cases, the involvement of specialists with projects or with development agencies is temporary, and they work as consultants or advisers for part of a project or a policy undertaking. Anthropologists are frequently hired to perform social impact analyses, for example, to do evaluation reports, or to design sections or parts of a project. There is a relatively high likelihood that an anthropological specialist will be recognized and referred to as an anthropologist by his or her colleagues.

Managers, on the other hand, are often considered generalists, even though they may have specialized degrees. They tend, on the whole, to find longer-term work within the agencies, as planners, analysts, project and program managers, and researchers. Often—although not always—the word "anthropologist" does not appear in the job title or terms of reference.

Managers deal not with one set of things, but with many. Managers must have—or develop—skills in planning and coordinating the activities of others. Managers work as team leaders, project directors, chiefs of party, and agency representatives. Although some managers also have specialized skills, they are usually employed to oversee all or part of a program or project or to serve as core staff in headquarters.

In your search for work, keep these distinctions in mind. If you portray yourself as a specialist, then your data collection and analysis skills, your command of a foreign language, or your knowledge of a particular area may be very helpful to you. They will also, obviously, restrict you—initially at least—to jobs that require those specific skills, and they will tend, for the most part, to get you into short-term assignments, unless there is a high, continuing demand for your specialty.

It is somewhat harder to promote oneself initially as a manager, and here, although anthropology is still very useful, it is secondary to the broader work skills outlined earlier. Although specialists tend to be put into the field fairly quickly—for the need is there—managers will often begin work for an agency by putting in time in the home office, learning the ropes, and writing reports or proposals. Only later will they be assigned to the field. Although this is not a rigid pattern, it is fairly commonplace.

One way to combine elements of both and to gain valuable experience is to seek work as a short-term consultant initially, using your technical skills, and move later into other, longer-term jobs of a more managerial nature. This allows you to build up experience and a track record, and to begin to evaluate the various long-term job possibilities. For many people, it is both expedient and attractive to do short-term consulting at the start of one's career. With the proper skills and background, it is not terribly difficult to land short assignments, and these are often the springboard to others.

NETWORKING

The best way to approach getting a job in the development industry is to *network*. Networking is a systematic method of creating and managing a web of professional relationships centered on a particular area or set of activities. Networking will help you:

- Meet people in the industry and present yourself to them as an aspiring professional
- Learn about the development industry and the opportunities it offers
- Discover what qualifications you need to take advantage of these opportunities

Networking is *focused* and *systematic*. Properly constructed, your professional network will provide you with information, insight, advice, and referrals, and will help you extend and refine your professional objectives. Your network will not only be helpful to you as you search for a job; it will be helpful later, as you develop professionally. With care, your network can be a lifelong resource for you, constantly appreciating in value.

Networking is particularly important in the development industry, for several reasons:

- The industry is difficult to break into for outsiders. The industry operates, to a much larger extent than most people realize, on word of mouth. Networking connects you to the grapevine.
- The industry contains a relatively small number of people. It is possible to network across vast geographical and organizational areas with just a few connection points. Everyone else in the industry has a network too. By establishing a connection with one person, you can often get quickly connected to the rest of his or her network.
- The industry relies at least as much on peer judgments as it does on formal qualifications in making decisions about who to hire. "Who you know" can be a very important factor in landing a job.
- Agencies inside the industry rely greatly on referrals from people in other agencies, particularly for short-term jobs. Someone who was unable to offer you a job in one organization may eventually be the key to getting you hired in another.
- People in the development industry move around, in and out of different parts of the industry and the world. As they move, your network expands and extends into new areas.

You should build your network from the inside out, beginning with friends, teachers, and classmates. Move out to include people you have met at work, in meetings, and at other professional gatherings. Then extend your search to people you don't yet know. Each person in your network can provide you with one or more of three essential things: people, information, and job leads.

Most of them will be able to connect you with other *people*. When you begin networking, you are mainly looking for people who know other people, as a way to build your network. Your first contacts may not know much personally about the development industry, but if they know people who do, then they become valuable links or nodes in your developing web.

Many of them can give you useful *information*. As you begin to develop your contacts, you will find people who have detailed knowledge of the development industry: how it works, what it does, what kinds of people are being hired. These are not necessarily the people who can give you jobs, but their knowledge and experience is very valuable.

A few of them, however, will indeed know of *job opportunities*, now or in the future. They will be able to describe the job's scope of work or terms of reference, and outline the qualifications and procedures necessary to compete for that job, or for similar ones.

Each person that you talk to will add detail to the picture of the development industry that you're developing. Each person's responses can be used to structure and refine later questions to other people. As your questions become more focused, the answers you get will be more useful to you.

The most valuable people in your network are those who:

- Understand what kind of an international opportunity you are looking for
- Have knowledge, information, connections, or power helpful to you in this regard
- Are willing to help you

You will use different "scripts" with different people as you network. But for anyone who you do not already know well, you should rehearse a short presentation consisting of two main elements: what you are looking for and why; and what your skills are. You should be able to deliver this smoothly and professionally in no more than two or three minutes.

Much of your networking will happen on the telephone. Here, you will be severely restricted in terms of time, and all of the body language signals that are so important when people talk will be missing. Your calls will rarely last more than ten or fifteen minutes, and for a busy manager, even this much time represents a big commitment.

They will want to know who you are, what you want, and why you called them instead of someone else. Nothing will put a busy person off more than someone who calls and in response to the question "What can I do for you?" gets a vague or general response.

It's much better to say something like this: "A mutual friend, Betty Smith, told me that you did some work with the World Bank in Pakistan several years ago. I'm thinking about applying to the Bank, and I wondered if you could talk with me for a few minutes about how I should proceed. I'm particularly interested in knowing whether I should go to Washington to talk directly with someone in the Bank, and who that might be."

A question like this, although fairly specific, is also open-ended in the sense that it allows your contact to be more forthcoming if they want to be. And it leads, hopefully, to useful information, more names, and possibly, news of a job opportunity.

As you network, you will be able to do two things: construct a vision for yourself of the job you want and identify organizations that are likely to have those jobs.

DEVELOPING YOUR VISION

Your future job situation—whatever it is—will have four main components. These are set out in Table 12.6.

Constructing a vision of your development job will help you answer the following questions:

- Where do I want to work, and what do I want to do?
- What development issues or problems will I be dealing with?
- Who are my coworkers and colleagues likely to be?
- What are the main benefits and rewards of this type of work?
- What's ahead for me professionally after this?

Your vision statement gives you a platform to build on. If you write your vision out in no more than three or four paragraphs, you can use this as you network. As your thinking develops, you can change the written description accordingly.

NARROWING THE FOCUS

Up until now, you've been networking across the development industry in general, gathering information and making contacts in a broad range of fields. This was essential preparation for helping you understand what possibilities the industry offers, and of these, which fit best with your qualifications.

Now it's time to focus even more sharply on:

- Agencies and organizations that have jobs available
- What types of jobs these are
- What qualifications are necessary to compete for these jobs
- What the procedures are for hiring

If you have been successful with your networking, you should now have a list of a dozen or more organizations that do the kinds of work you seek in suitable sectors and locations. These organizations constitute your "shortlist" of likely employers. For each of them, you can find out more about what the organization

TABLE 12.6 Components of a Future Job Assignment

Job Component	Description
Level of Effort	How much time and energy are you going to put into this? How much responsibility are you able and willing to take?
Functions	"Functions" refer to the skills, knowledge, and roles you want to use in your new assignment. Are you primarily thinking of being a technician or being a manager? Or some combination of the two? Are you working primarily with things or with people? These questions focus mainly on the kinds of things you do at work.
Sectors	What areas, sectors, disciplines, or contexts are you interested in? Are you in the field of enterprise development, public health, agriculture, education, famine relief, or what? These questions relate specifically to the type of work that you will eventually seek.
Community	Where are you living? Who are you working with? Are you in a remote, rural area, a big city, a small town? Are you in one place or moving around through several? These and similar questions relate to your environment and how you interact with it.

does, how extensive it is, what approach it takes to its work, where its main op-erations occur, and what its past history and likely future are.

INFORMATIONAL INTERVIEWING

You do this through *informational interviewing.* Keep in mind that informational interviewing is not really the same as a job interview. You should ensure that the person you are talking to understands that he or she is *not* being asked for a job, but only for information. Of course, employers know perfectly well that infor-mational interviews are often the prelude to a job application, but you will find them much more willing to talk with you and to share what they know if this el-ement is taken out during your initial meeting.

The reason for this is simple. If *you* are talking to them about a specific job, they will be focusing on *you,* and doing two things as the discussion proceeds: they will be evaluating you and they will be thinking of reasons not to employ you. Neither of these reactions is useful to you at this stage. Instead, you want to focus on *them,* on *their* needs, *their* working environment. There will be time later on to redirect the focus to yourself.

You can do your informational interviewing on the phone, or in person. In-person interviewing is much better, of course. You are interested in learning about where business takes place, and what the office environment looks and feels like. You are especially interested in looking directly at the people who have jobs to give you, and giving them a direct look back at you.

If most of the agencies that you have targeted for your search are in one city, such as Washington, New York, or Boston, you should consider making a "pilgrimage" and visiting as many organizations as possible. Allow two weeks for your pilgrimage if you can afford it. Plan for a week of scheduled appointments, with two to four interviews a day, and leave a second week free, if possible, for callbacks and following up new leads.

Do your preparation carefully. Make sure that you have already used your network to target the people you want, and call in advance to set things up. Have a backup person in mind for each organization, in case your primary contact is called away. Keep in mind that it is usually not the personnel officer that you want to see, but rather the person or persons who have managerial responsibility for operations. These will be the folks you wind up working for.

An informational interview isn't a chat, although it may be done in a relaxed, informal way. It's a semistructured interview, and you should approach it just as carefully as a professional anthropologist would. Depending on who you are talking to, you may want to think of your questions as falling into one or more of three basic groups: questions about the *person;* questions about the *organization;* and questions about *yourself.*

Questions About the Person

If your contact turns out to be someone who is willing to talk at some length, you may want to ask him or her about their own work in international development. One reason for doing this is to gain some insight into the sort of person you might turn into if *you* go overseas for development work. You might therefore try to elicit a sort of life history from them, focusing on broad concerns such as these:

- How did they decide to get into international development?
- How did they prepare for their career?
- What job strategies worked best for them?
- How did their careers develop over time?
- What did they learn from their work that you should know?
- What would they have done differently?

By asking someone to essentially tell you the story of their life in the development industry, you will learn much more than a mere chronology of events. You will learn something about the key or pivotal events in their career, what they considered to be problems and opportunities, and how these were dealt with.

Questions About the Organization

Your questions might include:

- What does this organization do and how does it do it? What sectors are they involved in? What kinds of activities do they engage in? How are they funded, and what is their overall approach or philosophy of work? Who are their clients or customers?
- What qualifications do people need to be considered for employment by this organization? What type of personality does well here? What skills or experience are people expected to bring when they are hired? What things are they expected to learn once they are hired?
- What are the working conditions like here? What are salary and benefit levels? How are these determined? What are the possibilities for promotion and advancement? What is a typical career path here?
- What are the procedures and criteria that this organization uses to hire people? Where are jobs advertised? What application forms and documentation are necessary? Who makes hiring decisions, and how?

Questions About Yourself

These might include:

- Does my previous career or preparation make sense if I want to work in this industry?
- Are my goals realistic?
- What trends should I be aware of?
- What kinds of people am I competing against, and how do my qualifications compare?
- Where should I seek to build skills or make improvements?

INTERVIEWING

Now it's time for the *job interview*. This is not an informational interview, but the real thing, for a specific job, with you as a candidate.

You and the interviewer are working toward the same goal—finding out whether your abilities match their needs—but the two of you are approaching it from entirely different directions. The interviewer is trying to find reasons to reject you. You, on the other hand, are trying to find ways to make them accept you.

You should prepare carefully for the interview. You do this in two ways:

- By reviewing and examining your own goals, skills, experience, and key strengths; and
- By collecting all the information you can about the organization and its work.

In this way you will be prepared to show the interviewer why and how you can meet their needs.

Anthropologists face a particular problem when they look for nonacademic work, and this problem has two aspects. On the one hand, most people—including many in the development industry itself—know less than they probably should about what anthropology is. On the other hand, many anthropology graduates tend to talk in their interviews more about anthropology itself than about what they as individuals can do with it in development work.

This last is a huge mistake. Anthropology may be your core skill, your passion, and your life, but it is *not* the main thing you talk about in a job interview. Van Willigen rightly observes: ". . . you will not be hired on the basis of your being the best anthropologist, they must see you as a skills-possessing problem solver that relates to their organizations' need to be more efficient, more sensitive, more effective, more responsive, or more profitable."[2]

You will be hired, in other words, for what you can do, not for what you have studied.

In the job market, you will be competing with people *not* trained as anthropologists. Because potential employers may not fully understand what anthropology is, or how it can benefit them, you will need to educate your market. You do this by explaining to them what you can do for them in functional, practical terms related to the needs of their specific policy, program, or project development concerns. Unless you have done your homework, you will not be able to do this.

Regardless of the form or structure of an interview, and regardless of how many different people actually participate in the interview, the organization that is interviewing you essentially wants to know four things:

- Why are you here? What are your motivations in seeking work in international development? What do you hope to gain from such work? Why did you come to us? What was it about the job that particularly attracted you, and why?
- What can you do for us? What are your skills and abilities, and how will these be useful to us? What in your background or experience is particularly relevant to our needs, now and in the future?
- What will you be like as a colleague? If we hire you, what will it be like to work with you? Are you a pleasant, mature person? What are your expectations, professionally and socially, of us? How are you likely to de-

velop over time? Besides wanting a job, are there other agendas or issues
that seem important to you here?
- What will it cost us? What are your salary expectations likely to be
(even though we might not discuss them in a first interview)? What
other things do you want or need from us? Do we run any risks in hiring
you? What changes in our present arrangements might we have to make
if we hire you?

Throughout the interview process, you should return whenever possible to
your comparative advantage; to the strong points that distinguish you from the
crowd. Your goal here is *not* to look like a superhero—far from it—but rather to
relate your abilities to their needs.

THE JOB OFFER

The formal terms of an offer vary greatly from one organization to another.
Some firms provide a very simple memorandum of agreement, whereas others
will draft a long contract for you to sign. All such offers, however they are written, should contain specific language about four main things:

- The *scope of work* or *terms of reference* under which you are being hired.
In other words, what is the nature of the job that you are expected to
do?
- The *conditions* under which the work is to be performed. This includes
information about your rights and responsibilities, reporting arrangements, timetables, locations, and other matters.
- Any *special considerations* that will affect your employment or your performance under the contract. These might include the availability of
project funding, security clearances, government approvals, and so
forth.
- The *salary and benefits* you will receive for performing the work.

AFTER THE FIRST JOB

Getting the first job assignment is only the beginning, of course. As time goes
on, most development anthropologists eventually find their career options
falling into four or five main categories.

- Staff members at a multilateral or bilateral agency. Although few agency
jobs are labeled "anthropologist," positions as managers, analysts, researchers, and writers give you ample opportunity to use anthropology
in your work. Agency work is reasonably well paid and secure, the work

is relatively predictable, and there are a variety of support services available. Agencies are, however, sometimes very bureaucratic. Furthermore, some development agencies in recent years have experienced budget and morale problems.

- Staff for an NGO or consulting firm. It is probably easier, on the whole, to find a position with an NGO than with a multilateral or bilateral agency, for the simple reason that there are many more of them. Although salary and benefits do not usually match those of the larger agencies, each NGO has its own institutional culture, and many of them are much less bureaucratic and more innovative.

- University staff or faculty. This is an ideal arrangement in theory, but somewhat difficult to realize in practice. As I've noted, full-time university positions usually involve traditional academic expectations and pressures, often made explicit in tenure requirements. To the extent that you can manage to fulfill both academic requirements (for example, teaching, research, publication, and service) *and* the demands of professional practice, you will be able to use the university as a base from which to organize periodic and temporary excursions into the development world. Alternatively, you can associate yourself with a university department as an adjunct, part-time, or soft-money member, giving you less security, perhaps, but more time and freedom for practice. Your involvement with development work, however, will almost always be short-term, given the academic demands.

- Freelance work. Although exciting at first, it is hard to continue freelance work on a long-term basis. The work of a short-term consultant is erratic and high-pressure, and few people can sustain the pace for more than a few years. Most practitioners eventually seek permanent jobs within an agency. Many if not most development anthropologists do freelance consulting, however, from time to time, and many of them began their careers this way.

- Forming your own company. At some stage, virtually all freelancers dream about having their own consulting firm. Here again, the work is hard and the market is both competitive and volatile. The firms that are successful in gathering large agency contracts tend to become highly specialized, and over time, it is the larger firms that survive.

WHAT WILL YOU DO
WITH THE REST OF YOUR LIFE?

To conclude, let's look briefly at the question of what it's all for. What are the broader purposes of your work? Beyond putting groceries on the table and having some fun, what else is there?

Let me suggest that there are four main tasks facing any development anthropologist today. I've referred to these in this book in various places, but let's look at them again. Although you'll have personal goals as a professional, what you do and how you do it will also have a direct effect on these four things.

- Changing our institutional structures. It's clear that new times need new organizations. Whether we scrap the old ones or reform them, a new approach to the organization of development efforts seems urgently needed. In your work, you'll be a part of this issue, whether you like it or not. You will need to make decisions about who you work for, who you work with, how you work, and whether you press for changes in the status quo or just go along with the existing arrangements.
- Learning the lessons of experience. Each development project, no matter how small, is an experiment to see what works in a particular sociocultural environment. The way in which the project developed, and its outcomes, constitute an invaluable fund of information for practitioners and academics alike. It is difficult to collect, analyze, and disseminate this information, both within the development industry and the academy. One of the most important tasks for practitioners, therefore, is to organize what we learn from development projects and discuss it with like-minded others.
- Widening our disciplinary boundaries. As we have seen, anthropology is somewhat marginal and self-isolated among the various sciences that contribute toward development. Both intellectually and as a practical matter, the discipline needs to be opened up to its surroundings, and made more responsive to them. This means making anthropology available to the public at large and to the development industry, but it also means getting anthropology more involved with other disciplines inside and outside the academy, to promote the kind of intellectual synergy needed for continued growth.
- Redefining development. Finally, there is the task of crafting a new paradigm for development. Although our former approaches have worked in some situations, their limitations are becoming increasingly apparent, and the development effort is in danger of stalling. As practitioners, we owe it to ourselves—and to future generations—to help recast the framework that guides our efforts. Anthropology will make a major contribution to this effort, and so—of course—will you.

ENDNOTES

1. van Willigen (1986: 215).
2. van Willigen (1986: 213).

glossary

Access Structure   A tool sometimes used by planners to outline how a service delivery project will actually work, by describing how beneficiaries will be chosen (Gate), how they will be served (Line), and what services or benefits they will actually obtain (Counter).

Accommodation   A negotiating posture or strategy based on a relatively low concern for the outcome of a negotiation, but a relatively high concern for the maintenance of the relationship with the negotiating partner.

Advocacy   Active support for a cause, idea, policy, or group of people. A role that anthropologists sometimes play with respect to indigenous groups, wherein the anthropologist puts skills and experience at the service of the group to advance their interests.

AID   The U.S. Agency for International Development.

Anthropologist Practitioner   An anthropologist employed outside an academic setting, whose work involves the application of anthropology to contemporary problems.

Applied Anthropology   The use of anthropology for problem solving outside the boundaries of the discipline itself.

Appraisal   Appraisal refers to the formal procedures undertaken by an agency or donor organization to assess the likely success of a project design, usually from multiple perspectives; for example, financial, environmental, socio-cultural, technical, an so on. Positive appraisals are usually necessary for project funding and implementation.

Approaches   Broad strategies or methodologies for planning and implementing projects.

Appropriate Imprecision   One of the so-called Chambers Principles of data collection and management, reminding planners to learn only as much about something as they need in order to make intelligent decisions of the moment.

Archaeology   Anthropology of the human past.

Baseline Data   Data relating to conditions in the project area before implementation begins. Baseline data are compared with monitoring and outcome data to determine what changed, when, and (if possible) why.

Bilateral Agencies   Development agencies of one particular country. These donor agencies form two-sided linkages with individual recipient countries.

Branching-Tree Diagrams   Also called a "problem tree," the branching tree is used by planners to break a problem area down into its constituents, and to arrange these in a hierarchy that indicates something of the cause-effect relationships operating in the project environment.

Bretton Woods Agreement   The agreement hammered out at the Bretton Woods meeting in 1944 that set up the IMF and the World Bank, and which paved the way for other multilateral organizations.

Collaboration   A negotiation strategy used when one partner has a strong interest in both the outcome of the negotiations themselves, and in the continuing relationship with the negotiating partner. In these cases, a collaborative strategy will encourage joint problem solving and the creation of solutions where both parties "win" part or all of what they need.

Compromise   A negotiation strategy used when one or both partners care about both the outcome and the relationship, but are not highly attached to either. This makes it possible for them to give up some of what they want, in order to get the rest of what they want. Although the results are not ideal, they are satisfactory for the moment.

Conditionality   "Strings" attached to development aid: financial, political, or managerial.

Conflict Resolution   The process by which differences between people are surfaced and resolved before they become destructive to the overall efforts of the group or organization.

Content Knowledge   The specific (and largely culture-free) details of processes, procedures, and operations.

Context Knowledge   The understanding of a specific cultural environment within which various forms of content knowledge are meant to operate.

Core Values   Value orientations that, although not held to the same degree by all members of a culture, are important for many members of that culture and help inform their reactions and responses to their surroundings.

Counterpart   Typically, a project counterpart will be someone from the local community or local government ministry assigned to work with a foreign manager or specialist on part or all of a project. Often, the expectation is that, through this type of pairing, the counterpart will learn how to do what the specialist/manager already knows how to do, and will take over that role when the foreign manager or specialist leaves.

Criteria   Measures or standards against which things are judged. In project development, criteria allow planners, for example, to distinguish good strategies from less good ones, better outcomes from worse, and so on.

Cultural Brokerage   Managing relationships between culturally different groups in such a way that differences are used in a positive and creative way to address common concerns.

Cultural Knowledge   The ways in which people in a given culture arrange and interpret the world. Cultural knowledge includes meanings, values, beliefs, categories, expectations, and other created understandings that shape overt behavior.

Culture   Culture is a shared worldview held by a group or organization. Cultures are distinctive, and have three main components: artifacts (the things people make and use); behavior (the things people do); and knowledge (the ways in which people think).

Development   Attempts to improve conditions of life for people, focusing on raising standards of living, building local capacity, and encouraging local participation and decisionmaking. Development almost always involves multiple groups, and therefore, multiple cultural perspectives.

Development Approaches   An "approach" in development planning refers to an overall strategy used to guide planning choices, given a particular issue, problem, or opportunity. Typical development approaches include "empowerment," "capacity-building," "basic needs provision," "intermediate technology," and so on. The approach helps determine how a problem will be addressed.

Development Assistance   Money and other resources (e.g., technicians) provided by donor agencies to poorer countries for development purposes.

Development Narratives   Development narratives are scripts or stories that planners tell each other to explain why the world is the way it is. These narratives are largely anecdotal, but they serve to guide thinking and decisionmaking.

Development Sectors   A sector is some area or part of a society or an economy that is targeted for development purposes. "Health" is a sector. So is "education," "transportation," or "agriculture."

Directive Planning   Also called "blueprint planning," this approach to project development is relatively rigid and linear. It works best when both techniques and the environment in which those techniques will be applied are well known.

Domain   An area of culture seen as significant to the members of that culture.

Domain Analysis   An anthropological method for investigating cultural domains by breaking them down into components, discovering the pattern and rationale for their arrangement, and looking at the way these categories are used in social interactions within and across groups. Doing a domain analysis usually leads to a better understanding of key areas of life important to project stakeholders.

Donor Fatigue   A term referring to a growing feeling among development agencies that their efforts are inappropriate and/or ineffective in terms of the relationship between the amounts of energy and funding expended and the results achieved.

Economic Support Fund   The ESF "advances economic and political foreign interests of the United States," according to AID. This money is often used for nondevelopment purposes, or for purposes that not everyone might define as "development related." For example, AID's 20001 budget request for ESF was some $2.3 billion, of which $1.8 billion was earmarked for "the Middle East peace process." The ESF replaced the earlier category of "Security Assistance."

Emergent Problem   An "emergent" problem is one whose outlines or true significance is not necessarily wholly apparent at first, but must be discovered through a series of investigations, interventions, and analyses.

Emic   An insider's view of a culture.

Ethics   Principles of proper conduct; the rules or standards that govern the behavior of individuals or members of a profession.

Ethnocentric   The attitude that your own culture's ways are best.

Ethnography   The detailed written description of a culture, or of significant aspects of a culture.

Ethnology   The cross-cultural analysis of different cultures, in the attempt to locate patterns, analyze differences and similarities, and build theory.

Etic   An outsider's view of culture.

Evaluation   Project evaluation is part of overall project assessment. "Evaluation" tends to refer to judgments made about project outcomes at various levels. Contrast this with "monitoring."

Food For Peace   Public Law 480 created this program as a way to dispose of American farm surpluses by exporting them to needy nations. Food for Peace provides agricultural commodities (i.e., food) to developing countries. PL 480 also funds a farmer-to-farmer exchange program and several grant programs to nongovernment organizations (NGOs).

Force Field Analysis   A technique often used by planners to help analyze the balance of forces that combine to produce a situation. If relevant forces can be identified, then planners can begin to look for points of likely intervention to promote change.

Formative Assessment Another term for "monitoring," meaning assessment carried out during the implementation phase of a project.

Formula-Detail Approach A strategy of negotiation that begins with a discussion of what is to be the focus of negotiation, proceeds to agreement on a formula to guide decisions, and finally, applies the formula to find mutually-agreeable solutions.

Framing Decisions Those decisions made very early in the development of a project that have the effect of setting the project's broad parameters in place and making initial decisions about what type of project it is to be. Once framing decisions have been made, detailed aspects of the project can be designed.

Globalization A term denoting the integration of financial and technical networks across the world.

Gross National Product The GNP is a measurement of the value of the total output of goods and services produced by a country, regardless of location. A slightly different measure, **GDP** (Gross Domestic Product) measures the value of total goods and services produced only within a country's borders (even though some of this production may be from foreign-owned businesses).

Goals In Logical Framework terms, the long-term, wide outcomes that are sought through a project.

Governance A term referring to a government's ability to provide conditions of peace, social justice, accountability, openness, and stability to its citizens, as well as economic growth and social security.

Grants Development assistance that does not need to be repaid. Grants can still be "tied," however.

High Context Part of Edward T. Hall's high/low context culture concept. A high context culture will communicate by paying attention to all aspects of the context or situation surrounding the communication (people, place, tone of voice, quality of relationship, and so on), not just on the words alone.

Holism The notion that parts of a culture are connected, often in ways that are not immediately apparent.

Inputs In Logical Framework terms, "inputs" refer to resources and activities that go into a project, and that are used to produce short-term and long-term results.

Integrated Rural Development   Popular in the 1970s and 80s, integrated rural development was an approach to project design that emphasized the interrelationship between changes in various sectors of a (usually) rural area. Thus, attempts to raise living standards would involve coordinated activities in several different sectors at once—for example, health, education, transportation, and agriculture.

Interactive Planning   An alternative to directive or "blueprint" planning, interactive planning attempts to discover salient aspects of the project environment, fitting plans to these as they are discovered. Project design, therefore, becomes more interactive, flexible and open-ended.

International Bank For Reconstruction And Development   One of the main agencies of the World Bank.

International Monetary Fund   One of the multilateral agencies created by the Bretton Woods agreement, whose main job has been to facilitate currency conversion.

Intervention Points   These are points or areas within a situation where projects may prove useful in promoting wider changes. By identifying likely intervention points, planners hope to ensure the success of projects, and to encourage positive changes in other, linked areas.

Key Decisions   In planning, "key" decisions are those that are critical or highly significant for project development. They tend to be decisions that affect many aspects of the project, and/or that are difficult to "undo" once made.

Linguistics   That branch of anthropology that is concerned with language, language structures and history, and language performance.

Loans   Development assistance that is given at a stated rate of interest (not necessarily at market rates) and that must in principle be repaid over time.

Local Practitioner Organizations   Groups of applied anthropologists, many of whom work in nonuniversity settings, who meet regularly to exchange information and discuss issues of common interest.

Logical Framework   A tool used by planners to check the internal consistency of a project design, by linking inputs to outputs, and outputs to results. The Logical Framework also helps define assessment requirements, and draws attention to salient aspects of the proximate and outer project environments that may affect performance and therefore success.

Low Context   In Edward T. Hall's formulation, low context cultures tend to pay more attention to the specific substance of communication; for example, to the words spoken, and less attention to the context in which those words are uttered.

Marshall Plan The Marshall Plan, begun in 1949, lasted for about three years and pumped about $13 billion of U.S. aid into Western Europe to help rebuild war-ravaged economies.

Monitoring Also known as "formative assessment," monitoring looks at results as a project is implemented, to track performance. It differs from evaluation, which looks primarily at end-of-project outcomes. Both monitoring and evaluation are necessary components of overall project assessment.

Multilateral Agencies Development agencies to which several nations belong.

Naive Realism The misconception that the way your own culture sees the world is the way the world really "is."

Negotiation A process of discussion and mutual problem solving intended to resolve differences between two or more partners.

New Directions This refers to legislation enacted in 1973 that required AID to focus its efforts primarily on helping "the poorest of the poor" in developing countries. New Directions helped create an increased demand for development anthropologists within AID and its associated agencies.

NGOs Nongovernment organizations, that include both for-profit and not-for-profit groups.

NonGovernment Organizations See NGOs.

Non-Profits Development groups or agencies that do not seek profit. Some are staffed by volunteers.

OECD The OECD, or Organization for Economic Cooperation and Development, is a collection of twenty-four (mainly) Western industrialized countries who collaborate on matters of policy and funding for development efforts. Countries include Australia, Austria, Belgium, Canada, Denmark, Finland, France, Germany, Greece, Iceland, Ireland, Italy, Japan, Luxembourg, the Netherlands, New Zealand, Norway, Portugal, Spain, Sweden, Switzerland, Turkey, the United Kingdom, and the United States.

Optimal Ignorance One of the so-called "Chambers Principles" of data management (see also appropriate imprecision), optimal ignorance means that planners should not spend time or energy trying to collect data about things that they do not need to know.

Organizational Culture Organizations, like societies, have cultures of their own. Although an organization's culture will incorporate major elements from the society in which it exists, it will differ in other ways. Organizations that contain members from different cultures will reflect these differences to some extent.

Outputs   In Logical Framework terms, outputs refer to the immediate results of the application of resources, or inputs, into the project.

Paradigm   A pattern or model that guides thinking and action.

Participant Observation   A research technique for gaining cultural information, in which the fieldworkers attempt in various ways to enter into the daily lives of the people around them.

Participation   In project development, "participation" refers to the various ways in which stakeholder groups are involved in the planning, implementation, and assessment of the project.

Physical Anthropology   That part of anthropology that looks at humans as physical organisms. Also called biological anthropology.

PL480   Public Law 480, the Agricultural Trade Development and Assistance Act of 1954, governs the Food for Peace Program. See Food for Peace.

Point Four   First announced in the Truman inauguration speech of 1949, Point Four became the start of the American foreign aid program.

Policy   An overall plan or course of action, usually based on clearly-stated values or beliefs, intended as a guide for decisions and plans.

Practice   Referring to those applications of anthropology conducted or performed by anthropologists who are not academically-based.

Practitioner   See anthropologist practitioner.

Program   A program is distinct from either a policy or a project. Programs operationalize broad (and sometimes vague) policy directives by collecting resources of various kinds, outlining sets of goals and objectives, and setting out timetables. Projects then further refine such plans, and apply them directly to the grass-roots level.

Project Camelot   A 1964 Defense Department project that proposed to employ anthropologists and other social scientists to study aspects of insurgency and counterinsurgency in Third World countries.

Project Development Cycle   This refers to the life-cycle of a project from the time it is initially conceived until it is completed. The project development cycle can be described in many different ways, but it always involves a design (or "framing") phase, an implementation/management phase, and an assessment phase.

Project Ethnography   Provides a detailed account of how a project developed over time primarily from the perspective of the various project stakeholders.

Project Hardware "Hardware" as used here refers to the hard-wired aspects of project design and delivery, such as the technical specifications of machinery, personnel regulations, laws, deadlines, and so on.

Project Software "Software" in this sense refers to the socio-cultural systems through which project arrangements must pass if they are to be effective.

Projects A development project is a planned collection of activities, bound in space and time, designed to achieve a stated set of objectives, using specific resources and employing stated strategies or rationales. Projects are the predominant way in which development assistance is delivered.

Proxy Measures Proxy measures are substitutes for data measures that are difficult, impossible, or inappropriate to obtain. They "stand in" for other measures.

Purposes Project purposes, in the Logical Framework, refer to the short-term results or outcomes of a project, and that lead, under normal circumstances, to wider and longer-term project goals.

Rapid Assessment Procedures Rapid assessment procedures, or RAP, refer to a broad collection of investigative techniques used by project planners—often with the participation of local stakeholders—that help them quickly get a sense of the local context and how it should be taken account of in project design.

Relativism An approach to cross-cultural discovery that is nonjudgmental, and that attempts to locate justifications for behaviors, beliefs, and so on, within the framework of that culture itself, instead of with reference to an outside framework.

Resources Resources, in project development, refer to project inputs: money, personnel, equipment, and so on, that are necessary in order to engage in the various activities planned under the project.

Sectors See development sector.

Security Assistance Security Assistance was formerly a major category of U.S. development aid, focused on helping to strengthen the military and police forces of recipient countries. Security assistance, still a substantial component of U.S. foreign aid, is now subsumed under a different rubric, that of the "Economic Support Fund."

Social / Cultural Anthropology That branch of anthropology concerned with beliefs, values, social structures, and patterns of behavior among contemporary peoples.

Social Impact Analysis See socio-cultural appraisal.

Socio-Cultural Appraisal   A socio-cultural appraisal, otherwise known as a social impact assessment, attempts to predict what the likely effects will be of the project as planned on the stakeholder populations.

Stakeholders   Groups or individuals who have an interest in a project or undertaking, and who also have some degree of influence or control over its outcome.

Stereotypes   Simplified images of members of another culture that may be partially based on experience, but that are too general, and are applied to all members of that group, regardless of their individual characteristics. Stereotypes are often, but not always, negative.

Strategies   In project design, a strategy refers to the approach, rationale, or overall methodology used to knit together resources and activities so that the project's objectives may be attained.

Structural Adjustment   Also called "policy-based lending," structural adjustment refers to development funding offered to recipient countries in exchange for major economic policy changes within that country, typically centering on interest and exchange rates, subsidies, interest and credit policies, import-export regulations, and so on.

Summative Assessment   A summative assessment looks at the outcomes or results of a project once the project itself is over. "Evaluation" is another name for summative assessment, and this aspect of assessment is distinguished from formative assessment, or "monitoring."

Sustainability   "Sustainability" in project design refers to how long project benefits last, and how these are maintained over time.

Symbols   A sign or object that stands for something else. A dove, for example, may stand for peace.

System Matrix   A technique used by planners to ascertain the degree of fit between a project design and its external environment. A system matrix looks specifically at where project inputs come from and where project outputs go, as well as what outside systems or organizations control what happens inside the project itself.

Technical Assistance   Technical assistance refers to the provision of expatriate personnel to help plan and manage development projects funded by international bilateral and multilateral donors.

Technicist   An approach characterized by economically-centered thinking, focused on growth in key output indicators such as GNP, relying on aggregate quantitative measures, and largely ignoring other factors.

Third World A term used to denote the collectivity of less-developed countries of the world. Originally, the term "Third World" referred to those countries which were neither Western-industrial-democratic (the "First World") nor part of the Soviet bloc (the "Second World").

Tied Aid Development aid that requires the recipient to do something specific, in addition to project or program purposes, such as purchasing commodities from the donor country, adopting specific policies, and so on. See "conditionality."

Time-Series Design A research design involving the collection of data at specified intervals throughout the life of a project, in order to provide a series of snapshots of change as project activities take place.

Triangulation "Triangulation," a term borrowed from navigation, refers to the practice of using multiple data-collection methods to achieve more relevant understanding of a socioeconomic context.

USAID The United States Agency for International Development. Now part of the U.S. State Department, USAID (or simply AID) is a bilateral development agency, the main U.S. organization involved in international development work.

Winner Take All A negotiating strategy characterized by a high level of concern for the outcome coupled with a low level of interest in any continuation of the relationship beyond the negotiation itself.

Withdrawal A negotiating strategy adopted when one or both of the partners value neither the outcome of the negotiation, nor the continuation of their relationship with each other.

World Bank A collection of agencies that are part of—but relatively separate from—the United Nations. The World Bank was set up in 1944 as part of the Bretton Woods agreement. Today, the World Bank is one of the largest and most influential multilateral agencies engaged in international development.

references

Adler, Nancy J. *International Dimensions of Organizational Behavior*. Kent International Business Series. Boston: Kent Publishing, 1986.

Angrosino, Michael, ed. *Do Applied Anthropologists Apply Anthropology?* Athens, Ga.: Southern Anthropological Society, University of Georgia Press, 1976.

Asad, Talal. *Anthropology and the Colonial Encounter*. New York: Humanities Press, 1973.

Austin, James E. *Managing in Developing Countries*. New York: The Free Press, 1990.

Autumn, Suzanne. "Anthropologists, Development and Situated Truth." *Human Organization* 55, no. 4 (1996): 480–484.

Ayres, Robert. *Banking on the Poor: The World Bank and World Poverty*. Cambridge, Mass.: MIT Press, 1983.

Bailey, F. G. *Stratagems and Spoils: A Social Anthropology of Politics*. Oxford: Basil Blackwell, 1969.

———. *The Tactical Uses of Passion*. Ithaca, N.Y.: Cornell University Press, 1983.

———. *Humbuggery and Manipulation: The Art of Leadership*. Ithaca, N.Y.: Cornell University Press, 1988.

———. *The Prevalence of Deceit*. Ithaca, N.Y.: Cornell University Press, 1991.

Bainton, Barry. "SOPA: Cultivating the Profession and Harvesting at the Grassroots Level." *Human Organization* 38, no. 3 (1979): 318–319.

Bandow, Doug, and Ian Vásquez, eds. *Perpetuating Poverty: The World Bank, the IMF, and the Developing World*. Washington, D.C.: The Cato Institute, 1994.

Baré, Jean-François. "Of Loans and Results: Elements for a Chronicle of Evaluation at the World Bank." *Human Organization* 57, no. 3 (1998): 319–325.

Barger, Ken, and Susan Hutton. "Personal Abilities in Applied Work and Training Programs in Anthropology." *Practicing Anthropology* 2, no. 3 (1980): 6–7, 24–25.

Barlett, Peggy, ed. *Agricultural Decision Making: Anthropological Contributions to Rural Development*. New York: Academic Press, 1980.

Barth, Fredrik. "Models of Social Organization." Occasional Paper no. 23, Royal Anthropological Institute, London, 1966.

Batalla, Guillermo Bonfil. "Conservative Thought in Applied Anthropology: A Critique." *Human Organization* 25, no. 2 (1966).

319

Beals, Ralph. *The Politics of Social Research: An Enquiry into the Ethics and Responsibilities of Social Scientists*. Chicago: Aldine, 1969.

Beebe, James. "Basic Concepts and Techniques of Rapid Appraisal." *Human Organization* 54, no. 1 (1995): 42–51.

———. *Rapid Assessment Process*. Boulder: Rowman and Littlefield, 2001.

Belshaw, Cyril. *The Sorcerer's Apprentice: An Anthropology of Public Policy*. New York: Pergamon, 1976.

Bennett, John. "Anthropology and Development: The Ambiguous Engagement." In *Production and Autonomy: Anthropological Studies and Critiques of Development*, edited by John Bennett and John Bowen, pp. 1–29. New York: University Press of America, 1988.

Bennett, John, and John Bowen, eds. *Production and Autonomy: Anthropological Studies and Critiques of Development*. New York: University Press of America, 1988.

Bentley, Jeffrey W., and Keith L. Andrews. "Pests, Peasants, and Publications: Anthropological and Entomological Views of an Integrated Pest Management Program for Small-Scale Honduran Farmers." *Human Organization* 50, no. 2 (1991): 113–124.

Bentley, Margaret, et al. "Rapid Ethnographic Assessment: Applications in a Diarrhea Management Program." *Social Science in Medicine* 27, no. 1 (1988): 107–116.

Bernard, H. Russell. "Scientists and Policy Makers: An Ethnography of Communication." *Human Organization* 33, no. 3 (1974): 261–275.

Berrios, Ruben. *Contracting for Development: The Role of For-Profit Contractors in U.S. Foreign Development Assistance*. Westport, Conn.: Praeger, 2000.

Bierce, Ambrose. *The Devil's Dictionary*. New York: Dover, 1958.

Bierschenk, Thomas, and Jean-Pierre Olivier de Sardan. "ECRIS: Rapid Collective Inquiry for the Identification of Conflicts and Strategic Groups." *Human Organization* 56, no. 2 (1997): 238–244.

Black, Jan Knippers. *Development in Theory and Practice*, 2d ed. Boulder: Westview, 1999.

Bodley, John H. *Anthropology and Contemporary Human Problems*, 2d ed. Palo Alto, Calif.: Mayfield, 1985.

———. *Tribal Peoples and Development Issues*, Mountain View, Calif.: Mayfield, 1988.

———. *Cultural Anthropology: Tribes, States, and the Global System*. Mountain View, Calif.: Mayfield, 1994.

Bohannon, Laura. "Shakespeare in the Bush." In *The Cultural Experience: Ethnography in a Complex Society*, edited by James Spradley and David McCurdy, pp. 35–44. Prospect Heights, Ill.: Waveland Press, 2000.

Bowers, C. A. *The Cultural Dimensions of Educational Computing: Understanding the Non-Neutrality of Technology*. New York: Columbia University, Teachers College Press, 1988.

Boyle, W. Philip. "On the Analysis of Organizational Culture in Development Project Planning." Binghamton, N.Y.: Institute for Development Anthropology, 1984.

Branch, Kristi, Douglas Hooper, James Thompson, and James Creighton. *Guide to Social Assessment*. Boulder: Westview, 1984.

Brecher, Jeremy, and Tim Costello. *Global Village or Global Pillage: Economic Reconstruction from the Bottom Up*. Boston: South End Press, 1994.

Brinkerhoff, Derick, and Marcus Ingle. "Integrating Blueprint and Process: A Structured Flexibility Approach to Development Management." Working Paper no. 100, International Development Management Center, University of Maryland, College Park, Md., 1987.

Brodhead, Tim. "NGOs: In One Year, Out the Other?" *World Development* 15, supplement (1987): 1–6.

Brokensha, David W. "IDA, the First Ten Years (1976–1986)." *Development Anthropology Network* 4, no. 2 (July 1986): 1–4.

Browne, Katherine E. "The Informal Economy in Martinique: Insights from the Field, Implications for Development Policy." *Human Organization* 55, no. 2 (1996): 225–234.

Browne, Stephen. *Foreign Aid in Practice*. New York: New York University Press, 1990.

Bruneau, Thomas C., Jan J. Jorgensen, and J. O. Ramsay. "C.I.D.A. The Organization of Canadian Overseas Assistance." Working Paper no. 24, Centre for Developing Area Studies, McGill University, Montreal, 1978.

Carley, Michael, and Eduardo Bustelo. *Social Impact Assessment and Monitoring: A Guide to the Literature*. Boulder: Westview, 1984.

Center for International and Security Studies at Maryland (CISSM), Program on International Policy Attitudes. *CISSM in Focus*. College Park, Md.: CISSM, 1995.

Cernea, Michael. "Entrance Points for Sociological Knowledge in Planned Rural Development." *Research in Rural Sociology and Development* 3 (1987): 1–25.

_____. "Social Organization and Development Anthropology (The 1995 Malinowski Award Lecture)." Environmentally Sustainable Development Studies and Monographs Series no. 6, Washington, D.C., World Bank, 1996.

Cernea, Michael, ed. *Putting People First*. New York: World Bank, Oxford University Press, 1985.

_____. *Putting People First*, 2d ed. New York: World Bank, Oxford University Press, 1991.

Cernea, Michael, and Scott Guggenheim, eds. *Anthropological Approaches to Resettlement: Policy, Practice and Theory*. Boulder: Westview, 1993.

Cernea, Michael, and Christopher McDowell, eds. *Reconstructing Livelihoods: Experiences with Resettlers and Refugees*. Washington, D.C.: World Bank, 2000.

Chambers, Erve. *Applied Anthropology: A Practical Guide*. Prospect Heights, Ill.: Waveland Press, 1985.

Chambers, Robert. *Managing Rural Development: Ideas and Experience from East Africa*. Uppsala: Scandinavian Institute of African Studies, 1974.

———. *Rural Development: Putting the Last First*. London: Longman, 1983.

———. "Shortcut Methods of Gathering Social Information for Rural Development Projects." In *Putting People First*, edited by Robert Cernea, pp. 397–415. New York: World Bank, Oxford University Press, 1985.

———. "Rapid Rural Appraisal: Rationale and Repertoire." IDS Discussion Paper No. 155, Brighton, England, Institute for Development Studies, 1988.

———. *Challenging the Professions: Frontiers for Rural Development*. London: Intermediate Technology Publications, 1993.

———. "Participatory Rural Appraisal (PRA): Analysis of Experience." *World Development* 22, no. 9 (1994a): 1253–1268.

———. "Participatory Rural Appraisal (PRA): Challenges, Potentials and Paradigms." *World Development* 22, no. 10 (1994b): 1437–1454.

———. "Editorial: Responsible Well-Being—A Personal Agenda for Development." *World Development* 25, no. 11 (1997a): 1743–1754.

———. *Whose Reality Counts? Putting the First Last*. London: Intermediate Technology Publications, 1997b.

Clements, Paul. "An Approach to Poverty Alleviation of Large International Development Agencies." *World Development* 21, no. 10 (1993): 1633–1646.

Cleveland, David. "Globalization and Anthropology: Expanding the Options." *Human Organization* 59, no. 3 (2000): 370–374.

Cobb, John, Jr. *The Earthist Challenge to Economism*. New York: St. Martin's Press, 1999.

Cochrane, Glynn. *Development Anthropology*. New York: Oxford University Press, 1971.

———. *What We Can Do for Each Other: An Interdisciplinary Approach to Development Anthropology*. Amsterdam: B. R. Gruner, 1976.

Cochrane, Glynn, and Raymond Noronha. "A Report with Recommendations on the Use of Anthropology in Project Operations of the World Bank Group." Washington: World Bank, 1973.

Conlin, S. "Anthropological Advice in a Government Context." In *Social Anthropology and Development Policy*, edited by Ralph Grillo and Alan Rew, pp. 73–87. ASA Monographs 23. London: Tavistock, 1985.

Cooper, Frederick, and Randall Packard, eds. *International Development and the Social Sciences: Essays on the History and Politics of Knowledge*. Berkeley: University of California Press, 1997.

Curtis, Donald. "Anthropology in Project Management: On Being Useful to Those Who Must Design and Operate Rural Water Supplies." In *Social Anthropology and Development Policy*, edited by Ralph Grillo and Alan Rew, pp. 102–116. ASA Monographs 23. London: Tavistock, 1985.

Danaher, Kevin, ed. *Fifty Years Is Enough: The Case Against the World Bank and the International Monetary Fund*. Boston: South End Press, 1994.

Delp, Peter, Arne Thesen, Juzar Motiwalla, and Neelakantan Seshadri. *Systems Tools for Project Planning.* Bloomington, Ind.: International Development Institute, 1977.

DeWalt, Billie R. "Anthropology, Sociology and Farming Systems Research." *Human Organization* 44, no. 2 (1985): 106–114.

_____. "Using Indigenous Knowledge to Improve Agriculture and Natural Resource Management." *Human Organization* 53, no. 2 (summer 1994): 123–131.

DiBella, Anthony J., and Edwin C. Nevis. *How Organizations Learn: An Integrated Strategy for Building Learning Capability.* San Francisco: Jossey-Bass, 1998.

Dichter, Thomas W. "The Changing World of Northern NGOs: Problems, Paradoxes and Possibilities." In *Strengthening the Poor: What Have We Learned?*, edited by John Lewis, pp. 177–188. New Brunswick, N.J.: Overseas Development Council, Transaction Books, 1988.

Dörner, Dietrich. *The Logic of Failure.* Reading, Mass.: Perseus Books, 1996.

Doughty, Paul. "Against the Odds: Collaboration and Development at Vicos." In *Collaborative Research and Social Change: Applied Anthropology in Action,* edited by Donald D. Stull and Jean Schensul, pp. 129–157. Boulder: Westview, 1987.

Douglas, Mary. *How Institutions Think.* Syracuse, N.Y.: Syracuse University Press, 1986.

Eade, Deborah. *Capacity-Building: An Approach to People-Centered Development.* London: Oxfam, 1997.

Epstein, T. Scarlett, and Akbar Ahmed. "Development Anthropology in Project Implementation." In *Training Manual in Development Anthropology,* edited by William Partridge. Washington, D.C.: Special Publication no. 17, American Anthropological Association, Society for Applied Anthropology, 1984.

Ervin, Alexander. *Applied Anthropology: Tools and Perspectives for Contemporary Practice.* Boston: Allyn and Bacon, 2000.

Escobar, Arturo. *Encountering Development: The Making and Unmaking of the Third World.* Princeton, N.J.: Princeton University Press, 1995.

Estroff, Sue. "Who Are You? Why Are You Here? Anthropology and Human Suffering." *Human Organization* 43, no. 4 (1984).

Feeney, Patricia. *Accountable Aid: Local Participation in Major Projects.* London: Oxfam, 1998.

Ferguson, James. *The Anti-Politics Machine: "Development," Depoliticization, and Bureaucratic Power in Lesotho.* New York: Cambridge University Press, 1990.

_____. "Anthropology and Its Evil Twin: 'Development' in the Constitution of a Discipline." In *International Development and the Social Sciences: Essays on the History and Politics of Knowledge,* edited by Frederick Cooper and Randall Packard, pp. 150–175. Berkeley: University of California Press, 1997.

Fetterman, David. "Guilty Knowledge, Dirty Hands, and Other Ethical Dilemmas: The Hazards of Contract Research." *Human Organization* 42, no. 3 (1983): 214–224.

Finan, Timothy. "Anthropological Research Methods in a Changing World." In *Transforming Societies, Transforming Anthropology*, edited by Emilio Moran, pp. 301–324. Ann Arbor, Mich.: University of Michigan Press, 1996.

Finger, Matthias, and Philomene Verlaan. "Learning Our Way Out: A Conceptual Framework for Socio-Environmental Learning." *World Development* 23, no. 3 (1995): 503–513.

Finnemore, Martha. "Redefining Development at the World Bank." In *International Development and the Social Sciences: Essays on the History and Politics of Knowledge*, edited by Frederick Cooper and Randall Packard, pp. 203–227. Berkeley: University of California Press, 1997.

Finsterbusch, Kurt. *Understanding Social Impacts*. Beverly Hills, Calif.: Sage, 1980.

Fisher, Glen. *Mindsets: The Role of Culture and Perception in International Relations*. Yarmouth, Maine: Intercultural Press, 1988.

Fisher, Roger, and Alan Sharp. *Getting it Done*. New York: HarperBusiness, 1998.

Fisher, Roger, and William Ury. *Getting to Yes: Negotiating Agreement Without Giving In*. Boston: Houghton Mifflin, 1981.

Fiske, Shirley. "Resource Management as People Management: Anthropology and Renewable Resources." *Renewable Resources Journal* (winter 1990): 16–20.

Fiske, Shirley, and Erve Chambers. "The Inventions of Practice." *Human Organization* 55, no. 1 (1996): 1–12.

Fleuret, Patrick. "Comment on "Natural Resource Anthropology." *Human Organization* 46, no. 3 (1987): 271–272.

Forde, Darryl. "Applied Anthropology in Government: British Africa." In *Anthropology Today: An Encyclopedic Inventory*, edited by A. L. Kroeber, pp. 841–865. Chicago: University of Chicago Press, 1953.

Foster, George, Thayer Scudder, and Elisabeth Colson, eds. *Long-Term Field Research in Social Anthropology*. New York: Academic Press, 1979.

Freedman, Jim, ed. *Transforming Development: Foreign Aid for a Changing World*. Toronto: University of Toronto Press, 2000.

Garber, Bill, and Penny Jenden. "Anthropologists or Anthropology? The Band Aid Perspective on Development Projects." In *Practising Development: Social Science Perspectives*, edited by Johan Pottier. London: Routledge, 1993.

Gardner, Katy, and David Lewis. *Anthropology, Development and the Post-Modern Challenge*. London: Pluto Press, 1996.

Gatter, Philip. "Anthropology in Farming Systems Research: A Participant Observer in Zambia." In *Practising Development: Social Science Perspectives*, edited by Johan Pottier, pp. 153–186. London: Routledge, 1993.

Gay, John. "Kpelle Farming Through Kpelle Eyes." In *The Cultural Dimension of Development: Indigenous Knowledge Systems*, edited by D. Michael Warren, L. Jan Slikkerveer, and David Brokensha, pp. 269–285. London: Intermediate Technology Publications, 1995.

Goffman, Erving. *The Presentation of Self in Everyday Life*. London: Allen Lane, 1969.

Goldman, Laurence, ed. *Social Impact Analysis: An Applied Anthropology Manual*. New York: Berg, 2000.

Goldschmidt, Walter, ed. *Anthropology and Public Policy*. Washington, D.C.: American Anthropological Association, 1986.

_____. "On the Unity of the Anthropological Sciences." Keynote address. Beijing: IUAES Inter-Congress, July 24, 2000.

Gorman, Robert, ed. *Private Voluntary Organizations as Agents of Development*. Boulder: Westview, 1984.

Gough, Kathleen. "Anthropology: Child of Imperialism." *Monthly Review* 19 (1968): 12–27.

Gould, Peter, and Rodney White. "Mental Maps." In *Urban Place and Process: Readings in the Anthropology of Cities*, edited by Irwin Press and M. Estellie Smith, pp. 96–104. New York: Macmillan, 1980.

Gow, David D. "Collaboration in Development Consulting: Stooges, Hired Guns, or Musketeers." *Human Organization* 50, no. 1 (1991): 1–15.

_____. "Anthropological Praxis and Development in a Postmodern Postcolonial World." Paper presented at the 93rd Annual Meeting of the American Anthropological Association, 1994.

Grant, Richard, and Jan Nijman. "The Foreign Aid Regime in Flux." In *The Global Crisis in Foreign Aid*, edited by Richard Grant and Jan Nijman, pp. 3–10. Syracuse, N.Y.: Syracuse University Press, 1998.

Grant, Richard, and Jan Nijman, eds. *The Global Crisis in Foreign Aid*. Syracuse, N.Y.: Syracuse University Press, 1998.

Grayzel, John. "Libido and Development: The Importance of Emotions in Development Work." In *Anthropology and Rural Development in West Africa*, edited by Michael Horowitz and Thomas Painter, pp. 147–165. Boulder: Westview, 1986.

Green, Edward C. "The Planning of Health Education Strategies in Swaziland." In *Anthropological Praxis: Translating Knowledge into Action*, edited by Robert Wulff and Shirley Fiske, pp. 15–25. Boulder: Westview, 1987.

Greenwood, Ernest. "Attributes of a Profession." *Social Work* 2 (1957): 44–55.

Greider, William. *One World, Ready or Not: The Manic Logic of Global Capitalism*. New York: Simon and Schuster, 1997.

Grenier, Louise. *Working with Indigenous Knowledge*. Ottawa: International Development Research Centre, 1998.

Griesgraber, Jo Marie, and Bernhard Gunter, eds. *Development: New Paradigms and Principles for the Twenty-First Century*. London: Pluto Press, 1996.

Griffith, Geoffrey. "Shaviyani Nights." *Anthropology Today* (1987–1991).

Grillo, Ralph, and Alan Rew, eds. *Social Anthropology and Development Policy.* ASA Monographs 23. London: Tavistock, 1985.

Grimm, Curt D. "Anthropology at the U.S. Agency for International Development: Are the Best Years Behind Us?" *Development Anthropologist* 16, nos. 1–2 (1998): 22–25.

Grindle, Merilee. "Divergent Cultures? When Public Organizations Perform Well in Developing Countries." *World Development* 25, no. 4 (1997): 481–495.

Grindle, Merilee S., ed. *Politics and Policy Implementation in the Third World.* Princeton, N.J.: Princeton University Press, 1980.

Hackenberg, Robert, and Beverly Hackenberg. "You CAN Do Something! Forming Policy from Applied Projects, Then and Now." *Human Organization* 58, no. 1 (1999): 1–15.

Hall, Edward T., and Mildred R. Hall. *Understanding Cultural Differences.* Yarmouth, Maine: Intercultural Press, 1989.

Halstead, John, Robert Chase, Steve Murdock, and Larry Leistritz. *Socioeconomic Impact Management: Design and Implementation.* Boulder: Westview, 1984.

Hamilton, James W. "Problems in Government Anthropology." In *Anthropology Beyond the University*, edited by A. Redfield, pp. 120–131. Southern Anthropological Society Proceedings No. 7, Athens, GA., University of Georgia Press, 1973.

Hanchette, Suzanne. "Anthropology and Development: The 1998 ICAES Discussion." *Practicing Anthropology* 21, no. 1 (1999): 45.

Hancock, Graham. *Lords of Poverty: The Power, Prestige and Corruption of the International Aid Business.* New York: Atlantic Monthly Press, 1989.

Harman, Willis, and Maya Porter, eds. *The New Business of Business: Sharing Responsibility for a Positive Global Future.* San Francisco: Berrett-Koehler, 1997.

Harris, Philip D., and Robert T. Moran. *Managing Cultural Differences*, 3d ed. Houston: Gulf Publishing, 1991.

Hellinger, Stephen, Douglas Hellinger, and Fred M. O'Regan. *Aid for Just Development.* Boulder: Lynne Rienner, 1988.

Hoben, Allan. "Agricultural Decision-Making in Foreign Assistance: An Anthropological Analysis." In *Agricultural Decision Making: Anthropological Contributions to Rural Development*, edited by Peggy Barlett, pp. 337–369. New York: Academic Press, 1980.

_____. "Anthropologists and Development." *Annual Review of Anthropology* 11 (1982): 349–375.

_____. "The Role of the Anthropologist in Development Work: An Overview." In *Training Manual in Development Anthropology*, edited by William Partridge. Washington, D.C.: Special Publication no. 17, American Anthropological Association, Society for Applied Anthropology, 1984.

_____. "Assessing the Social Feasibility of a Settlement Project in North Cameroon." In *Anthropology and Rural Development in West Africa*, edited by Michael Horowitz and Thomas Painter, pp. 169–194. Boulder: Westview, 1986.

_____. "Paradigms and Politics: The Cultural Construction of Environmental Policy in Ethiopia." *World Development* 23, no. 6 (1995): 1007–1021.

Hoben, Allan, and Robert Hefner. "The Integrative Revolution Revisited." *World Development* 19, no. 1 (1991): 17–30.

Honadle, George. "Rapid Reconnaissance for Development Administration: Mapping and Moulding Organizational Landscapes." *World Development* 10, no. 8 (1982): 633–649.

Honadle, George, and Lauren Cooper. "Beyond Coordination and Control: An Interorganizational Approach to Structural Adjustment, Service Delivery, and Natural Resource Management." *World Development* 17, no. 10 (1989): 1531–1541.

Honadle, George, and J. K. Rosengard. "Putting 'Projectized' Development in Perspective." *Public Administration and Development* 3 (1983): 299–305.

Honadle, George, and Jerry Van Sant. *Implementation for Sustainability.* West Hartford, Conn.: Kumarian Press, 1985.

Hook, Steven. "Introduction: Foreign Aid in a Transformed World." In *Foreign Aid Toward the Millennium*, edited by Steven Hook, pp. 1–16. Boulder: Lynne Rienner, 1996.

Hook, Steven, ed. *Foreign Aid Toward the Millennium.* Boulder: Lynne Rienner, 1996.

Horowitz, Irving. "The Life and Death of Project Camelot." *Transaction* 3 (1965): 44–47.

_____. *The Rise and Fall of Project Camelot.* Cambridge, Mass.: MIT Press, 1967.

Horowitz, Michael. "Development Anthropology in the Mid-1990s." *Development Anthropology Network* 12, nos. 1–2 (1994): 1–14.

_____. "On Not Offending the Borrower: (Self?) Ghettoization of Anthropology at the World Bank." *Development Anthropologist* 14, nos. 1–2 (1996a): 1, 3–12.

_____. "Thoughts on Development Anthropology After Twenty Years." In *Transforming Societies, Transforming Anthropology*, edited by Emilio Moran, pp. 325–351. Ann Arbor, Mich.: University of Michigan Press, 1996b.

_____. "Development and the Anthropological Encounter in the 21st Century." *Development Anthropologist* 16, nos. 1–2 (1998a): 1–35.

_____. "Development and the Anthropological Encounter: A Reflective Underview." *Development Anthropologist* 16, nos. 1–2 (1998b): 44–50.

Horowitz, Michael, and Thomas Painter, eds. *Anthropology and Rural Development in West Africa.* Boulder: Westview, 1967.

Hyden, Goran. "The Changing Context of Institutional Development in Sub-Saharan Africa." In *Institutional and Sociopolitical Issues*, vol. 3 of *Background Papers: The Long-Term Perspective Study of Sub-Saharan Africa.* Washington, D.C.: World Bank, 1990.

Hyland, Stanley, and Sean Kirkpatrick. *Guide to Training Programs in Applied Anthropology.* Memphis, Tenn.: Society for Applied Anthropology, 1989.

Hymes, Dell, ed. *Reinventing Anthropology*. New York: Vintage Books, 1972.

Ilchman, Warren, and Norman Uphoff. *The Political Economy of Change*. Berkeley: University of California Press, 1969.

International Rice Research Institute, ed. *The Role of Anthropologists and Other Social Scientists in Interdisciplinary Teams Developing Improved Food Production Technology*. Manila: IRRI, 1982.

Iyer, Pico. "Strangers in a Small World." *Harper's Magazine* (September 1994): 13–16.

Jones, Delmos. "Social Responsibilities and the Belief in Basic Research: An Example from Thailand." *Current Anthropology* 12 (1971): 347–350.

Jones, James C. "Development: Reflections from Bolivia." *Human Organization* 56, no. 1 (1997): 111–120.

Jordan, Ann. *Practicing Anthropology in Corporate America: Consulting on Organizational Culture*. NAPA Bulletin 14, American Anthropological Association, 1994.

Kaplan, Robert D. "Was Democracy Just a Moment?" *Atlantic Monthly* (December 1997): 55–60, 80.

Kardam, Nüket. "Development Approaches and the Role of Policy Advocacy: The Case of the World Bank." *World Development* 21, no. 11 (1993): 1773–1786.

Kemper, Robert V., and Anya P. Royce. "Ethical Issues for Social Anthropologists: A North American Perspective on Long-Term Research in Mexico." *Human Organization* 56, no. 4 (1997): 479–483.

Kennedy, Paul. *Preparing for the Twenty-First Century*. New York: Random House, 1993.

Khon Kaen University. *Proceedings of the 1985 International Conference on Rapid Rural Appraisal*. Khon Kaen, Thailand: Khon Kaen University, 1987.

Kirk, Jerome, and Marc Miller. *Reliability and Validity in Qualitative Research*. Beverly Hills, Calif.: Sage, 1986.

Klitgaard, Robert. *Tropical Gangsters*. New York: Basic Books, 1990.

_____. "'Unanticipated Consequences' in Anti-Poverty Programs." *World Development* 25, no. 12 (1997): 1963–1972.

Koenig, Dolores. "The Culture and Social Organization of USAID Development Projects in West Africa." In *Production and Autonomy: Anthropological Studies and Critiques of Development*, edited by John Bennett and John Bowen, pp. 345–364. New York: University Press of America, 1988.

Korten, David. "Community Organization and Rural Development: A Learning Process Approach." *Public Administration Review* 40, no. 5 (1980): 480–511.

_____. "Rethinking Development and the Meaning of Progress." In *The New Business of Business: Sharing Responsibility for a Positive Global Future*, edited by Willis Harman and Maya Porter, pp. 157–167. San Francisco: Berrett-Koehler, 1997.

Korten, David, and Rudi Klauss, eds. *People-Centered Development: Contributions*

Toward Theory and Planning Frameworks. West Hartford, Conn.: Kumarian Press, 1984.

Kottak, Conrad Philip. "When People Don't Come First: Some Sociological Lessons from Completed Projects." In *Putting People First*, 2d ed., edited by Michael Cernea, pp. 431–464. New York: World Bank, Oxford University Press, 1991.

Kroeber, A. L., ed. *Anthropology Today: An Encyclopedic Inventory*. Chicago: University of Chicago Press, 1953.

Labrecque, Marie France. "Social Research as an Agent of Transformation." In *Transforming Development: Foreign Aid for a Changing World*, edited by Jim Freedman, pp. 211–221. Toronto: University of Toronto Press, 2000.

Landes, David S. "Why Are We So Rich and They So Poor?" In *Developing Areas: A Book of Readings and Research*, edited by Vijayan Pillai and Lyle Shannon, pp. 74–86. Oxford: Berg, 1995.

Lappé, Francis Moore, Rachel Schurman, and Kevin Danaher. *Betraying the National Interest*. New York: Grove Press, 1987.

Lecompte, Bernard. *Project Aid: Limitations and Alternatives*. Paris: OECD, 1986.

Lederer, William J., and Eugene Burdick. *The Ugly American*. New York: W. W. Norton, 1958.

Leeson, P., and M. Minogue, eds. *Perspectives on Development: Cross-Disciplinary Theses in Development Studies*. Manchester, England: Manchester University Press, 1988.

Lethem, Francis, and Lauren Cooper. "Managing Project-Related Technical Assistance." World Bank Staff Working Paper no. 586. Washington, D.C.: World Bank, 1983.

Lewellen, Ted. *Dependency and Development*. Westport, Conn.: Bergin and Garvey, 1995.

Lewis, John, ed. *Strengthening the Poor: What Have We Learned?* Overseas Development Council. New Brunswick, N.J.: Transaction Books, 1988.

Mangin, William. "Thoughts on Twenty-Four Years of Work in Peru: The Vicos Project and Me." In *Long-Term Field Research in Social Anthropology*, edited by George Foster, Thayer Scudder, and Elisabeth Colson. New York: Academic Press, 1979.

Maren, Michael. *The Road to Hell: The Ravaging Effects of Foreign Aid and International Charity*. New York: The Free Press, 1997.

McMichael, Philip. *Development and Social Change: A Global Perspective*. Thousand Oaks, Calif.: Pine Forge Press, 1996.

McNeil, Desmond. *The Contradictions of Foreign Aid*. London: Croom Helm, 1981.

Mickelwait, Donald. "Terms of Reference: The AID Consulting Industry." Washington, D.C., Development Alternatives, nd.

Moerman, Michael. *Agricultural Change and Peasant Choice in a Thai Village*. Berkeley: University of California Press, 1968.

Molnar, Augusta. "Rapid Rural Appraisal Methodology Applied to Project

Planning and Implementation in Natural Resource Management." In *Soundings: Rapid and Reliable Research Methods for Practicing Anthropologists*, edited by John van Willigen and Timothy Finan, pp. 11–23. NAPA Bulletin no 10. Washington, D.C.: American Anthropological Association, 1991.

Moran, Emilio. "Goals and Indices of Development: An Anthropological Perspective." In *Transforming Societies, Transforming Anthropology*, edited by Emilio Moran, pp. 211–240. Ann Arbor, Mich.: University of Michigan Press, 1996.

Moran, Emilio, ed. *Transforming Societies, Transforming Anthropology*. Ann Arbor, Mich.: University of Michigan Press, 1996.

Morey, Nancy, and Robert Morey. "Organizational Culture: The Management Approach." In *Practicing Anthropology in Corporate America: Consulting on Organizational Culture*, edited by Ann Jordan, pp. 17–26. NAPA Bulletin 14, American Anthropological Association, 1994.

Moris, Jon. "A Case in Rural Development: The Masai Range Development Project." In *Managing Induced Rural Development*, edited by Jon Moris, pp. 99–113. International Development Institute, Bloomington, Ind.: University of Indiana Press, 1981a.

———. *Managing Induced Rural Development*. International Development Institute, Bloomington, Ind.: University of Indiana Press, 1981b.

Moris, Jon, and James Copestake. *Qualitative Enquiry for Rural Development*. London: Intermediate Technology Publications, 1993.

Moris, Jon, and C. Hatfield. "A New Reality: Western Technology Faces Pastoralism in the Maasai Project." In *The Role of Anthropologists and Other Social Scientists in Interdisciplinary Teams Developing Improved Food Production Technology*, edited by the International Rice Research Institute, pp. 43–61. Manila: IRRI, 1982.

Mosley, Paul, Jane Harrigan, and John Toye. *Aid and Power: The World Bank and Policy-Based Lending*. Vol. 1: *Analysis and Policy Proposals*, 2d ed. London: Routledge, 1991.

Murray, Gerald F. "The Domestication of Wood in Haiti: A Case Study in Applied Evolution." In *Anthropological Praxis: Translating Knowledge into Action*, edited by Robert Wulff and Shirley Fiske, pp. 223–240. Boulder: Westview, 1987.

Naylor, Larry L. *Culture and Change: An Introduction*. Westport, Conn.: Bergin and Garvey, 1996.

Nolan, Riall. *Bassari Migrations: The Quiet Revolution*. Boulder: Westview, 1986.

———. "If You Don't Know Who You Are, Try Being Someone Else for a While: Senegal and the Making of an Applied Anthropologist." *Practicing Anthropology* 19, no. 1 (1997).

———. Review of Jean-François Baré, ed., *Les Applications de l'Anthropologie*, Paris: Éditions Karthala. In *Practicing Anthropology* 20, no. 2 (spring 1998): 40.

——— *Communicating and Adapting Across Cultures*. Westport, Conn.: Bergin and Garvey, 1999.

Oakley, Peter. *Projects with People: The Practice of Participation in Rural Development*. Geneva: International Labour Office, 1991.

OECD. *DAC Principles for Effective Aid*. Paris: OECD, 1992.

O'Hanlon, Michael, and Carol Graham. *A Half Penny on the Federal Dollar: The Future of Development Aid*. Washington, D.C.: Brookings Institution Press, 1997.

Overseas Development Council and InterAction. *What Americans Think: Views on Development and U.S.–Third World Relations*. New York: Overseas Development Council, 1987.

Paddock, William, and Elizabeth Paddock. *We Don't Know How: An Independent Audit of What They Call Success in Foreign Assistance*. Ames, Iowa: Iowa State University Press, 1973.

Partridge, William. "Anthropology and Development Planning." *Practicing Anthropology* 1, nos. 5–6 (1979): 6, 26–27.

_____. "Toward a Theory of Practice." *American Behavioral Scientist* 29, no. 2 (1985): 139–163.

Partridge, William, ed. *Training Manual in Development Anthropology*. Special Publication no. 17. Washington, D.C.: American Anthropological Association and the Society for Applied Anthropology, 1984.

Paul, Samuel, and Arturo Israel. *Nongovernmental Organizations and the World Bank: Cooperation for Development*. Washington, D.C.: World Bank, 1991.

Payer, Cheryl. *The World Bank: A Critical Analysis*. New York: Monthly Review Press, 1982.

Peace Corps. *Bureaucratic Effectiveness and Working with Counterparts*. Washington, D.C.: Information Collection and Exchange, 1983.

Peattie, Lisa. "Drama and Advocacy Planning." *Journal of the American Institute of Planners* 36 (1970): 405–410.

Perrett, Heli, and Francis Lethem. *Human Factors in Project Work*. Washington, D.C.: World Bank, 1980.

Pigg, Stacey. "Found in Most Traditional Societies." In *International Development and the Social Sciences: Essays on the History and Politics of Knowledge*, edited by Frederick Cooper and Randall Packard, p. 270. Berkeley: University of California Press, 1997.

Pillai, Vijayan, and Lyle Shannon, eds. *Developing Areas: A Book of Readings and Research*. Oxford: Berg, 1995.

Pillsbury, Barbara. "Making a Difference: Anthropologists in International Development." In *Anthropology and Public Policy*, edited by Walter Goldschmidt, pp. 10–28. Washington, D.C.: American Anthropological Association, 1986.

Porter, David. *U.S. Economic Foreign Aid: A Case Study of the United States Agency for International Development*. New York: Garland Publishing, 1990.

Posz, Gary, Jong Jun, and William Storm. *Administrative Alternatives in Development Assistance*. Cambridge, Mass.: Ballinger Publishing, 1973.

Pottier, Johan. "The Role of Ethnography in Project Appraisal." In *Practising*

Development: Social Science Perspectives, edited by Johan Pottier, pp. 13–33. London: Routledge, 1993a.

Pottier, Johan, ed. *Practising Development: Social Science Perspectives*. London: Routledge, 1993b.

Press, Irwin, and M. Estellie Smith, eds. *Urban Place and Process: Readings in the Anthropology of Cities*. New York: Macmillan, 1980.

Pressman, Jeffrey, and Aaron B. Wildavsky. *Implementation*. Oakland Project Series. Berkeley: University of California Press, 1973.

Rapley, John. *Understanding Development*. Boulder: Lynne Rienner, 1996.

Redfield, A., ed. *Anthropology Beyond the University*. Southern Anthropological Society Proceedings 7. Athens, Ga.: University of Georgia Press, 1973.

Rew, Alan. "The Organizational Connection: Multi-Disciplinary Practice and Anthropological Theory." In *Social Anthropology and Development Policy*, edited by Ralph Grillo and Alan Rew, pp. 185–197. ASA Monographs 23. London: Tavistock, 1985.

Rhoades, R. "Using Anthropology in Improving Food Production: Problems and Prospects." *Agricultural Administration* 22 (1986): 57–78.

Rich, Bruce. *Mortgaging the Earth: The World Bank, Environmental Impoverishment and the Crisis of Development*. Boston: Beacon Press, 1994.

Roche, Chris. *Impact Assessment for Development Agencies*. Oxford: Oxfam, 1999.

Roe, Emery. "Development Narratives, of Making the Best of Blueprint Development." *World Development* 19, no. 4 (1991): 287–300.

———. "Except-Africa: Postscript to a Special Section on Development Narratives." *World Development* 23, no. 6 (1995): 1065–1069.

Rondinelli, Dennis. *Development Projects as Policy Experiments*. New York: Methuen, 1983.

———. "Development Administration and American Foreign Assistance Policy: An Assessment of Theory and Practice in Aid." *Canadian Journal of Development Studies* 6, no. 2 (1985): 211–240.

———. "UNDP Assistance for Urban Development: An Assessment of Institution-Building Efforts in Developing Countries." *International Review of Administrative Sciences*, SAGE 58 (1992): 519–537.

Rostow, W. W. *The Stages of Economic Growth, a Non-Communist Manifesto*. Cambridge: Cambridge University Press, 1960.

Roxas, Sixto. "Principles for Institutional Reform." In *Development: New Paradigms and Principles for the Twenty-First Century*, edited by Jo Marie Griesgraber and Bernhard Gunter, pp. 1–26. London: Pluto Press, 1996.

Rubenstein, Robert A. "Reflections on Action Anthropology: Some Developmental Dynamics of an Anthropological Tradition." *Human Organization* 45, no. 3 (1986): 270–279.

Ryan, Richard. "Rural Poverty and Rural Development Tourism: Getting Data for Effective Projects and Programs." PASTAM Design Note no. 23, Indiana University, Bloomington, 1981.

Sagasti, Francisco. "Editorial: Development, Knowledge and the Baconian Age." *World Development* 25, no. 10 (1997): 1561–1568.

Samoff, Joel. "Chaos and Certainty in Development." *World Development* 24, no. 4 (1996): 611–633.

Schein, Edgar H. *Process Consultation: Its Role in Organization Development.* Reading, Mass.: Addison-Wesley, 1969.

Schön, Donald A. *The Reflective Practitioner.* New York: Basic Books, 1983.

Scott-Stevens, Susan. *Foreign Consultants and Counterparts: Problems in Technology Transfer.* Boulder: Westview, 1987.

Scrimshaw, Nevin, and Gary Gleason, eds. *RAP Rapid Assessment Procedures: Qualitative Methodologies for Planning and Evaluation of Health Related Programmes.* Boston: International Nutrition Foundation for Developing Countries, 1992.

Scrimshaw, Susan, and E. Hurtado. *Rapid Assessment Procedures for Nutrition and Primary Health Care: Anthropological Approaches for Improving Program Effectiveness.* Tokyo: United Nations University, 1987.

Scudder, Thayer. "The Institute for Development Anthropology: The Case of Anthropological Participation in the Development Process." In *Production and Autonomy: Anthropological Studies and Critiques of Development,* edited by John Bennett and John Bowen, pp. 365–385. New York: University Press of America, 1988.

Senge, Peter. *The Fifth Discipline: The Art and Practice of the Learning Organization.* New York: Doubleday, 1990.

Serageldin, Ismail. *Nurturing Development: Aid and Cooperation in Today's Changing World.* Washington, D.C.: World Bank, 1995.

Sharp, Lauriston. "Steel Axes for Stone-Age Australians." In *Human Problems in Technological Change,* edited by Edward Spicer, pp. 69–72. New York: Russell Sage Foundation, 1952.

Shaw, George Bernard. *Two Plays for Puritans.* New York: Heritage Press, 1966.

Shore, Chris, and Susan Wright. "British Anthropology in Policy and Practice: A Review of Current Work." *Human Organization* 55, no. 4 (1996): 475–480.

Siffin, William. "Intelligent Rural Development Project Design." PASTAM Design Notes no. 22, Bloomington, International Development Institute, University of Indiana at Bloomington, 1981.

Silverman, Jerry M. *Technical Assistance and Aid Agency Staff: Alternative Techniques for Greater Effectiveness.* World Bank Technical Paper no. 28. Washington, D.C.: World Bank, 1984.

Simmonds, Norman W. *Farming Systems Research: A Review.* World Bank Technical Paper no. 43. Washington, D.C.: World Bank, 1985.

Sjoberg, Gideon. "Project Camelot: Selected Reactions and Personal Reflections." In *Ethics, Politics and Social Research,* edited by Gideon Sjoberg, pp. 141–161. Cambridge, Mass.: Schenkman, 1967.

Sjoberg, Gideon, ed. *Ethics, Politics and Social Research.* Cambridge, Mass.: Schenkman, 1967.

Smillie, Ian. *The Alms Bazaar*. London: Intermediate Technology Publications, 1995.

Smillie, Ian, and Henny Helmich, eds. *Public Attitudes and International Development Cooperation*. Paris: OECD, 1998.

Soetoro, Ann. "Prosperity Indicators for Java." Washington, D.C.: Development Alternatives Incorporated, 1979.

Spicer, Edward. "Anthropology and the Policy Process." In *Do Applied Anthropologists Apply Anthropology?*, edited by Michael Angrosino, pp. 118–133. Athens, Ga.: Southern Anthropological Society, University of Georgia Press, 1976.

Spicer, Edward, ed. *Human Problems in Technological Change*. New York: Russell Sage Foundation, 1952.

Spradley, James. "Adaptive Strategies of Urban Nomads: The Ethnoscience of Tramp Culture." In *The Anthropology of Urban Environments*, edited by Thomas Weaver and Douglas White, pp. 21–38. Society for Applied Anthropology Monograph Series, no. 11, 1972.

_____. *The Ethnographic Interview*. New York: Holt, Rinehart and Winston, 1979.

_____. *Participant Observation*. New York: Holt, Rinehart and Winston, 1980.

Spradley, James, ed. *Culture and Cognition: Rules, Maps and Adaptive Processes*. Prospect Heights, Ill.: Waveland Press, 1972.

Spradley, James, and David McCurdy, eds. *The Cultural Experience: Ethnography in a Complex Society* Prospect Heights, Ill.: Waveland Press, 1972.

_____. *Conformity and Conflict: Readings in Cultural Anthropology*, 10th ed. Boston: Allyn and Bacon, 2000.

Staudt, Kathleen. *Managing Development: State, Society, and International Contexts*. Newbury Park, Calif.: Sage, 1991.

Stone, Linda. "Cultural Crossroads of Community Participation in Development: A Case from Nepal." *Human Organization* 48, no. 3 (1989): 206–213.

Stull, Donald D., and Jean Schensul, eds. *Collaborative Research and Social Change: Applied Anthropology in Action*. Boulder: Westview, 1987.

Tendler, Judith. *Inside Foreign Aid*. Baltimore: Johns Hopkins University Press, 1975.

Tilman, Martin. "How Do We Feel About Foreign Aid?" *International Educator* (winter 1995): 42–43.

Tisch, Sarah, and Michael Wallace. *Dilemmas of Development Assistance*. Boulder: Westview, 1994.

Trotter, R., ed. *Anthropology for Tomorrow*. AA/NAPA Publication no. 24. Washington, D.C.: American Anthropological Association, 1988.

Turton, David. "Anthropology and Development." In *Perspectives on Development: Cross-Disciplinary Theses in Development Studies*, edited by P. Leeson and M. Minogue, pp. 126–159. Manchester, England: Manchester University Press, 1988.

Uphoff, Norman. "Fitting Projects to People." In *Putting People First,* edited by Michael Cernea, pp. 359–395. New York: World Bank, Oxford University Press, 1985.

_____. "Paraprojects as New Modes of International Development Assistance." *World Development* 18, no. 10 (1990): 1401–1411.

USAID. "Why Foreign Aid?" Washington, D.C.: Agency for International Development, 1998.

_____. "Fiscal Year 1999 Budget Request Summary." *www.info.usaid.gov.*

van Willigen, John. "Truth and Effectiveness: An Essay on the Relationships Between Information, Policy and Action in Applied Anthropology." *Human Organization* 43, no. 3 (1984): 277–282.

_____. *Applied Anthropology: An Introduction.* South Hadley, Mass.: Bergin and Garvey, 1986.

van Willigen, John, and Timothy Finan, eds. *Soundings: Rapid and Reliable Research Methods for Practicing Anthropologists.* NAPA Bulletin no. 10. Washington, D.C.: American Anthropological Association, 1991.

Warren, D. Michael, L. Jan Slikkerveer, and David Brokensha, eds. *The Cultural Dimension of Development: Indigenous Knowledge Systems.* London: Intermediate Technology Publications, 1995.

Watkins, Eric. *Anthropology Goes to War.* Madison, Wisc.: University of Wisconsin Center for Southeast Asia Studies, Monograph Series 6, 1992.

Wax, Murray. "Review of the Best Laid Schemes, S. J. Deitchman, 1976, Cambridge, MIT Press." *Human Organization* 37, no. 4 (1978): 400–412.

Weaver, Thomas. "Anthropology as a Policy Science: Part I, a Critique." *Human Organization* 44, no. 2 (1985): 97–104.

Weaver, Thomas, and Douglas White, eds. *The Anthropology of Urban Environments.* The Society for Applied Anthropology Monograph Series, no. 11, 1972.

Wedel, Janine R. *Collision and Collusion: The Strange Case of Western Aid to Eastern Europe 1989–1998.* New York: St. Martin's Press, 1998.

Wilk, Richard, and Stephen Miller. "Some Methodological Issues in Counting Communities and Households." *Human Organization* 56, no. 1 (1997): 64–70.

Wilson, Ruth P. "The Role of Anthropologists as Short-Term Consultants." *Human Organization* 57, no. 2 (1998): 245–252.

Winthrop, Robert. "Fools Walk In: Engaging Globalization." *Practicing Anthropology* 20, no. 2 (1998): 38–39.

Wolcott, Harry F. "A Malay Village that Progress Chose: Sungai Lui and the Institute of Cultural Affairs." *Human Organization* 42, no. 1 (1983): 72–81.

Wolf, Eric, and Joe Jorgenson. "Anthropology on the Warpath in Thailand." *New York Review of Books* 15, no. 9 (1970): 26–35.

World Bank. *Annual Report.* Washington, D.C.: The World Bank, 1988.

_____. *World Development Report* (Executive Summary). Washington, D.C.: World Bank, 1995.

_____. *Assessing Aid: What Works, What Doesn't and Why.* Washington, D.C.: World Bank, 1998.

_____. *World Bank Atlas 1999.* Washington, D.C.: World Bank, 1999.

_____. *World Bank Information Briefs* A.04.4.94.

Wulff, Robert, and Shirley Fiske. *Anthropological Praxis: Translating Knowledge into Action.* Boulder: Westview, 1987.

Yoder, Amos. *International Politics and Policymakers' Ideas,* rev. ed. Brunswick, Ohio: King's Court Communications, 1988.

Zakaria, Fareed. "Our Hollow Hegemony: Why Foreign Policy Can't Be Left to the Market." *NY Times Magazine* (November 1, 1998): 44–47, 74–80.

Zimmerman, Robert, and Steven Hook. "The Assault on U.S. Foreign Aid." In *Foreign Aid Toward the Millennium,* edited by Steven Hook, pp. 57–73. Boulder: Lynne Rienner, 1996.

Index